REVELATION AND THEOLOGY

Revelation and Theology
The Gospel as Narrated Promise

RONALD F. THIEMANN

Wipf & Stock
PUBLISHERS
Eugene, Oregon

Wipf and Stock Publishers
199 W 8th Ave, Suite 3
Eugene, OR 97401

Revelation and Theology
The Gospel as Narrated Promise
By Thiemann, Ronald F.
Copyright©1985 by Thiemann, Ronald F.
ISBN: 1-59752-358-5
Previously published by University of Notre Dame Press, 1985

FOR MY PARENTS

Frank Joseph and Marie Magdalene Thiemann

Contents

Acknowledgments

Writing can be a lonely task, and so I am eager to acknowledge those friends and colleagues who by their encouragement and friendly criticism provided a community of support for me during the conception, gestation, and birth of this book. An early draft of the first chapters was vigorously discussed at the inaugural meeting of the Yale-Washington Theology Group. I am grateful to the group members for their insightful criticisms, for their continued interest in the project, and for their sustaining friendship. Tom Tracy was a particularly helpful guide through the thicket of the philosophy of agency. George Hunsinger and Mike Root read the entirety of the revised manuscript and offered copious helpful comments.

Gil Meilaender, a close friend and conversation partner for nearly two decades, has had a deep and abiding influence on my theological development. Though we often disagree on matters theological, I treasure our happy adversarial relationship. I have profited enormously from our countless amicable debates and count him among my most important teachers (even though he does not always properly distinguish law and gospel!). Bill Werpehowski gave generously of his time and advice, reading each chapter with a sympathetic and critical eye. He provided invaluable intellectual and personal support during the period in which this manuscript took shape. For that, for his constant collegiality, and for his companionship at Phillies baseball and Big East basketball games I am deeply grateful.

Haverford College provides a marvelous context for serious scholarly work. Richard Luman has been a stimulating departmental colleague during the last eight years and has taught me much about teaching and writing. A careful analyst of style, he has helped me eliminate the "Teutonic" turns of phrase which so often characterize the prose of those of us who spend our time reading German theologians. Dick Bernstein and Aryeh Kosman have been appreciative philosophical critics of my work. Dick read the entire manuscript and helped me to refine my philosophical critiques of foundationalism. Aryeh recognized some infelicities in my use of speech-act theory and helped me to strengthen my concluding hermeneutical arguments. Such interdisciplinary exchange is commonplace at Haverford, an institution which continues to exemplify the ideals of a liberal arts college. My students have been a constant source of stimulation. Many of the ideas which are central to this book first developed in classroom debate and discussion. Shirley Averill, my secretary, assisted me in the typing and editing of the manuscript and continually buoyed my spirits with her remarkable good cheer. Finally, the college administration, and particularly our former provost, Bob Gavin, provided both moral and monetary support for this project. I am grateful for grants from the Whitehead Fund and the Mellon Foundation which supported my research and writing.

Two other persons deserve special mention. The influence of Hans Frei is evident throughout this book. He has been a wonderful theological mentor, a teacher who has formed my thinking even as he encouraged my independence. I continue to benefit from his wise counsel. Richard Hoyer, friend and pastor, has given me, through his preaching, a constant lively sense of God's narrated promise. His ministry at the Lutheran Church of the Redeemer has helped to create a community committed to the nurturance of Christian character.

Finally I want to acknowledge the support of my family. My wife, Beth, has been a continual gentle reminder that there is more to life than the stuff of scholarship. With enormous patience and good humor she has helped us all survive the disruptions which a major writing project inevitably brings to family life. My daughters, Sarah and Laura, continue to devise ways to surprise and delight their father in even his most somber moods. Along with Karli, our household hound, they have helped me to keep this project in its proper perspective. To my parents, from whom I first heard the promise of the Gospel, I want to express my thanks for their unfailing love and trust. Though such devotion deserves a more costly gift, this book is dedicated to them.

R.F.T.
Epiphany, 1985

A Doctrine of Revelation: Worth the Trouble

"The very idea that the Bible is revealed . . . is a claim that creates more trouble than it is worth."[1] That statement, made almost as an aside by Stanley Hauerwas in an article on the Bible's moral authority, captures well a growing consensus among contemporary theologians. The debates about revelation, natural knowledge of God, *Anknüpfungspunkten*, and the like, which dominated theology from the 1920s to the 1960s, seem to have led the discipline into a blind alley. Despite the prominence of doctrines of revelation in nearly every modern theology written prior to 1960, very little clarity has emerged regarding the possibility and nature of human knowledge of God. Indeed, most discussions of revelation have created complex conceptual and epistemological tangles that are difficult to understand and nearly impossible to unravel. A sense of revelation-weariness has settled over the discipline and most theologians have happily moved to other topics of inquiry.

A number of important studies written in the last two decades have called for a moratorium on the use of the term *revelation*, arguing that it is, among other things, "unbiblical," "unintelligible," and "incoherent."[2] F. Gerald Downing has stated the case most bluntly.

> The word 'revelation' is a source of great confusion. A theology based on it is inadequate for the exposition of the traditional faith of Christians. . . . "God" cannot be said to be 'known' without very heavy qualifications. He cannot be said to have 'revealed' himself, unless the word 'reveal' is evacuated of most if not all meaning. . . . It is surely nonsense, even pernicious nonsense, to pretend that [revelation] is a present fact.[3]

Downing and James Barr[4] have produced exegetical studies to show that theologians have no scriptural warrant for their broad and loose

1

use of the term *revelation*. David Kelsey has shown that doctrines of revelation give a false and misleadingly narrow view of the diverse ways theologians use Scripture to authorize theological proposals.[5] Gordon Kaufman has argued that the notion of revelation suggests a naively realistic view of God's reality and of the theological task.[6] The list of critics and their criticisms could be extended considerably.

The range of opinion and the weight of argument against revelation appear to be decisive. A horse as moribund as this one would hardly seem worth beating and any attempt to revive the beast would appear foolhardy. And yet a nagging sense remains that Christian theology will lose something essential if the doctrine of revelation and its associated notions are simply jettisoned. If the notion of revelation is to be removed from the theological lexicon we need to know more precisely both *what* we are discarding and *why* we are discarding it. We need to gain a clearer sense of the theological issues at stake in traditional conceptions of revelation. What essential Christian convictions did the framers of the modern doctrine of revelation seek to defend? Which concerns (if any) of the traditional doctrine ought to be preserved and defended under a new conceptuality? More particularly, what is the relation between a doctrine of revelation and the Christian belief in the priority or prevenience of God's grace? Can belief in God's prevenience be maintained if the doctrine of revelation is discarded?

Christian theology has traditionally been guided by the conviction that faith's knowledge of God is a gift bestowed through God's free grace. Our thought and speech about God are not simply the free creations of human imagination but are developed in obedient response to God's prior initiative.[7] Theologians have commonly referred to this prior act of God as revelation. Thus Martin Luther writes in his greater Galatians commentary,

> We continually teach that knowledge of Christ and of faith is not a human work but utterly a divine gift. . . . What the Gospel teaches and shows me is a divine work given to me by sheer grace. . . . I accept this gift by faith alone. . . . This sort of doctrine which reveals the Son of God . . . is revealed by God, first by the external Word and then inwardly through the Spirit.[8]

Some four centuries later Karl Barth expressed similar sentiments.

Revelation in the Christian sense is a revelation which [is] completely new . . . which comes to all men with equal strangeness from outside. . . . [It] is the realization of a possibility which lies wholly in the place where revelation takes place, not in the human realm. . . . The biblical writers testify that the revelation came to them with a supreme authoritativeness of its own. . . . They *answered* something that came *to* them, not from them.[9]

Despite important differences in rhetoric Luther and Barth give common witness to the central Christian conviction that faith's knowledge of God is a gift of God's grace. Whatever their manifest flaws, modern doctrines of revelation have attempted to restate that central Christian conviction. Luther's insistence that faith "is not a human work but utterly a divine gift" has been recast in the modern discussion to stress that faith's knowledge is not a natural human possession but a new possibility granted through the graciousness of the giver. Both positions stress the *prevenience* of God's grace, the conviction that we are enabled to have access to God solely through God's prior action.

Even the most vigorous critics of revelation admit that the prevenience of God's grace must "be accepted in some form if there is any desire at all to remain in the historic Christian tradition."[10] But if the traditional defense of God's prevenience, the doctrine of revelation, is judged to be incoherent, then how can that constitutive Christian belief be justified? Contemporary theologians have, I believe, been much too sanguine in assuming that belief in God's prevenience can survive the demise of a doctrine of revelation.

Many theologians who refuse to employ the concept of revelation still undertake to defend belief in God's prevenience by an argument which asserts the universality of a "religious dimension" of human experience. These arguments for *homo religiosus* serve as the functional equivalents of doctrines of revelation because, like the classic modern doctrine, they are theoretical justifications for Christian belief in the priority of God's gracious reality. Theologians who employ these arguments seek to demonstrate that human beings are inherently in relation to God. Human existence, they argue, possesses an ontological depth or root which is irreducibly religious. "Religion" is not an empirically specifiable component of ordinary experience but is rather a hidden dimension of the everyday. That religious dimension becomes manifest in certain "boundary" or "limit" situations where in an ecstatic moment "we experience a reality simply given, gifted, happened."[11] That experience further "discloses a reality . . . which functions as a final, now gracious, now frightening, now trustworthy, now absurd, always uncontrollable limit-of the very meaning of existence itself. . . . [T]he objective referent of all such language and experience is that reality which religious human beings mean when they say 'God.' "[12] To be human is to be religious, and to be religious is to be in relation to God. Such an argument functions in the broadest sense as an account or doctrine of revelation.

Few theologians then are willing to argue that theology can dispense with such defenses of God's prior reality, and yet most theologians apparently want to discard the doctrine of revelation. But without further conceptual clarification it is not clear how the former can be affirmed while the latter is denied. Most critics of revelation appear to resist particular forms of the doctrine, e.g., those which rely on metaphors like Word of God, God speaking, God acting in history, and the like. But they often fail to see that the swords they wield against those metaphors can be directed against their own alternative accounts of revelation.[13] The problem of revelation is not simply a problem associated with particular outmoded objectivist metaphors for speaking of God's reality. The problem is whether *any* coherent argument can be made which establishes God's prior reality. That more profound problem is expressed with characteristic power (albeit with typical verbosity) by Ludwig Feuerbach.

> The belief in revelation exhibits in the clearest manner the characteristic illusion of the religious consciousness. The general premiss of this belief is: man can of himself know nothing of God; all his knowledge is merely vain, earthly human. But God is a superhuman being; God is known only by himself. Thus we know nothing of God beyond what he reveals to us. . . . By means of revelation, therefore, we know God through himself; for revelation is the word of God—God declaring himself. Hence, in the belief in revelation man makes himself a negation, he goes out of and above himself; he places revelation in opposition to human knowledge and opinion. . . . But nevertheless the divine revelation is determined by the human nature. God speaks not to brutes or angels but to men; hence he uses human speech and human conceptions. . . . God is indeed free in will; he can reveal himself or not; but

he is not free as to the understanding; he cannot reveal to man whatever he will but only what is adapted to man, what is commensurate with his nature such as it actually is; he reveals what he must reveal, if his revelation is to be a revelation for man. . . . Thus, between the divine revelation and the so-called human reason or nature, there is no other than an illusory distinction; — the contents of the divine revelation are of human origin, for they have proceeded not from God as God, but from God as determined by human reason, human wants, that is, directly from human reason and human wants. And so in revelation man goes out of himself, in order, by a circuitous path, to return to himself! Here we have a striking confirmation of the position that the secret of theology is nothing else than anthropology — the knowledge of God nothing else than a knowledge of man![14]

Modern theologians seek to assert God's prior reality in an intellectual and cultural atmosphere in which that reality is no longer assumed. No only has the theistic consensus collapsed but powerful nontheistic alternatives have been proposed. Modern theologians are confronted not only by the logical possibility of atheism, but by its apparent instantiation in those who claim, with Pascal's interlocutor, "I am so made that I cannot believe."[15] The crisis of revelation has occurred within a cultural context decisively marked by radical pluralism. The modern defender of God's reality must seek to show how God is both in relation and prior to those human concepts by which we seek to grasp his reality. He or she must do so by an argument which resists the reduction of God's priority to his relation, i.e., which avoids the reduction of theology to anthropology. Such arguments must be made in the full recognition that these matters can be conceived otherwise, i.e., that God's reality is not a self-evident assumption of modern or postmodern culture. Ironically, the most prevalent defenses of God's prevenience, those theologies which eschew the term *revelation* but seek to show the necessary religiousness of human existence, are least able to confront the phenomenon of radical atheism.

The most powerful of all such arguments, Schubert Ogden's ingenious defense of the correlative reality of faith and God, asserts that atheism "is not the absence of faith, but the presence of faith in a deficient or distorted mode. It is . . . faith in God in the perverted form of *idolatry*."[16] Ogden and those who follow his lead seek to demonstrate the necessity of faith and of its objective ground, God, thereby showing the logical impossibility of atheism. By defining faith as "our ineradicable confidence in the final worth of our existence" and God as "whatever it is about this experienced whole that calls forth and justifies our original and inescapable trust,"[17] Ogden comes as close as one can to providing an adequate defense of God's prevenience through añ argument for *homo religiosus*. But this approach manifests two deficiencies that cannot be ignored.

First, the argument seeks to cut atheism off at the root by asserting its logical impossibility. Thus the atheist cannot be considered an equal partner in debate whose particular arguments for a nontheistic interpretation of reality and against theism need to be heard and refuted. Rather, the atheist must from the beginning be considered to be a perverted or distorted theist. That is, it seems to me, an odd position for theologians who celebrate cultural pluralism to adopt, for their argument denies the possibility of that phenomenon which lies at the heart of modern pluralism, namely, atheism. An acceptance of radical cultural pluralism seems to demand acknowledgement of the *possibility* that atheism may be the truth about reality.[18] Second, the movement from faith's necessity to God's reality requires, as David Tracy's recent work shows, a transcendental argument which demonstrates "the reality of God as the one necessary existent [who] can validate . . . our primordial and unconquerable basic faith in the ultimate worthwhileness of our existence."[19] It is, I believe, unlikely that such a transcendental argument can be coherently articulated independent of the conceptual flaws of epistemological foundationalism.[20] But even if the problems of foundationalism could be avoided, an argument for God's necessary existence would have to overturn a formidable tradition of philosophical criticism.[21] The prospects for a successful transcendental argument of this sort are dim indeed.

The problem of revelation, i.e., the attempt to assert both the priority and relation of God's reality to our linguistic framework, is not a problem simply for those theologies which rely on traditional language about God's word, speech, or action. It is a problem for all modern theologies which seek to affirm God's prevenience.[22] The key issue remains: how can belief in God's prevenience be justified independent of the conceptual confusions which plague the modern doctrine of revelation? Can that belief be justified in a way which takes seriously the radical pluralism of contemporary culture? Can the intention of the doctrine to affirm the priority of God's grace be salvaged as the epistemological and conceptual confusions of the doctrine are relegated to the theological scrap heap? I am convinced that such a salvage operation is possible only if the incoherence which pervades the modern conception of revelation is recognized and rooted out. I will argue that the fatal flaw which haunts the modern doctrine of revelation (in both its explicit and implicit forms) is the epistemological foundationalism which theologians employ in order to provide the theoretical justification for Christian belief in God's prevenience. This foundationalism, which relies on an incoherent notion of non-inferential intuition as the means of asserting the priority of God's gracious reality, can be seen in theologians as diverse as John Locke, Friedrich Schleiermacher, and Thomas Torrance. The first three chapters of this book attempt to show the pervasive hold foundationalism has on the modern theological mind and to demonstrate the logical incoherence of this conceptuality.

If claims regarding the priority of God's gracious reality are to be rescued from hopeless confusion, they must be separated from the foundational conceptuality. Thus in the succeeding chapters, I offer a nonfoundational view of the theological task (chapter 4) and then seek to show how nonfoundational resources can be used to defend belief in God's prevenience (chapters 5 through 7). Specifically, I will argue that the category of "narrated promise" offers a way of reconceptualizing the Christian doctrine of revelation so that it can display the intelligibility and truth of Christian claims concerning God's relation and priority to our theological framework. A doctrine of revelation ought not be conceived as an epistemological theory but as an account which justifies a set of Christian convictions concerning God's gracious identity and reality. That account is grounded in Christian-specific reasons and arguments but is open to scrutiny by those who stand outside those commitments. Consequently it seeks to demonstrate neither the necessity of Christian theism nor the impossibility of atheism. It does assert the intelligibility and truth of Christian claims and thus invites discussion and debate with other diverse and opposing positions within a pluralistic culture. Such a Christian doctrine of revelation is finally nothing more or less than a reasoned theological account of Christian faith and hope. And that, it seems to me, is decidedly not "a claim that creates more trouble than it is worth."

CHAPTER ONE

The Modern Doctrine of Revelation: Faith Seeking Foundation

The rehabilitation of a doctrine of revelation cannot be undertaken without careful examination of its current malaise. The modern doctrine has developed under the peculiar pressures of the Enlightenment ethos, and its present shape differs considerably from its Reformation predecessor. If the doctrine's malady is located not in its intention to uphold the prevenience of grace but in its incoherent conceptuality, then it is essential to understand the origin of its current form. To do that we must examine the decisive shift in sensibility which occurred between the sixteenth and seventeenth centuries.

Modern theologians have used the notion of revelation to restate in epistemological categories the traditional Christian emphasis on the prevenience of God's grace. The joining of the categories of grace and knowledge may have been a fateful error, especially at a time when epistemology had become a technical philosophical specialty, but the uniting of the two categories is hardly surprising, particularly in Protestant theology. The theme of the prevenience of God's grace predominates in the thought of the reformers, and Calvin particularly stresses the act of God's grace by which he bestows knowledge of himself upon the creature. Though Luther is less prone to stress faith's cognitive aspect, he regularly speaks of God being revealed in Christ and the gospel.[1] Thus it is perfectly natural that modern Protestant theologians, seeking to reassert the prevenience of God's grace, should employ the concept "revelation."

And yet the sixteenth-century idea of revelation cannot simply be repristinated in a post-Enlightenment culture. Calvin speaks of revelation of the knowledge of God in the *Institutes* as part of a larger Reformation program to stress the priority of God's grace in all his dealings with his creatures. Human beings depend for their very lives on God's creating and sustaining grace, and for their growth in love and hope on God's sanctifying grace. Calvin's focus on knowledge of God and revelation simply emphasizes one key aspect of this larger pattern. It would be misleading to say that Calvin offers an epistemology in the *Institutes*, because he has no interest in placing knowledge of God in a general theory of human knowing.[2] He is interested in faith's particular knowledge of God and the fact that all such knowledge is a gift of God's grace. But modern theologians find themselves in a vastly different situation and cannot use the categories of knowledge so easily. Philosophy in the modern era has been fixated on epistemology, and ever since John Locke gave us *An Essay Concerning Human Understanding*,[3] questions about the ground and nature of knowing in general have dominated philosophical discourse.[4] Philosophers, overhearing Christian claims to knowledge of God, have been quick to ask how such knowledge relates to other kinds of knowledge carried in their epistemological kit bags. And theologians have by and large been more than willling to provide appropriate answers.

To provide answers to such epistemological queries involves a much broader approach to questions of knowledge than that characteristic of the Reformation period. Modern theologians have been asked to justify the claim to knowledge of God and to the God-given character of that knowledge with reference to epistemologies developed independent of the Christian faith. Theologians have rightly been reluctant to forego talk of God's grace-given knowledge, not only for the sake of continuity with the Reformation traditions, but because silence on this topic could appear to suggest an unseemly agnosticism. Historically, Christians have without embarrassment spoken of knowledge of God, and the mere fact of the emergence of secular epistemologies has seemed to most theologians insufficient provocation to warrant silence about such matters. Rather, theology has taken on the additional task of showing how such language is warranted with reference to the reigning epistemology of the day. That has often involved criticism and/or expansion of such a theory to allow the inclusion of theological claims to knowledge, but the revisions in the theory have been made, so theologians claim, without contradicting the theory's basic principles.

Modern doctrines of revelation have thus become in part theoretical justifications for the Christian claim to knowledge of God. While that task can be seen as continuing the Reformation emphasis on the primacy of God's grace, the modern doctrine has departed from the sixteenth-century conception of revelation in at least one decisive way. The reformers did not attempt to demonstrate that knowledge of God is a gift of God's grace; they simply assumed that it was the case. This shift from assumption to argument may be slight, but it is not trivial. Calvin writes in the *Institutes*,

> There is within the human mind, and indeed by natural instinct, an awareness of divinity. . . . God himself has implanted in all men a certain understanding of his divine majesty. . . . Men one and all perceive that there is a God and that he is their Maker.[5]

This position, Calvin asserts, "we take to be beyond controversy."[6] That all human beings possess a knowledge of God is assumed; the theological task is to explicate the content of that knowledge. In the course of that explication it is common for pre-modern theologians to distinguish between truths known to reason (natural knowledge) and truths known by revelation (saving knowledge). But the reason/revelation contrast does not distinguish those things known independent of grace from those known through the gift of grace. The reason/revelation distinction simply contrasts the knowledge of God implanted by God's grace in all of his creatures and that saving knowledge which comes only by the testimony of the Spirit through scripture. The unassailable axiom of the entire discussion is that *all* human knowledge is a gift of God's grace.

The belief that all knowledge of God is given by God functions for the reformers as a basic conviction or background belief.[7] Every coherent system of belief rests upon certain convictions which are assumed to be true and thus provide stability for the whole framework. These beliefs are *basic* because the coherence of many other beliefs depends on the acceptance of these beliefs as true, and they are *background* because their axiomatic status makes explicit justification of them unnecessary. While these background beliefs are not immune to revision, they must remain relatively fixed in order for the framework to remain stable. Revision or suspension of a background belief requires a rearrangement of all dependent beliefs and possible rejection of some. Calvin can speak of God's gracious implanting of knowledge of his majesty in his creatures as "beyond controversy" precisely because it functions as a background belief.

In modern doctrines of revelation the reformers' basic conviction regarding the prevenience of God's grace no longer functions as a background belief. The shift from assumption to argument indicates that the belief that knowledge of God is given by God loses its axiomatic status. It becomes a dependent belief which must be justified in relation to new basic convictions independent of the Christian faith. While this change in status is clearly evident at the end of the eighteenth century when Kant writes *Religion Within the Limits of Reason Alone*,[8] it is already anticipated at the beginning of the seventeenth century in Descartes's *Meditations*.[9]

Descartes obviously holds many beliefs in common with the reformers, particularly regarding the God-given character of our knowledge of God. In his introductory letter to the theological faculty of Paris he writes:

> It is absolutely true, both that we must believe that there is a God because it is taught in the Holy Scriptures, and, on the other hand, that we must believe the Holy Scriptures because they come from God. The reason for this is that faith is a gift of God, and the very God that gives us the faith to believe other things can also give us the faith to believe that he exists.[10]

Had he concluded his comments here Descartes could easily be read as a medieval or Reformation theologian. But he goes on to say:

> Nevertheless, we could hardly offer this argument to those without faith, for they might suppose that we were committing the fallacy that logicians call circular reasoning. . . . For although it may suffice us faithful ones to believe by faith that there is a God and that the human soul does not perish with the body, certainly it does not seem possible ever to persuade those without faith to accept any religion, nor even perhaps any moral virtue, unless they can first be shown these two things by means of natural reason.[11]

Descartes is not simply offering a seventeenth-century variation of a traditional apologetic strategy. The rational demonstration to those without faith is not an adjunct to the theological task but, with reference to God and the soul, its replacement. These two principal questions, he argues, "should be demonstrated by rational philosophy rather than theology."[12] Descartes's pattern of argument clearly indicates that for him the God-given nature of our knowledge of God is no longer a background belief but a dependent belief which is justified in relation to a more basic conviction.

Descartes believes that human beings are so dependent upon God the "supreme and perfect Being" that "everything in us necessarily comes from him."[13] This bold assertion of human dependence upon God is, however, surely not "beyond controversy." It is the conclusion of an involved rational argument warranted by beliefs more basic than the conclusion itself. Descartes draws his conclusion about human dependence only after he has demonstrated both his own existence as "a thing that thinks"[14] and God's existence as the source and ground of his idea of God.[15] The arguments for God's existence and human dependence upon God cannot be generated at all without the prior argument concerning the existence of the ego. Descartes's epistemological vertigo induced by his methodic doubt[16] is not eliminated until he has established the one indubitable foundational proposition, "I think therefore I am." That necessary truth is logically prior to the argument for God's existence, an argument which begins with the premise that among the ideas the thinking thing possesses is the idea of God. The argument proceeds to its conclusion via the distinction between formal and objective reality and an argument from causality, but the most important observation for our purposes is that the argument could not begin at all without the establishment of the ego's necessary existence. That necessary truth constitutes the essential background belief, the "general principle that everything we conceive very clearly and very distinctly is wholly true."[17]

Descartes's belief in the ontological priority of God's being is justified by an argument in which logical priority is granted to a claim concerning the human self. In the *ordo essendi* the prevenience of God's being is asserted, but that assertion is justified by a more basic conviction within the *ordo cognoscendi*. Moreover, the *ordo cognoscendi* is ruled by a general epistemological principle derived from the basic conviction concerning the ego's necessary existence. While Descartes affirms with the reformers the belief that our knowledge of God derives from God, the logical function he assigns to that belief is decisively different. Its justification depends on its inferential connection to general background principles which apply to all ostensible claims to truth. That conviction can no longer be assumed to be true, i.e., it can no longer function as a background belief; its truth must be demonstrated in relation to more fundamental convictions about human reason.

Note also the change in status of the reigning background belief. The conviction concerning God's prevenience functioned axiomatically in the Reformation because all parties in the Reformation disputes accepted the belief as true. Beginning with Descartes, however, the essential background belief, e.g., any clear and distinct idea is necessarily true, has axiomatic status not by virtue of its universal acceptance, but because it is established by a universal and necessary argument. Thus there is an important readjustment in the relation of a claim to truth, the arguments in support of that claim, and communal acceptance of the claim. While the reformers could accept a claim as true simply because it was widely accepted as true in the community, Descartes and his successors insisted that claims to truth must ultimately be grounded in necessarily true arguments. For modern thinkers communal acceptance must always follow philosophical demonstration. A faith which assumes the truth of its background beliefs and seeks simply to understand them cannot flourish in an atmosphere which demands justification prior to belief. Under these changed modern circumstances faith seeking understanding inevitably becomes faith seeking foundation.

The shift in the logical status of background beliefs, and particularly the belief in God's prevenience, has enormous consequences for modern doctrines of revelation. When the assertion of God's prevenience functions as a background belief, a doctrine of revelation simply explicates the content of that knowledge given by God's grace. Issues concerning the possibility or actuality of God's revelation simply do not arise, because theologians begin from the "givenness" of our knowledge of God. But when the assertion becomes a dependent belief justifiable by general epistemological principles, its apparent self-evidence dissolves. Claims about knowledge of God must be demonstrated to be in accord with (or at least not contrary to) the ruling epistemological theory. In light of that demand, doctrines of revelation must do more than simply explicate the content of a "given" revelation; they must justify both the content of particular claims to knowledge and the prior assertion that these claims are given by God. Not only must each particular assertion pass muster before the epistemological theory, but the very possibility of the idea of knowledge of God must be justified by such general principles. While that idea may possess *prima facie* plausibility in a Cartesian world populated by innate ideas and disembodied egos, it becomes considerably more problematic in an epistemology grounded in perception and sensible intuition.

Given the enormity of the task presented to modern doctrines of revelation, it is remarkable how many theologians have attempted to meet the demand. In the following chapter I will examine three distinctive religious thinkers and their attempts to formulate doctrines of revelation. Though they differ decisively on many issues, John Locke, Friedrich Schleiermacher, and Thomas Torrance all exemplify the standard procedures adopted by modern theologians in reformulating doctrines of revelation.[18] Each theologian 1) follows Descartes rather than the reformers in construing claims to knowledge of God not as axiomatic background beliefs but as dependent beliefs in need of justification, 2) adopts a foundational epistemological theory to justify the possibility of revelation, and 3) employs the notion of "intuition" to justify the claim that knowledge of God is a gift of God's grace. The apologetic strategy exemplified by these three procedures has lead to the confusing impasse which plagues current discussions of revelation. Clarity on this matter will not be forthcoming until the claim concerning God's prevenient grace is separated from the incoherent conceptuality within which most modern doctrines of revelation are framed.

CHAPTER TWO

Revelation and Reasonableness: Three Case Studies

In order to justify Christian claims to revelation modern theologians have commonly adopted a dual strategy. Following the Cartesian pattern, they have assumed that claims to revelation must be "reasonable," at least in the sense of not being contrary to reason, if theologians are to avoid the charge of "special pleading." On the other hand, they have argued that revelation designates a special category of truths undergirded by a unique mode of knowing. Truths of revelation are distinctive because they cannot be known through ordinary uses of reason. The justification of Christian claims to knowledge of God depends upon an argument which shows both the similarity and dissimilarity between the content of revelation and the content of ordinary knowledge as discerned through the use of reason.

Such arguments require unusual intellectual dexterity, for two limiting dangers constantly threaten the coherence of the argument. The theologian must assert just enough distinctiveness to establish the irreducibility of Christian claims and sufficient similarity to guard against the charge of irrationality or unintelligibility. The precariousness of the task has been enough to challenge the most dexterous dialectician, and such arguments, no matter how skillfully drawn, have rarely survived rigorous scrutiny. The fragile balance between distinctiveness and similarity has been almost impossible to maintain, and arguments for revelation regularly succumb to one of the two limiting dangers. Theologians who are primarily concerned to guard the distinctiveness of revelation are commonly forced to adopt arguments which assert revelation's absolute uniqueness. They are then hard pressed to show how a unique content discerned by a unique mode of knowing can be justified with reference to an ordinary philosophical epistemology. Revelation is gained in such positions at the expense of reasonableness. Theologians who, by contrast, strive to show the consistent conformability of revelation to reason commonly deny the distinctiveness of the very claims they set out to justify. If Christian beliefs can be fully justified by a philosophical theory of knowledge, it is no longer clear that the claim to revelation is warranted. Revelation connotes a uniqueness in source and content which cannot be maintained in a position fully justified by general epistemological principles.

The enormous difficulties facing the modern doctrine of revelation are clearly exemplified in the thought of the father of this apologetic strategy, John Locke. Locke not only founded the discipline of epistemology; he also formulated the classical strategy for defending Christian claims to revelation in the modern era. His inability to maintain a distinctive role for truths of revelation in light of his own epistemology presages the difficulties faced by virtually every modern doctrine of revelation in the succeeding three centuries.

John Locke: The Fragile Case for Revelation

> *Reason*, therefore, here, as contradistinguished to *faith* I take to be the discovery of the certainty or probability of such propositions or truths, which the mind arrives at by deduction made from such ideas, which it has got by the use of its natural faculties; viz. by sensation or reflection.
>
> *Faith*, on the other side, is the assent to any proposition, not thus made out by the deductions of reason, but upon the credit of the proposer, as coming from God, in some extraordinary way of communication. This way of discovering truths to men, we call *revelation*.[1]

In this famous passage from the *Essay Concerning Human Understanding* Locke distinguishes truths of revelation from truths of reason as the first step in an argument by which he hopes to demonstrate the reasonableness of revelation. Locke had earlier stated that revealed truths are "above reason" and thus differ in kind from truths "according to reason" (p. 413). The two kinds of truths differ in three basic ways. They stem from dissimilar sources (sense ideas/God's "extraordinary way of communication"); they are grasped by different mental processes (the deductions of reason/accepting the credit of the proposer); and they elicit distinctive kinds of assent (certainty or probability/mere assent). Reason cannot discover the truths of faith, nor justify them by deduction.

This sharp separation of the truths of faith and reason can work to faith's advantage as long as reason is considered the inferior faculty. But Locke clearly believes reason to be the central human faculty, "Our last judge and guide in everything" (p. 438). Consequently, he must *justify* his claim that the truths of faith are both above reason and worthy of our assent. That is no easy task, for according to Locke's own principles such truths are not so much "above reason" as "beyond knowledge," for "whatever comes short of [intuition or demonstration] . . . is but of *faith* or *opinion*, but not knowledge" (p. 185). Faith is thus an assent given to propositions which are at best probable.

> Probability is likeliness to be true. . . . The entertainment the mind gives this sort of proposition is called *belief, assent,* or *opinion* which is the admitting or receiving any proposition for true . . . without certain knowledge that it is so. And herein lies the difference between *probability* and *certainty, faith* and *knowledge,* that in all the parts of knowledge there is intuition; each immediate idea, each step has its visible and certain connexion; in belief not so. (p 365)

Given his equation of faith and opinion, Locke's designation of revelation as "above reason" seems misleading. Belief, assent, and opinion might more accurately be categorized as "below reason," since they fall short of "true and certain knowledge." Locke makes this point himself when he analyzes the religious belief in finite spirits or angels. Although revelation teaches that angels exist, we cannot know they exist, because our senses cannot discover them. "For however true it may be, v.g., that all the intelligent spirits that God ever created do still exist, yet it can never make a part of our certain knowledge. These and like propositions we may assent to, as highly probable, but are not, I fear, in this state capable of knowing" (pp. 337–338). Revelation thus communicates truths which, being beyond reason, cannot be known with certainty. Revelation on Locke's account cannot communicate *knowledge* of God. Insofar as the preposition "above" implies that truths of faith are of a higher order than the truths of reason, the phrase "above reason" seems unwarranted on Locke's own epistemological principles.

Locke appears to have provided a very modest justification for revelation. Given the empirical basis of his epistemology and his high regard for intuition and deduction as guides to certain knowledge, revelation must be barred access from the realm of knowledge. Yet

he insists that revelation bears truth, and that we are justified in giving our assent to its propositions. But on what ground? "A firm assent of the mind," Locke argues, "which, if it be regulated, as is our
duty, cannot be afforded to anything but upon good reason" (p. 413).
What good reason have we to assent to the truth of a revelation which
can at best be shown to be probable? If we apportion our assent to
the degree of evidence, then faith ought to be most qualified and tentative, hardly "a firm assent of the mind." Yet Locke asserts that "faith
is a settled and sure principle of assent and assurance, and leaves no
manner of room for doubt or hesitation. . . . It [is] nothing else but
an assent founded on the highest reason" (pp. 383–384).

Locke finds himself faced by a tangled epistemological problem
of his own making. He wants to assert the irreducible uniqueness of
revealed truths, while also claiming that reason is warranted in assenting firmly to them. But his argument for revelation's uniqueness has
robbed reason of its ordinary grounds for granting assent. If his position is to escape the charge of utter incoherence, Locke must provide
other grounds which will replace the intuition and deduction that usually guide reason's firm assent. He attempts to do this with the key
notion of "the credit of the proposer, as coming from God." Since
the pattern of deduction characteristic of rational demonstration is not
available to faith, faith's assurance must rest upon the conviction that
a belief or proposition comes from God. But that conviction itself,
Locke asserts, must be guided and justified by the deliberations of
reason. Locke is acutely aware of the dangers of enthusiasm, the belief
that "whatever groundless opinion comes to settle itself strongly upon
[one's] fancies is an illumination from the Spirit of God" (p. 432).
The key question guiding reason's deliberation is "How do I know that
God is the revealer of this to me; that this impression is made upon
my mind by his Holy Spirit; and that therefore I ought to obey it?"
(p. 435). One cannot simply appeal to the strength of one's conviction as the warrant for assent, for reason's assent must be grounded
on "nothing else but the evidence of the truth of any proposition,"
(pp. 436–437) and its assurance can be no greater "than the proofs
it is built upon will warrant" (p. 429).

The appeal to "the credit of the proposer" has hardly assisted Locke
in solving his dilemma. The truths of faith lack rational certainty
because they are neither self-evidently true nor deducible from premises
known to be self-evident. Yet reason is justified in assenting to such

a truth, *if* it knows that the truth is revealed by God. A proposition must manifest its truth "either by its own self-evidence to reason, or by the rational proofs that make it out to be so" (pp. 436–437). But Locke has already argued that self-evidence and proof are by definition not available to truths of faith. Therefore it appears that reason can never know if a truth comes from God, and thus can never properly assent to an ostensible truth of faith.

Locke attempts to rescue his argument for revelation by an appeal to God's "extraordinary way of communication," i.e., by an appeal to miracles. The truth of a revealed proposition cannot be established by the inner light of one's own conviction, but it can be established "by some marks which reason cannot be mistaken in" (p. 438), i.e., by the external visible signs which God provides to vouch for his revelation. Locke's treatment of miracles in the *Essay* is strikingly brief and undeveloped, given the weight an appeal to miracle bears in his argument for revelation.[2] Reason is warranted, he claims, in assenting to a proposition as a revelation from God if the proposition manifests the power of God as confirmed by external signs. Miracles attest to the credit of the proposer and confirm that the proposer's testimony comes from God. Where an ostensible revelation is confirmed by miracle, reason ought to give its assent to such a proposition as coming from God.

> The holy men of old, who had revelations from God, had something else besides that internal light of assurance in their own minds, to testify to them that it was from God. They were not left to their own persuasions alone, that those persuasions were from God, but had *outward signs* to convince them of the Author of those revelations. And when they were to convince others, they had a power given them to justify the truth of their commission from heaven, and by visible signs to assert the divine authority of a message they were sent with. (p. 439)

If this argument had come from the hand of Hume a century later, we might well suspect that this conclusion was meant to be ironic, because it appears to undermine the very truth it purports to demonstrate. A proposition is to be accepted as a revelation of God if and only if it is accompanied by miraculous signs. That demand seems reasonable enough when applied to the "original revelation" as received and transmitted by the prophets and apostles. Moses and Gideon received miraculous confirmation that their commissions truly came from God. They in turn provided miraculous signs to convince others of their divine authority. Thus Moses, Gideon, and the people of Israel were warranted in receiving the propositions given to them as divine revelation. But that original situation is irrelevant for the question Locke poses so sharply. The issue is not how "the holy men of old" discerned God's revelation, but how the present generation is to recognize a proposition as coming from God. Locke's argument from miracles applies only if the Anglican divine is expected to provide an extraordinary sign during the public reading of Scripture! Locke surely cannot have expected that, so either his appeal to miracle fails to rescue his argument or he must rest his case, as he sometimes does, on an unexamined assumption that Scripture as word of God "is attested revelation . . . and we may safely receive it for true" (p. 439). Either way the argument is insufficient to meet reason's demand for "marks which reason cannot be mistaken in."

Locke's dilemma is a familiar one. Having drawn a principled distinction between truths of reason and truths of revelation, he is unable to provide a convincing argument in support of reason's assent to faith's ostensible truths, and he falls dramatically short of supporting his claim that faith is "an assent founded on the highest reason." Locke's failure might not have been so striking had he developed hints in the *Essay* and in other writings that reason's assent to revelation might be guided by signs other than those provided by miracles. Miracles, Locke argues at one point, "do not only find credit themselves, but give it also to *other truths which need such confirmation*" (p. 382). Are there truths which can be received as revelation on their own account without the external confirmation of miracles? Apparently so, though he speaks of them only briefly and enigmatically.

> There is one sort of propositions that challenge [sic] the highest degree of our assent, *upon bare testimony*. . . . The reason whereof is, because the testimony is of such an one as cannot deceive nor be deceived: and that is of God himself. This carries with it an assurance beyond doubt, evidence beyond exception. This is called by a peculiar name, *revelation*, and our assent to it, *faith*, which as absolutely determines our minds and as perfectly excludes all wavering as our knowledge itself. . . . *Only we must be sure that it be a divine revelation, and that we under-*

stand it right: Else we shall expose ourselves to all the extravagancy of enthusiasm. . . . Our assent can be rationally no higher than the evidence of its being a revelation. (p. 383, first emphasis added)

What are these propositions which convince us that they come from God "upon bare testimony?" What marks show us "the evidence of its being a revelation?" No clear answer is forthcoming in the rest of the *Essay*. Locke provides criteria which eliminate purported claims to revelation. "No man inspired by God can by any revelation communicate to others any new simple ideas which they had not before from sensation or reflection. . . . No proposition can be received for divine revelation . . . if it be contradictory to our clear intuitive knowledge" (pp. 416, 420–421). He also argues that "revelation, where God has been pleased to give it, must carry against the probable conjecture of reason" (p. 423). But he never provides a fuller account of how *we* can recognize when God is pleased to give us revelation.

One notion which Locke mentions but does not develop in his account of revelation is the idea of "power" or "authority."[3] The prophets "had a power given them to justify the truth of their commission from heaven" (p. 439), a power confirmed by visible signs. Locke seems to toy with the idea that some propositions possess an inherent power to convince. Thus he argues in *A Third Letter Concerning Toleration* that "true religion is able to prevail now, as it did at first, and has done since, in many places, without assistance from the [political] powers in being, *by its own beauty, force, and reasonableness.*"[4] Scripture in particular possesses that inherent ability to persuade independent of the external force of governments or the confirming presence of miracles. Locke appears to be seeking an argument which will establish a form of religious intuition, an assent given to a proposition "upon bare testimony" due to its own "beauty, force, and reasonableness." The ground of assent would not be (contra enthusiasm) the firmness of the conviction but the irresistibility of the proposition's truth. Such truths would be "above reason" in a way similar to intuitive sense knowledge, of which Locke says, "In the discovery of and assent to these truths, there is no use of the discursive faculty, *no need of reasoning*, but they are known by a superior and higher degree of evidence" (p. 407). If Locke had made an argument for the presence of this religious intuition, then his claim that truths of faith are "above reason" would have had much stronger support. But he never explicitly makes such an argument, and consequently his assertion of faith's firm and reasonable assent remains unwarranted.

One can surmise that Locke's deep mistrust of enthusiasm kept him from developing the idea that faith is an organ of religious intuition. Locke consistently understands faith as *reason's* assent to propositions revealed by God. If the implicit argument regarding religious intuition is patient of elaboration, it must be expanded with reference to the luminous object and not to the perceiving subject. The philosopher can either present a general argument designating the indubitable marks of the self-evident religious object or simply display the beauty, force, and reasonableness of a particular religion and trust that the intuitive firm assent will be forthcoming. Locke adopts the latter strategy in *The Reasonableness of Christianity*. Christian scripture, he argues implicitly, is reasonable in that it does not violate the negative criteria for revelation and should thus "carry against the probable conjectures of reason." But most importantly the reasonableness of Christianity is shown by its inherent beauty and force which immediately call forth our highest degree of assent.

If this reconstruction of Locke's implied argument is correct, then *The Reasonableness of Christianity* should be seen as Locke's attempt to display the inherent power of Christian Scripture in order to elicit the reader's immediate and firm assent to its truth.[5] Despite the ingenuity of this approach and its clear superiority to the argument from miracles, it too falls short of meeting Locke's own criteria for recognizing a proposition as revelatory. The difference between an immediate recognition of the color yellow and a similar recognition of scripture's divine origin is obvious. It is difficult to conceive of an effective argument in support of scripture's luminous self-evidence. Should such an argument be logically possible, Locke surely does not provide it either in the *Essay* or in *Reasonableness*.

But without that argument or a more general account of religious intuition, it is impossible for Locke to sustain his high view of revelation and of the reasonableness of reason's assent to it. Without these arguments revelation appears on Locke's own account to be a collection of opinions, based on ancient and unreliable testimony, eliciting the most qualified and tentative assent. Locke's assertion of revelation's uniqueness, set against the demands of his own epistemology, renders his argument for its reasonableness impotent. The fragile structure of the claim to revelation consequently collapses under the pressures of his own theory of knowledge.[6] His failure to demonstrate both the uniqueness and reasonableness of revelation is not simply the result of faulty execution. The demands of the task are so great that a doctrine which seeks to satisfy those demands inevitably drifts toward incoherence.

Locke's struggle to formulate a doctrine of revelation is significant because it anticipates the more mature doctrines which appear in the nineteenth and twentieth centuries. Locke's successors reaffirm his intention to provide a rational justification of the Christian claim to revelation by appealing to the distinctive origin of Christian beliefs and the distinctive process by which they are known. Moreover, they seek to complete the argument for religious intuition which Locke executes only in part. The irony of the subsequent history is that the completion of Locke's task creates a new set of insoluble logical puzzles for the doctrine's formulators. Locke's general epistemology is built upon a foundation of ostensibly self-evident sense intuitions, but his religious thought makes only the most tentative moves toward a foundation in religious intuition. Nineteenth- and twentieth-century theologians complete the move to religious foundationalism, but in so doing they demonstrate that the foundational strategy for upholding the uniqueness and reasonableness of revelation simply does not work. Locke's tentativeness about religious intuition, motivated by his fears of enthusiasm, introduces intolerable tension into his thought, but those reservations, seen in light of the ensuing development of the concept revelation, appear to be the product of a wise and sensible mind.

Friedrich Schleiermacher: Revelation as Universal Religious Experience

John Locke's case for revelation, despite its ultimate failure, provides the pattern which most modern doctrines of revelation have emulated. Locke sets out to provide a theoretical justification for the Christian claim to revelation but falls considerably short of his goal. The classic formulation of the modern doctrine is not achieved until the beginning of the nineteenth century in the theology of Friedrich Schleiermacher. In the intervening century Immanuel Kant had sharply

challenged the intelligibility of all claims to knowledge of God by arguing that the scope of knowledge is limited by the mind's categorial
structure and its interaction with the sensible manifold.[7] The idea of
God, the transcendental ideal, is the highest and most inclusive idea
the mind can form, but it is a purely regulative concept which guides
the mind's movement toward conceptual generality and universality.
The transcendental ideal cannot be made the object of human knowledge, nor can we know whether it corresponds to an existent transcendent being. God lies beyond the limits of human knowledge.

One might have expected Kant's first critique to have stunted
the development of doctrines of revelation; in fact the doctrine has
flourished in the intellectual atmosphere permeated by Kant's challenge
to knowledge of God. In light of the Kantian critique a theoretical
justification for the Christian claim to revelation has seemed all the
more important. Since Kant challenged the possibility of knowledge
of God, the theologian's most pressing task has become the development of an argument defending the possibility of revelation. Modern
theologians have often been willing to concede Kant his victory over
knowledge of God, but they have worked all the harder to demonstrate
the possibility and actuality of God's revelation. This separation between knowledge of God and revelation is anticipated in Locke's pioneering work. Locke uses the term *revelation* to designate the divine
source of the truths of faith, even though he denies that those truths
yield knowledge. Schleiermacher and his successors follow Locke's lead
in attempting to demonstrate the possibility of human access to God's
revelation, while denying that revelation grants knowledge of God.

The modern doctrine of revelation in its classic post-Kantian form
attempts to provide a theoretical justification for revelation by formulating a universally valid argument for a unique mode of access to God's
reality. Schleiermacher is clearly the father of the mature modern doctrine, and his account of revelation marks the pinnacle of achievement
in this tradition. Schleiermacher's turn to human consciousness as the
locus for God's revelation uncovers a rich terrain which theologians
are still plowing in search of an argument demonstrating the possibility
of that revelation. Schleiermacher's argument for revelation exhibits
the elements which have become the standard components of the
modern doctrine. Beginning from the particular content of the Christian self-consciousness he attempts to show that Christian beliefs are

grounded in a deeper universal form of human self-consciousness. Christian revelation is ultimately validated by an intuitive universal religious experience.

Schleiermacher shares with Locke the conviction that Christian revelation, though distinctive, does not violate the basic standards of rationality. In contrast to Locke, however, Schleiermacher does not insist that revelation has a *unique* source and content, and thus he softens the sharp contrast between reason and revelation which ultimately undermines Locke's position.[8] Schleiermacher's belief in the basic compatibility of Christian faith and rational inquiry[9] shows itself in his treatment of revelation. "The appearance of the Redeemer in history is, as divine revelation, neither an absolutely supernatural nor an absolutely supra-rational thing" (p. 62). The word *revelation* signifies the distinctive origin of a religious community's beliefs, i.e., "there is an inner experience to which they may all be traced; they rest upon a *given*; and apart from this they could not have arisen, by deduction or synthesis, from universally recognized and communicable propositions" (p. 67). Because Christian beliefs arise from a distinctive inner experience, it is proper to use the word *revelation* to denote "a divine communication and declaration" (p. 50). But the initiating divine act always works through means which are fully natural and rational.

Schleiermacher's insistence on the natural and rational means of revelation is especially important for his understanding of Christ's role as redeemer. Since Christ redeems humanity by sharing his perfectly regnant God-consciousness, "there must reside in human nature the possibility of taking up the divine into itself, just as did happen in Christ" (p. 64). Schleiermacher readily admits that "the actual implanting therein of the divine element must be purely a divine and therefore an eternal act" (p. 64), but the implanting could not take place at all without the prior human capacity or possibility. Revelation is thus given to consciousness by divine initiative, but it is received by consciousness in a way conformable to the universal structure of human nature. With regard to its origin revelation is supernatural and supra-rational;[10] with regard to its reception revelation actualizes a universal human possibility.

Schleiermacher's formal discussion of revelation does little more than formulate a negative rule for eliminating spurious claims to revelation. Whatever can be deduced from universal propositions or fully understood by historical explanation cannot be a revelation. On the other hand, revelation cannot violate the ordinary canons of rationality; once it is given it must be comprehended by natural human capacities. The key characteristic of revelation, then, is that it originates from a divine source and thus could not have been discovered by natural means. "The idea of revelation signifies the *originality* of the fact which lies at the foundation of a religious communion, in the sense that this fact . . . cannot in turn be explained by the historical chain which precedes it" (p. 50).[11] In order for this definition of revelation to be plausible Schleiermacher must give a fuller account of the marks which specify an experience as stemming from a divine origin.

Schleiermacher attempts to give such an account by appealing to the peculiar quality of a divinely originating experience. Nonrevelatory experiences are apprehended by ordinary means of knowing. We synthesize new experiences through the normal categories which regulate our knowledge and action. The new becomes familiar through an inferential extension of our previous ordinary experience. There is nothing revelatory in this ordinary expansion of our experience.[12] Revelation, by contrast, occurs when we have an immediate experience of an other which we apprehend not inferentially but directly. Revelation can "only be apprehended . . . as a moment of the life of a thinking being who acts upon us directly as a distinctive existence by means of his total impression on us" (p. 50). Revelation is a self-conscious experience, but it does not directly engage our knowing and doing but our self-conscious states of feeling, i.e., our *immediate* self-consciousness.

Schleiermacher's defense of revelation rests upon his famous argument for absolute dependence in paragraph 4 of *The Christian Faith*.[13] The pattern of his argument in this crucial paragraph reduplicates the distinctions and principles which guide his overall conception of revelation. He sets out to ground his belief in Christian revelation in an argument which demonstrates that the possibility of an innate God-relation is *plausible* because it is a particular expression of a universal human *possibility*. Schleiermacher surely does not set out to demonstrate the truth of Christian revelation; nor does he deduce the content of Christian self-consciousness from a philosophically derived universal religious self-consciousness.[14] He begins from the particular content of Christian beliefs and attempts to discern the universal structure of consciousness which underlies those beliefs. In his second letter to Dr. Lücke, Schleiermacher defends himself against the charge "that I try to explain Christian piety on the basis of a universal human consciousness of piety." The correct statement of his position is that "I try to specify the distinctive place Christianity occupies among the various modifications of that common consciousness."[15] Nonetheless, the plausibility of the Christian claim to revelation in both its supra-rational and rational dimensions rests on the success of the argument which demonstrates the very possibility of God-consciousness.

> The common element in all howsoever diverse expressions of piety . . . or, in other words, the self-identical essence of piety, is this: the consciousness of being absolutely dependent, or, which is the same thing, of being in relation to God. (p.12)

Using the resources of philosophical theology[16] Schleiermacher seeks to discover "the self-identical essence of piety"from among its "diverse expressions" within Christianity and other historical religions. He does this by an analysis of the two coexisting elements of all human self-consciousness, receptivity and activity. In all finite moments of existence we experience receptivity and activity in reciprocal relation, i.e., we experience ourselves as simultaneously dependent and free. We can have no sense of absolute freedom because we always experience ourselves in relation to an other given to us. Nor do we have an experience in any finite moment of absolute dependence, for we are always aware of our reciprocal response to the other, even if our response is limited to mere acknowledgement. But when we consider the totality of our active and passive existence we are struck by "a consciousness of absolute dependence . . . the consciousness that the whole of our spontaneous activity comes from a source outside us" (p. 16). That source is, of course, no finite object or person, but God—"the Whence of our receptive and active existence" (p. 16). Human nature is in its basic universal structure related to God.

Though he begins with the particulars of Christian belief and of Christian self-consciousness, Schleiermacher claims to have discerned the formal, universal, precognitive shape of piety-as-such, prior to its combination with particular historical or cultural elements.[17] In historical experience the universal God-consciousness is always linked to some particular which gives each religious community its peculiar identity, but the essential shape of piety, the experience of absolute dependence, remains the same. That experience is one of feeling or immediate self-consciousness, and cannot be grasped under the ordinary categories which shape knowing and doing. The feeling of absolute dependence removes one from the world of particular times and places, of distinct subjects and objects, and allows an immediate relation to God through the transparent tissue of feeling. Because immediate self-consciousness is beyond knowledge and action, it is precognitive. Once it is schematized through ordinary concepts it loses its pristine quality.[18]

The Christian claim to revelation rests finally on the authenticity of the feeling of absolute dependence. If such a feeling is a universal human possibility, then talk of an original experience not reducible to ordinary categories is warranted, and the Christian claim to such revelation is rendered plausible. Schleiermacher does not take the Christian claim to revelation to be "beyond controversy"; its plausibility must be shown by an appeal to a formal, universal, precognitive form of experience which serves as the logical foundation for the particular Christian claim. Moreover, the foundational belief is established by an appeal to religious intuition, a self-authenticating claim to immediate self-consciousness. The immediacy of the feeling of absolute dependence establishes its extra-ordinary character, its divine origin. Like the reformers, Schleiermacher believes that our relation to God is given by God's grace, but he feels compelled to defend that conviction by arguing *first* that the God-relation is a universal element of human nature and *second* that the grace-given character of the relation is established by the marks of immediacy. The argument from absolute dependence is Schleiermacher's attempt to put the Christian belief in the prevenience of God's grace on a firmer universal footing.

Does Schleiermacher's appeal to the feeling of absolute dependence provide sufficient justification for the Christian claim to revelation? Schleiermacher's case for revelation depends on three closely interrelated claims. 1) The distinction between inferential and non-inferential experiences and beliefs (e.g., between immediate and non-immediate states of consciousness) is justified. 2) Non-inferential experiences are direct, immediate, and thus self-authenticating. 3) The feeling of absolute dependence as an immediate non-inferential experience is a self-authenticating experience of God. Schleiermacher defends the first claim at length in the Second Speech[19] and more briefly in paragraph 3 of *The Christian Faith*.[20] The division between feeling and knowing/doing depends on the non-inferential/inferential distinction. The second claim is established in his discussion of feeling as immediate self-consciousness and by the logic of his argument in paragraph 4. The third claim is implied in his equation of absolute dependence and relation to God. The relation to God is not inferred from a prior experience of absolute dependence but is given directly in the experience.

The distinction between inferential and non-inferential beliefs is difficult either to establish or overturn as a general distinction.[21] One must simply analyze and evaluate the arguments and evidence brought forward in support of the more obscure category—the non-inferential beliefs. Schleiermacher attempts to establish such beliefs by referring to peculiar qualities of the experience which generates the beliefs, i.e., their direct, immediate, and self-authenticating qualities. "Piety is immediate, raised above all error and misunderstanding. . . . All is immediately true in religion."[22] Schleiermacher's insistence that feeling is a realm which transcends the distinction between true and false because in piety "all is immediately true," is an argument for the self-evident truth of immediate experience. But how is the self-evidence or indubitability of an experience to be established? As Locke clearly saw, the mere fervor of the experience is hardly an infallible guide to its meaning. We are rarely infallible interpreters of our own feelings, as we regularly mistake a passing depression for *Weltschmerz* or momentary lust for authentic affection. Schleiermacher would undoubtedly argue that immediate self-consciousness differs in kind from such superficial and dubitable experiences, but until he gives us a clearer account of the characteristics which mark the experience as self-evident, we are justified in withholding our assent. Unless we are *aware of* and *in control of* all conditions which might introduce discrepancies between the apparent and real nature of an experience, we cannot claim that the experience is indubitable. Schleiermacher does not give us a sufficiently complete account of immediate self-consciousness to convince us of its self-evidence and indubitability. My statement "I am having an experience of absolute dependence" cannot be an indubitable self-evident claim based on the account Schleiermacher gives us. If the statement were reformulated to read, "I seem to be having an experience of absolute dependence" it might gain indubitability as a report about my "seeming" but not as a report about the experience itself.

Even if these objections were answered, they still point to an insoluble problem in Schleiermacher's position. What warrants his identification of the experience of absolute dependence with an experience of God? What warrants the move from a self-referential claim to a referential claim concerning a distinct other? Schleiermacher appears to have only two options available to him. Either he must insist that the immediately self-conscious self is God, and thus to recognize one is perforce to recognize the other, or he must provide some "identification procedures"[23] by which to distinguish God and the self and which warrant the mind's movement from one to the other. In his first letter to Lücke Schleiermacher reacts with horror to the suggestion that he equates God and the self (or even that the consciousness of God implies that God is "in" the self).[24] Rather he is asserting "a common inner experience"[25] which is "an immediate existential relation"[26] between the self and God. But Schleiermacher never clearly indicates how one distinguishes between an experience of the self's relationship to itself and the self's relationship to God. The mere invocation of self-authentification or self-evidence will not do. That an experience of absolute dependence is an experience of God is a judgment which must be warranted. Appeals to perceived uniqueness or degree of intensity are insufficient to establish the veridical character of the claim. Such appeals only establish the indubitability of the report of my own feelings ("I seem to be encountering God") but hardly suffice to justify a claim to *revelation*.

Schleiermacher follows Locke in grounding the idea of revelation in the divine source or origin of certain experiences and beliefs, but in contrast to Locke he provides a much fuller account of the self's intuitive grasp of that divine source. Nonetheless, upon careful examination his defense of revelation founders on the incoherence of the notion of intuition or immediate self-consciousness. Without a more plausible account of the nature of immediate experience and of the equation of immediate self-consciousness and God-consciousness the very idea of a non-inferential experience or belief is rendered suspect. But without a clear distinction between the inferential and non-inferential Schleiermacher cannot defend the supra-rational, i.e., the revelatory, nature of Christian beliefs. Thus Schleiermacher's case for revelation, though more complete than Locke's, also succumbs to its own internal incoherence. Schleiermacher's attempt to ground revelation in universal religious experience is thwarted by his inability to demonstrate that the experience stems from a divine origin. Thus the classic modern defense of revelation fails to justify that belief which seemed to the reformers "beyond controversy."

Thomas Torrance: Revelation as Divine Imposition

Though Friedrich Schleiermacher has provided modern theology with the classic model for revelation, his method certainly does not stand alone among modern articulations of the doctrine. Indeed, those theologians in the twentieth century who have granted the category of revelation its most exalted status trace their heritage not to Schleiermacher but to Søren Kierkegaard[27] and the early work of Karl Barth.[28] These theologians are convinced that the prevenience of God's grace is not asserted forcefully enough in a position which begins from the assumption that God's revelation must be conformable to universal standards of rationality. In order to maintain the absolute prevenience of grace, they argue, revelation must be conceived as that "impossible possibility" granted to the believer in a "moment of crisis." Revelation shatters the autonomous structure of human reason and communicates that which lies beyond reason's grasp. Theologians attracted to this crisis model begin from the conviction that the content of revelation, seen from the point of view of autonomous reason, is absolutely supra-rational. Nonetheless, God in his grace creates in the human subject a capacity for receiving revelation through faith. Some theologians, most notably Kierkegaard himself, assert the absolute contrast between faith and reason and seem almost to revel in revelation's utter non-rationality. Other theologians who accept the absolute contrast between revelation and autonomous reason argue, nonetheless, that faith's grasp of revelation is reasonable. This argument requires both a criticism of the Enlightenment notion of reason's autonomy and an account of revelation's reasonableness which maintains the absolute prevenience of God's grace.

Undoubtedly the most fully developed twentieth-century proposal of this sort comes in the work of the Scottish theologian Thomas Torrance.[29] Torrance's position is especially interesting because he attempts to assert both the absolute uniqueness and the rationality of revelation. To reach this conclusion he reverses Schleiermacher's method. Beginning from the background conviction of revelation's uniqueness, he proceeds to show that a believer's understanding of this unique content is fully rational. Ironically this reverse procedure leads Torrance into the same impasse which snared both Locke and Schleiermacher. Though he proceeds from a very different premise from that of his predecessors,[30] Torrance attempts to ground both the uniqueness and the rationality of revelation in the intuitive self-evident nature of a revelatory experience. Torrance's argument for the prevenience and rationality of God's grace rests on the same incoherent notion of intuition which undermined his predecessors' defense of revelation.

Torrance's argument moves in deft dialectical fashion. On the one hand he boldly asserts the absolute autonomy and prevenience of God's revelation. On the other hand he argues that theology's acceptance of that autonomy is perfectly rational and scientific. His argument for the reasonableness of revelation focuses on the rationality of the discipline of theology. Torrance poses this question: Can a discipline which accepts the absolute primacy of its object of inquiry be considered rational or scientific? Appealing to a model of rationality derived from the natural sciences he answers with a resounding "yes." In attending so carefully to its unique object theology exhibits the key characteristics of scientific objectivity—faithfulness to the nature of the object of inquiry and freedom from presuppositions foreign to its particular discipline. Because of the peculiar characteristics of its object, theology must submit more radically than other scientific disciplines, but its more radical submission is still congruent with its status as a "special science." This is an ingenious argument, because it makes theology's most obvious flaw, its apparent heteronomous obedience to God, into the virtue which grants theology scientific and thus rational status. Such ingenuity deserves our careful scrutiny.

Torrance begins with a bold but carefully worded statement of the absolute prevenience of revelation.

> In divine revelation we have to do with a Word of God which is what it is as Word of God in its own reality independent of our recognition of it, and we have to do with a Truth of God which is what it is as Truth of God before we come to know it to be true. That means that in all our response to God's self-revelation . . . we must seek to understand and interpret it in accordance with its intrinsic requirements and under the constraint of the truth which bears upon our minds in and through it.[31]

Both elements of Torrance's overall argument are present in this quotation. Torrance takes a more radical view of revelation than either of his predecessors. He does not simply insist that the content of revelation cannot be discovered through the mind's ordinary processes and thus must be given by divine initiative; he claims that the content of revelation is true in itself, independent of our recognition of its truth. That odd claim allows him to skirt the problem Locke could not solve, viz., how can human subjects accept as true propositions which cannot be known by ordinary means? According to Torrance revelation is true independent of the process by which we come to know it. But such a peculiar claim must surely establish the non-rationality, if not the irrationality, of faith's grasp of revelation. Not so, argues Torrance, because theologians "seek to understand and interpret" revelation in accordance with "its intrinsic requirements." In so doing theology is simply following the formal rules which guide all scientific inquiries.

Torrance's assertion of revelation's "*Wahrheit-an-sich*" sounds so strange because it directly contradicts the modern epistemological "turn to the subject." Philosophical investigation into the nature of human knowledge has, since Descartes, focused on the subjective process by which we come to know. The centrality of human subjectivity in the formation of knowledge was apparently established by Kant's argument that knowledge results from the imposition of the mind's categorial structure upon the formless sensible manifold. After Kant one can no longer speak of objects or phenomena independent of the mind's schematizing function. A *fortiori* one cannot speak of the truth of propositions independent of the human subjects' justification of those propositions, so the standard epistemological wisdom argues.

Torrance is not a pre-critical thinker who blithely ignores Kant's Copernican revolution; he is aware and sharply critical of the modern fixation on human subjectivity as the key to knowledge. Torrance does not deny that knowledge results from the mind's interaction with that which is given to it; he simply rejects the absolute priority Kant grants to the structure of reason in the formation of knowledge.

> We must violently disagree with Kant . . . in his attempt to convert the fact that nature only yields her secrets to us when we constrain her to act within limits we impose . . . into a general principle, in which the conformity of the object to the mind of the knowing subject is attributed to our power of knowing or is predicated of our human nature.
> (p. 89)

To some extent Torrance is lodging a common contemporary charge against Kant's epistemology. The categories of the mind are not, as Kant believed, the necessary and universal conditions for all possible experience.[32] They are rather the appropriate philosophical conditions for understanding the world in terms of Newtonian physics. Advances in quantum physics, for example, have shown the clear limitations of the Kantian scheme. The categorial scheme must be revised to reflect the new conceptuality of modern science. In contrast to most critics of Kantianism, however, Torrance does not argue for a historical and cultural relativizing of Kant's categories. He rather asserts that a reassessment of the Kantian system allows a renewed appreciation of the *object's* role in forming our knowledge. A recognition of Kantianism's weaknesses is the first step toward a reassertion of realism in epistemology. That key claim sets Torrance against the stream of current opinion in philosophy of science, but Torrance is convinced that most modern philosophical conceptions of scientific method overlook the realism implied in actual scientific procedure.

Torrance does not undertake a full-scale criticism of post-Kantian epistemology and philosophy of science. He rather constructs his own account of scientific rationality designed to show that theology's subservience to its own object is neither unscientific or irrational. That account depends on a clear distinction between criteria of rationality applicable to *scientia generalis* and those which apply to a particular *scientia specialis*.[33] Many modern philosophers have failed to heed this distinction and attempt to raise the criteria appropriate to a specific science to universal status. But the norms of physics do not apply equally to biology and geology, and yet it would be absurd to deny scientific status to the latter disciplines. General criteria of rationality must be purely formal so that they can be applied uniformly to all rational disciplines. Scientific activity, Torrance argues, is "vigorous, disciplined, methodological" (p. 116) devotion to the appropriate object of inquiry. True scientific behavior is characterized by humility, openness, and self-criticism; it refuses to be tied to a rigid *a priori* framework and maintains a capacity for wonder and an openness to the radically new. Science's devotion to its object requires a method and a set of organizing concepts which are responsive to the nature and behavior of the object. Scientific objectivity does not connote detachment from the object of inquiry but from presuppositions foreign to its own discipline. Because each science has a distinct object, "each special science has its own mode of rationality or objectivity, and its own aim and method as a *scientia specialis*" (p. 113).

Torrance has made two important points with this ingenious argument. First, he has defined rationality as consistent adherence to criteria internal to a particular discipline. Second, he has further specified those criteria as adherence to the *object* of inquiry, thereby gaining a degree of realism not available to accounts of knowledge which focus primarily on the subject's formative action. Torrance's very way of stating the issue sets up a greater reciprocity between subject and object in the knowing process. If science is characterized by disciplined but open devotion to its object, then the scientist must be prepared to revise both method and organizing concepts when the behavior of the object demands it.

But is Torrance's easy talk about "object" appropriate, especially for a discipline like theology which inquires after a unique transcendent object? Torrance defends the language of objectivity by asserting that theology has a right to the prerogatives of a scientific discipline until it has shown itself in violation of general norms of rationality. Theology's object surely differs from those of physics or history or economics, but that fact alone does not place any special burden of proof on theology. To demand that theology establish the actuality of its object prior to its investigation places "unscientific" constraints on the discipline.

> Each special science . . . presupposes the reality and accessibility of its own proper object and the possibility of knowing it further, and refuses to justify itself as a science by stepping outside of its own actuality, but leaves the question of its justificaton to be answered by its own special content and inner rationality. (p.3)

Having argued theology's general rationality, Torrance turns to examine its peculiar characteristics as a special science. Theology's particular rational qualities stem from the uniqueness of its object.

> The ultimate fact with which we have to come to terms in all theological and biblical interpretation [is] . . . that divine revelation is God himself, for it is not just something of himself that God reveals to us but his very own Self, his own ultimate being as God.[34]

Revelation is the object of theological interpretation, but revelation consists not simply of propositions *about* God. Revelation is the very being of God made present through words. Thus God in his "second-ary objectivity" is the proper object of theological inquiry.[35] Theology remains rational as long as it constructs a vigorous disciplined method appropriate to the nature of that object.

Theology's object differs from the object of every other scientific discipline in that it is "not a mute fact" (p. 29) but a self-disclosing, self-communicating subject. The objects of other sciences "speak," i.e., become understandable, only as they interact with the assumed concepts and categories of the science. Knowledge emerges from the reciprocal interaction of object and schematizing subject. To some extent the investigator must coerce the object to conform with an extant conceptual scheme if understanding is to occur. But that cannot be the case in theology.

> We cannot coerce God. . . . We are never allowed to impose ourselves with our notions upon Him. . . . Knowledge of Him arises and increases out of obedient conformity to Him and the way He takes with us in revealing Himself to us. . . . In theology we are concerned with statements that are pronounced primarily by God and only pronounced after Him by human subjects as hearers of his Word. (pp. 97–98)

Torrance characterizes this form of knowing as an "epistemological in-version" (p. 131) in which we think within the "inner compulsion" (p. 129) of God's gracious self-revelation. All statements about God are finally "statements of God [i.e., God's statements] and have their reference from a centre in God and not in ourselves; they are derived from God" (p. 14). Rational interpretation takes place only as we subor-dinate our subjectivity to God's objectivity and allow God to be his own interpreter. Rational normative interpretation is finally God's self-interpretation.

This radical argument is essential to Torrance's defense of the ab-solute prevenience of God's grace. The account of theology's rational-ity cannot undermine that basic theological convicton. But his argu-ments for revelations's uniqueness and rationality appear to contradict one another. In his criticism of Kant, Torrance acknowledged that a *reciprocal* relation between subject and object is a general characteristic of all rational inquiry. His definitions of realism and objectivity in science depend upon acceptance of that reciprocity. But in defending the uniqueness of theology's object, Torrance denies that such reciproc-ity characterizes the relation between the theologian and God. How can the claim that theology is a rational discipline be maintained if theology fails to exemplify that characteristic of scientific activity which establishes a discipline as objective? If Torrance consistently denies that human subjectivity has a reciprocal effect on the divine object, then either he must deny theology's rationality or he must use the terms *knowledge* and *rationality* equivocally.

This apparent contradiction threatens to undermine the most ingenious aspect of Torrance's position. His simultaneous assertion of theology's uniqueness and reasonableness depends upon his claim that theology exemplifies the formal characteristics of a rational discipline. This argument, if valid, shifts the burden of proof to those who would deny theology its scientific standing. In the absence of falsifying arguments, theology and the revelation it seeks to investigate are rationally justified. But Torrance's own account of theology's unique object appears to undermine the argument for formal rationality, thus providing the falsifying argument his critics seek. The argument for reciprocity, which establishes the subject-object framework, cannot be discarded when attention shifts to the peculiar nature of the theological object. Torrance cannot deny subject-object reciprocity and continue to claim that rationality and truth reside solely in the object without also denying theology's rationality. Torrance is faced with the following inconsistent triad.

1. Theology is a rational discipline exemplifying the characteristics of a true science.
2. The reciprocal relation between the investigating subject and the object of inquiry is a general characteristic of rational scientific activity.
3. Theology's unique object is the truth which imposes itself on the subject independent of the subject's reciprocal influence.

The assertion of any two of these propositions demands the denial of the third. Since Torrance's argument requires all three assertions, his position appears doomed to inconsistency.

Torrance attempts to rescue his position from this potentially devastating charge through an appeal to intuition. Human subjectivity, Torrance argues, plays an essential but nonconstitutive role in the revelatory relationship; revelation does not deny human subjectivity but reforms it so that it corresponds to revelation's essential structure. We do approach the theological object with our own categories and

concepts, but they are remolded until finally they are united with God's
self-interpretation.

> In order to set out our theological thinking in a coherent sequence that
> faithfully reflects the nature and pattern of the Truth itself, we have
> to re-live the encounter with the object, allowing ourselves to be re-
> addressed by Him, re-thinking His Word to us . . . and at the same
> time translate that into our statements in such a way that their necess-
> ity does not lie in themselves but in the object. (p. 127)

The theologian must penetrate to the inner reality of God's secondary
objectivity and thereby trace the "logic of grace" (p. 128). Only if the
theologian thinks with the "inner compulsion" of God's self-revelation
can theological concepts be adequate to their revealed object. Through
that process the theologian finally gains "an intuitive apprehension
of the whole pattern of faith. . . . In natural science this is spoken
of as *discovery*, in theology this is spoken of as *revelation*" (pp. 129–
131).

    This appeal to revelation as intuition leads Torrance to claim that
the theologian can apprehend God's essential reality. Intuitive revelation yields a non-inferential "direct apprehension of reality,"[36] which
allows a distinction between "existence-statements" (those statements
known to be true by virtue of their direct correspondence to an existent reality) and "coherence-statements" (which are true by implication and inference from the foundational existence statements).[37] The
correspondence between our language and God's reality is established
by the intuitive experience in which God's reality is imposed upon us.

> We can only "convince" others of the truth of our existence-statements
> if we can get them to see or hear the reality they refer to as we see or
> hear it. . . . They must be brought to share our *intuition* of the object
> given. . . . To intuit an object in a way appropriate to its nature and
> to be convinced of its external reality coincide. . . . Thus behind ex-
> istence-statements there are acts of intuition in which the mind is always
> open to the reality beyond. (pp. 165-166)

The experience of revelation unifies our interpretation and God's self-
interpretation and establishes a correspondence between our assertions
and God's reality. All that takes place through an act of intuition in
which we apprehend God's reality directly.

    Once again the weight of an argument for revelation comes to rest on the frail concept of intuition. Torrance's understanding of intuition, however, is not equivalent to that of Schleiermacher. For Schleiermacher intuition connotes an immediate precognitive experience which is prior to the formation of judgments about the object known. Immediate knowing is primary and direct; judgment or propositional knowing is by contrast derivative and indirect. Torrance's language concerning the "direct experience" by which we "re-live the encounter" with God reminds one of Schleiermacher's immediate self-consciousness, but one aspect of the experience is quite different. Torrance explicitly denies the validity of precognitive experiences in an extended polemic against the common distinction between personal and propositional revelation.[38] God reveals himself in his Word as mediated through the words of scripture. All personal revelation is propositional. There can be no non-propositional revelation of God.

The direct experience of God of which Torrance speaks is not precognitive but rather signifies God's direct imposition of true propositions on the mind of the believer. Torrance believes that the imposition of truth which occurs in revelation is unique to theology, but in fact it is characteristic of all foundational epistemologies.

> The notion of 'foundations of knowledge' — truths which are certain because of their causes rather than because of the arguments given for them — is the fruit of the Greek (and specifically Platonic) analogy between perceiving and knowing. The essential feature of the analogy is that knowing a proposition to be true is to be identified with being caused to do something by an object. The object which the proposition is about *imposes* the proposition's truth.[39]

Torrance uses the term *intuition* to signify the indubitability and incorrigibility of this causally imposed knowledge. Torrance wants human subjects to be involved in the act of revelation; he simply does not want their reception of revelation to influence the absolute certainty of its content. Thus human beings must be the passive recipients of a self-evident truth. But this appeal to intuition surely does not resolve the inconsistency in the logic of Torrance's position; it simply makes the nature of his difficulties more apparent. Despite his non-foundational Kierkegaardian starting point, Torrance's defense of revelation commits him to a form of theological foundationalism.[40]

Torrance's insistence that revelation is always linguistic in character seals the inconsistency of his position. Like all foundationalists Torrance distinguishes between inferential and non-inferential propositions (e.g., existence-statements and coherence-statements). Inferential beliefs are those which depend logically on a battery of interconnected concepts, i.e., on a conceptual framework. Non-inferential beliefs by contrast are established independent of any such framework, i.e., by direct relation to the objects they represent. Torrance makes this point explicitly when he speaks of the "epistemological inversion" which characterizes theological knowing, in which God, the object-as-subject, reconstructs our subjectivity to correspond with revelation. Our knowledge of God does not depend on the conceptual framework we bring to the divine object; rather the concept-independent object establishes the framework. The propositions which ground the conceptual framework must be true independent of the concepts for which it serves as the foundation.

But Torrance still has not provided a sufficient argument to justify his claim that the non-inferential propositions of revelation deserve the title knowledge. *Knowledge* is the term we ordinarily apply to justified true beliefs, i.e., those beliefs demonstrated as true with reference to the conceptual frame. What then warrants the use of the same term to describe beliefs established independent of that frame? Why should the term *knowledge* be attributed to this ostensibly independent apprehension? "Knowledge" like "rationality" appears to be used equivocally by Torrance. The problem facing Torrance has been most clearly stated by Wilfred Sellars in his criticism of sense-datum theorists.

> The concept of *looking green*, the ability to recognize that something *looks green*, presupposes the concept of *being green*, and . . . the latter concept involves the ability to tell what colours objects have by looking at them—which in turn involves knowing in what circumstances to place an object to ascertain its colour by looking at it. . . . One can have the concept of green only by having a whole battery of concepts of which it is one element. . . . One could not have the observational knowledge of *any* fact unless one knew many *other* things as well. . . . The point is specifically that observational knowlege of any particular fact, e.g., that this is green, presupposes that one knows general facts of the form *X is a reliable symptom of Y*. And to admit this requires an abandonment of the traditional empiricist idea that observational language stands on its own feet.[41]

The appeal to an ostensible revelatory experience to which human consciousness makes no contribution is fraught with the same difficulties. In order to recognize an experience as revelatory one must possess a general concept of the form *X is a reliable symptom of Y.* But to admit that is to grant that the "revelatory" experience yields knowledge precisely because it can be integrated into a conceptual framework. But that in turn is a denial of the non-inferential quality of revelatory experience!

Torrance's defense of revelation's self-evidence and his correlative denial of the contribution of the human subject to knowlege of God is reminiscent of the problem which plagued Karl Barth in his *Epistle to the Romans.* A position which stresses both God's sovereign transcendence and his knowability is hard pressed to give an account of how we can come to know such a God. Barth's solution (of which Torrance's position is an updated version) is to grant to God's Spirit the mediating power to bring divine object and human subject together. The Spirit of God dwells within the believing interpreter and bestows the capacity to know the unknowable. But God's Spirit is finally not the human subject but the "not-I" which dwells within.[42] Thus "I" know God only insofar as I conform my subjectivity to the power of the Spirit; only as the God within knows the God without can true interpretation take place. Human subjectivity then becomes nothing more than the vessel through which God knows himself. Whenever I contribute anything to the interpretation of God's being, it is the contribution of sin and falsity. True interpretation comes at the expense of the denial of the goodness of creaturely reality. The human self remains hopelessly bifurcated in the act of knowing God. While Torrance does not explicitly draw this anthropological conclusion, he seems bound to assert some version of it, if he hopes to maintain the self-evident incorrigibility of revelation.

Torrance's defense of revelation collapses when he appeals to intuition, i.e., a non-inferential knowing of God. His admittedly sophisticated and carefully argued position does not solve the problem of revelation but restates it in its sharpest form. How can we claim to have knowledge of God? If we bring God into a context dominated by our categories and concepts, we treat him as if he were simply another object among the many objects we know through rational schematization. If we set God outside that framework and allow him to create his own conditions and content of knowlege, then we cannot say how it is that *we* know him. The former option denies God his divinity; the latter denies us our humanity.

The modern strategy for justifying the Christian claim to revelation fails to survive careful scrutiny. The essential elements of that strategy are present in all three theologians examined in this chapter. Locke, Schleiermacher, and Torrance all seek to provide explicit justification for the Christian belief in God's prevenience by showing both the reasonableness and the distinctiveness of Christian beliefs. Each operates against the background of an accepted epistemology and seeks to adjust that epistemology to make room for transcendent claims. In every case these theologians argue that the distinctiveness of Christian beliefs resides in their divine origin. Though they can be grasped within the categories of the reigning epistemology, they cannot have originated from within that conceptual frame. Christian beliefs are revealed because they stem from a unique source, God. Revelation then refers not primarily to the content or logic of particular beliefs but to their origin. If that is the case, then the justification of Christian belief must attend to that process by which God shares himself with us by affecting our concepts and categories. That is to say, the defense of God's prevenience takes the form of an account of how we come to know God. Modern doctrines of revelation inevitably become epistemological doctrines. The key theological task becomes the devising of a category which will be congenial to a general epistemology and yet establish the uniqueness of the process of religious knowing. For all three theologians that category is intuition, a notion which grants to God ultimate causal responsibility for our knowlege of him.

I have tried to show that this common strategy, exemplified in different ways in these three theologies, in each case collapses into conceptual confusion. By way of conclusion I want to give a more general account of the failure of this modern *apologia*. The modern epistemological defense of God's prevenience fails because it confuses *rational justification* and *causal explanation*.[43] Ordinarily we think a belief to be justified when sufficient reasons have been offered in its support. What determines the sufficiency of reasons will vary from case to case, depending on the difficulty of the belief and the person or persons to be convinced. In practice we define sufficient reason to be reason enough to convince the relevant party. But epistemological doctrines seek a more stringent definition of sufficient reason. Proponents of such doctrines fear that unless some *ultimately* sufficient reason is discovered, then all other reasons will be groundless and without foundation. Appeals to "reason enough" will be arbitrary unless some final Sufficient Reason is discerned. Reasons may ordinarily depend on other reasons for their support, but the entire network of interrelated reasons will be without justification unless grounded in an ultimate reason. Thomas Aquinas argued similarly in the "five ways" that the whole pattern of contingency, or causation, or motion must be grounded in a higher order—in necessary existence, or self-caused cause, or unmoved mover—if infinite regress is to be avoided.[44] Likewise, the pattern of interconnected inferential beliefs must be grounded in some non-inferential belief or reality if ultimate rational justification is to be achieved.

The desire for a foundation of reasoning-as-such naturally leads to a conception of rational justification as a species of causal explanation. The ultimate justifying reason is the first cause; a belief is justified only when its origin, source, and cause has been identified. The causal explanation model has become influential in modern theology both because of its long theological history and because it has seemed an appropriate means of providing explicit theoretical justification for belief in God's prevenience. But the adoption of that model is, I have tried to argue, the very move which undermines that defense. The logical difficulties facing the defenders of revelation are not unlike those which plague causal arguments for God's existence. What finally justifies the leap from causal chain to self-caused cause, from inferential beliefs to non-inferential reality? In both cases the arguments move from ordinary experience or ordinary reasoning to the extra-ordinary cause of both. But the very argument which attempts to establish the extraordinary cause contradicts the pattern of reasoning which precedes it. Causal arguments for God's existence assert that either one must posit a self-caused cause or fail to provide an explanation of causality-as-such. Epistemological foundationalists argue that there must be self-evident, non-inferential beliefs or the whole pattern of inference is undermined. But both arguments assume that if we cannot demonstrate the necessity of the ultimate sufficient reason or the first cause, then the entire causal chain or reasoning process stands without causal explanation.[45] Surely that is not a self-evident implication, but, more importantly, every attempt to formulate an argument for a first cause appears to collapse into contradiction.

The foundationalist claim runs as follows: Ordinary knowledge rests upon that intricate web of inferential beliefs we call a conceptual framework. Knowledge is justified true belief, and justification consists in tracing the pattern of inference supporting the belief in question until we find those true beliefs on which the questioned belief rests. If we accept those beliefs to be true, and if the pattern of inference is valid, then we can assert the belief in question to be a justified true belief. But, the foundationalist adds, we are not *theoretically* justified in bringing our inquiry to an end until we have discovered a self-evident, non-inferential belief, i.e., a belief that must be *universally* accepted as true. Positivists, idealists, and revelationalists alike accept this account of theoretical justification. But the arguments they propose to establish the non-inferential beliefs, usually through an appeal to intuition, inevitably conflict with their arguments for ordinary knowledge. Once again the problem can be illustrated by use of an inconsistent triad.[46]

1. *X intuits the self-caused nature of y* entails *X non-inferentially knows that y is a first cause.*
2. The ability to know first causes is given in the moment of discernment, independent of a conceptual frame.
3. The ability to know facts of the form *x is* φ is a skill acquired through the use of a conceptual frame.

Foundationalists want to affirm all three propositions, but they cannot without using the word *know* equivocally. If knowing that y is a first cause is a fact of the form *x is* φ, then it follows from proposition 3 that it is dependent on a conceptual frame. But if that is the case, then proposition 2 must be denied, and then the foundationalist's case crumples altogether. If the foundationalist insists on affirming proposition 2, then a different account of *x intuits the self-caused nature of y* must be given from that offered in proposition 1. But it is difficult to conceive of such an account that continues to uphold proposition 3, while still claiming that intuition is a form of knowing. In short the foundationalist position cannot be given self-consistent formulation.

The modern epistemological doctrine of revelation must be adjudged a failure not because of inept execution or insufficient imagination on the part of its defenders, but because of the impossible logical demands of the project itself. The belief in God's prevenience has not and cannot be adequately defended by an argument for God's causal and thus epistemological priority. If the modern doctrine is rightly described as faith seeking foundation, then modern theology has yet to discover a sufficiently stable substructure on which to erect its theological edifice.

CHAPTER THREE

Theology without Revelation?

The pictures or images which influence theologians are as important as the arguments theologians present in defense of their positions. The central modern theological question has been: How can human beings with our finite concepts and categories have access to a God who is ontologically other? That question has seemed urgent in part because God's otherness or transcendence has been pictured spatially. God is other in that he stands "outside" the human realm. If communication between God and humanity is to occur then God must somehow "enter" the human situation and make himself known. In Kierkegaardian-Barthian conceptions of revelation the spatial distance between God and humanity is so stressed as to create an infinite qualitative gap which only God can bridge. In views of revelation influenced by Schleiermacher, God's otherness is placed not beyond the human realm but on its boundary. Ordinary experience becomes the vehicle of the extraordinary disclosure of God. Though the path to God is decidedly human, in the moment of revelation God alone acts and human subjects are passive. The otherness of revelation is established in that intuitive encounter. Despite their important differences both conceptions of revelation picture the divine-human relation in terms of spatial categories. God is transcendent insofar as he stands outside of or on the boundary of ordinary human existence.

If communication between God and humanity is to occur, i.e., if revelation is to be possible, then God must act upon that human realm which he transcends. The natural way to relate two objects standing in spatial relation to one another is to conceive of them in causal relation. The causal model has seemed especially relevant for the problem of revelation, because the cause and effect relation embodies the active-passive distinction necessary to preserve God's prevenience. Since the notion of causation seems an appropriate way to understand *creatio ex nihilo*, and since the medieval tradition often highlighted God's causal relation to the universe, the extension of causation to the problem of revelation has seemed reasonable. But while causation might well describe God's original act of creation, it is not clear that it is an apt notion either for an understanding of *creatio continua* or for conceiving of the process by which we become aware of our ultimate dependence upon God. To conceive either of the latter two relations under the notion of causation is to threaten the freedom which is an essential part of responsible human action.[1] The problem is how to preserve authentic human agency while granting priority to God's action in the moment of revelation. The modern solution has been to grant the autonomy of human action within the realm of the ordinary but to create an extraordinary sphere in which God is the supreme causal agent. Revelation occurs when God alone is agent and human beings are purely passive subjects (or in the more radical positions, passive objects), the effects of God's causative action.

I have argued in the preceding chapter that this way of picturing the relation between God and humanity is radically inconsistent. Theologians have been unable to justify the claim of a unique situation in which human action is stilled and yet human beings become aware of or know God. Theologians' failure to give self-consistent formulation to the notion of intuition has meant the collapse of the very causal model which undergirds the doctrine of revelation. However powerful the picture of God as external causal agent might be, it cannot be given a coherent rational defense as an epistemological doctrine. But just as importantly, the causal model has troubling religious implications. For the reformers God's grace stands at the center of human life. Human beings are created, sustained, redeemed, and sanctified through God's gracious action. Life in all its dimensions is a gift from the hand of a gracious giver. But when God's grace is conceived under the category of revelation, i.e., as the epistemological bridging of a spatial gap, then grace becomes a rare and extraordinary aspect of human life. Grace is located in the boundary situation or in an extraordinary moment of crisis, while the everyday and ordinary are given over to autonomous human activity. Such a view grants too much to human action and too little to God's reconciling grace. But as long as the prevenience of grace is defended by a conception of God's causal and thus epistemological priority, God's grace will have merely an extrinsic relation to human life.

A different conception of the divine-human relation and of the role of grace in that relation is necessary if theology is to move beyond its current methodological impasse. Two current theological options, both of which reject the view of God as external causative object, offer alternatives to modern revelation theology. The one option, influenced by Kant, maintains the general epistemological orientation of modern theology but assigns a very different role to the concept "God" and to theological reflection. God is conceived not as a transcendent object but as a transcendental ideal, a regulative concept within the conceptual framework. Since theological thinking no longer has an external object to describe, it must content itself with the imaginative construction of theological concepts. This neo-Kantian option, represented most clearly by Gordon Kaufman,[2] argues that theology must carry on without revelation and ought not be conceived as a response to the prevenient grace of God. The incoherence of doctrines of revelation implies the indefensibility of the conviction those doctrines sought to defend. The second option, influenced by Wittgenstein, suggests the general futility of epistemological questions and seeks solace in the various uses of theological language. This neo-Wittgensteinian option, represented by David Kelsey[3] and Charles Wood,[4] clearly rejects revelation as an epistemological doctrine and offers a functional view of authority in its place. Whether these theologians want to maintain a non-epistemological function for revelation is unclear, and whether they can maintain a place for God's prevenience is even more uncertain. Since both these positions offer alternatives to the modern doctrine of revelation and represent important contemporary options in American theology, they deserve our serious attention. An examination of Kaufman's "hard" rejection of revelation and the functionalists' "mixed" view will set the stage for my own proposal concerning revelation and theology.

Theology as Imaginative Construction: Epistemology Revised

Immanuel Kant anticipated (or perhaps precipitated) the problem of revelation in his first critique.[5] If God is, as Christian theists have confessed, "that than which nothing greater can be conceived," "the beginning and end of all things," he cannot be one of the ordinary objects schematized by the mind's categorial structure. As the source and ground of both being and rationality God must transcend any conceptual framework within which we seek to know him. That does not, however, mean that God should be conceived as an external

object in causal relation to the conceptual framework. Kant's criticisms
of the arguments for God's existence and his analysis of the antinomies
of reason anticipate the critique of foundationalism developed by
Sellars, Rorty, and others. God is not a special transcendent object to
be known by a special form of speculative knowledge. God must, rather,
be beyond the reach of our knowledge, since, according to Kant, knowledge results only from the interaction of the sense manifold and the
categorial scheme. "God" is rather the "transcendental ideal," the
highest most inclusive regulative concept the mind possesses. In its
ineluctable movement toward unity and totality the mind conceives
of "the idea of the sum total of all possible predicates, containing *a
priori* the data for all particular possibilities."[6] The idea of God is simply
the unconditioned condition of all particular predicates, but since the
idea is neither derived from experience nor required for the experience
of any object in the world, it functions purely to regulate the mind's
speculative tendencies. We cannot on the basis of pure reason demonstrate God's existence or assert a correspondence between the transcendental ideal and a transcendent object. Revelation understood as
speculative knowledge of God is impossible.

This Kantian approach maintains an epistemological framework
but reconceives the place of God in relation to it. God no longer occupies a problematic position outside our web of beliefs but is absorbed
within it as the transcendental ideal. It is important to remember, however, that Kant continues the epistemological tradition of distinguishing
the categorial scheme from that which lies outside it. There is something
"beyond" the framework which is *given* to the mind, namely, the sensible manifold, but we come to know the "given" only as the manifold
is schematized through the forms of sensibility and the categories.[7]
"God", however, is not one of those external but knowable objects
outside the framework, and thus theology ought not be conceived according to the epistemological model applicable to the sciences.

The clearest representative of the Kantian position in contemporary theology is Gordon Kaufman. Against the Kantian background
Kaufman makes the following claims. 1) Theology has no access to
a transcendent divine being, and thus its claims can neither be founded
upon nor authorized by an appeal to divine revelation. 2) Theology
has no given content to describe, and its concepts do not correspond
to a transcendent reality; theology is a purely constructive activity of
the human imagination. 3) Theological concepts are constructed not

primarily from the parochial tradition of a particular religious community but from the linguistic heritage of the broader cultural community. 4) The word *God* does not refer or correspond to a transcendent being who is the object of theological knowledge; rather, "God" functions as the focal point of an all-encompassing framework of interpretation. 5) The criteria by which theological claims are to be assessed are not those of correspondence but are thoroughly pragmatic in character.

It is important to note that though Kaufman is sharply critical of revelation theology, his criticism rests on epistemological grounds. Kaufman does not fault revelation theologians for construing the divine-human relation in epistemological terms but for using an inappropriate epistemological model, one derived from the sciences.[8] Thus Kaufman accepts the Kantian critique of revelation, but he does not follow Kant in construing theology as an ineluctable adjunct of moral reasoning. Nor does he adopt Kant's view of the close relation between theology and practical reason. Theology is for Kaufman a theoretical activity, the function of which is determined by epistemological considerations. It is simply a theoretical activity which has no determinate object to describe, and thus must be understood as purely constructive.

Kaufman's argument against revelation and his case for theology as imaginative construction both stem from his commitment to a basic epistemological assumption, what we might call the dogma of divided truths. This dogma teaches that truth

> should be thought of as divided into a lower and an upper division, the division between (in Plato's terms) mere opinion and genuine knowledge. It is the work of the Philosopher to establish an invidious distinction between such statements as "It rained yesterday" and "Men should try to be just in their dealings." For Plato the former sort of statement was second-rate, mere *pistis* or *doxa*. The latter, if perhaps not yet *episteme*, was at least a plausible candidate.[9]

Kaufman's position depends upon the dichotomies implied by the dogma of divided truths. Revelation theologians, he argues, are mistaken in assuming that knowledge of God is somehow akin to knowledge of the object of perception. Theology is in fact qualitatively different from disciplines grounded in perception because "there is no percept that corresponds directly to our concept of God. . . . Little wonder, then, that the concept does not correspond to anything we can directly perceive or know, and that it must be constructed in the mind and through history *by processes quite different from those which produce an ordinary concept*" (p. 25, emphasis added). This dichotomy of concepts yields a further sharp distinction between the epistemological activities of description and construction. The predicate *descriptive* is warranted only in those disciplines where there is a correspondence between "ordinary concepts" and their "percepts," i.e., only in the natural sciences. Since theology can claim neither percepts nor correspondence, "the theologians' claim of a direct revelatory foundation for their work is . . . a myth."[10]

Ironically Kaufman's commitment to the dogma of divided truths places his position in formal parallel to that of Thomas Torrance. Kaufman's argument concerning the descriptive character of science could just as easily have been made by Torrance. In fact Torrance presented a similar argument *in defense of* a theology of revelation. Ultimately Kaufman and Torrance share the same epistemological framework, though they represent opposite poles within it. Both are agreed that the nature of theology is determined by its relation to the descriptive sciences. Both agree that a correspondence between concepts and percepts, or existence statements and existing reality, is the distinguishing mark of a descriptive science. They disagree, however, on whether theology exhibits the characteristics of a science. For Torrance theology is a descriptive and thus rational science; for Kaufman theology cannot be descriptive and must therefore be a purely constructive discipline. "Theology . . . is fundamentally an activity of construction not of description" (p. x).

To his credit Kaufman does not dismiss the claims of nondescriptive disciplines as "mere opinion." Indeed, his project is designed to show that theological construction has a discernible formal shape and a rationally conceived method. His argument is, nonetheless, determined by the dogma of divided truths, and thus he remains committed to an epistemological explanation of theological activity. Kaufman does not extract theology from the epistemological maze created by the modern doctrine of revelation; he simply suggests that the discipline ought to move in the "opposite" direction. Human imagination, not divine revelation, is the *source* of theological concepts. Though Kaufman is not a foundationalist in quite the same way as sense-datum theorists or a revelation theologian like Torrance, he is ineluctably drawn to the metaphor of foundation, because he is describing the epistemological process of how theological concepts come to be.[11] As the following quotation indicates, Kaufman has not so much denied as reversed the procedure of revelation theology.

> [Theological] concepts have been created and developed in and through human processes of reflection in life and interpretation of experience. . . . The question about the determining moves that ground theology is the question about how and why such concepts were created and shaped in the first place, and how they can be sustained and reconstructed now. . . . Theological terms are concepts rooted in the wide experience and history of a whole culture, or a mixture of cultures, and until we discern the way in which theological reflection is grounded upon and built up out of this broader cultural experience, we have not gotten back to its real foundation. . . . The order of knowing with respect to God will have to be uncovered psychologically and epistemologically; and it may not correspond at all to the order of being, since it depends in large measure on the capacities of our cognitive apparatus. We must find the point at which human reflection can and does begin, and then we must trace the course through which it passes as it develops. (pp. 2-4)

Kaufman is well aware that a *genetic* account of how theological concepts arise does not provide the *normative* account of theology he seeks. His historicist orientation makes the strong causal explanation of traditional epistemology unacceptable, and so he seeks rather to discern the universal formal "moments of theological construction" which characterize all theistic theology whatever its diverse content.[12] Kaufman wants to show that there is a universal structure to the process by which theological concepts are created. The theologian, he argues, begins by constructing a concept of world, i.e., "the context within which all experience falls" (p. 46). Moving from that concept by "an imaginative leap," the constructive theologian then creates an idea of God which "limits and relativizes" the former notion. Finally the theologian returns to the topics of world and experience "thoroughly reconceiving them now in the light of this concept of God" (p. 46). These are the three formal and thus universal aspects of all proper theological thinking.

If nondescriptive lower-level truths are not to be dismissed as mere opinion, then both the rational method by which they are created and the rational criteria by which they are to be evaluated must be clearly stated. Kaufman's "three moments" provide a formal account of how theological concepts come to be, though it is surely a softer account than the causal explanation model of the descriptive sciences. Nonetheless, it does provide a discernible rational method for theological thinking. The more difficult problem is to provide material criteria of evaluation to replace the criterion of correspondence which constructive disciplines must forego. Kaufman appeals to pragmatic criteria of truth as the final test for theological concepts. The concepts "world" and "God" are regulative ideas in the Kantian sense, i.e., "they articulate the human imagination's attempt to grasp and understand and interpret the *whole* within which human life falls."[13] A regulative concept is true only "if it in fact leads to a fruitful life, in the broadest and fullest and most comprehensive sense possible." (p. 76). To ask whether a concept of God is true, is to ask whether an entire conceptual framework "provides proper orientation for human life."[14]

Despite this pragmatic turn, Kaufman is unwilling to follow Kant's proposal that theology is an inevitable part of practical or moral reasoning. He clearly does not find Kant's argument concerning the postulates of practical reason compelling, and yet he seeks pragmatic criteria for evaluating theological proposals. Kaufman suggests that there is a "criterion of humanization"[15] which can be useful in this regard. His most extensive account of the criterion is as follows:

> Whatever tends to enhance and strengthen those culture-creating processes through which our original animality is transformed into humanity is good; whatever tends to corrupt, block, or destroy these processes of humanization—for any human beings, regardless of race, class, or sex—is evil; whatever rescues us from or otherwise overcomes such evil processes, powers, or events is salvific.[16]

This statement of the criterion is far too general and abstract to provide rational guidance for choice between competing proposals for humanization, especially since Kaufman admits that "there is little agreement among religious traditions on conceptions of the human or on the understanding of what constitutes human fulfillment."[17] The criterion of humanization in its present form of development does not provide an adequate alternative to the lost criterion of correspondence. The danger that theological concepts may again appear as "mere opinion" looms large. Unfortunately Kaufman enhances that suspicion when he invokes a kind of decisionism as a way of dealing with the problem of diverse conceptions of humanization. The problem arises even within a particular tradition like Christianity where diverse conceptions of Jesus compete with one another. Kaufman argues "that in the man Jesus is to be found the normative paradigm or model for understanding who or what God is and what true humanity is."[18] And yet the final ground of this normative paradigm is simply "our decision." "The question, then, of who Jesus is (or was) and how we should interpret him theologically must be entirely and explicitly *our* decision. . . . We [must] decide to make our own choice about how we will understand Jesus' significance."[19] While such a decision is surely unavoidable, it cannot of itself be the basis for rational decision-making. Until Kaufman offers greater clarity on that issue the appeal to "our decision" will appear very much like an appeal to "our opinion."

These difficulties may not be insuperable. Gordon Kaufman remains an important and influential contributor to American theology, and he may offer a more detailed defense of the criterion of humanization. But I want to argue that the problems Kaufman faces are not surprising given his commitment to an epistemological paradigm for theological method. An account of the origin of theological concepts which dismisses both the divine source and the strong causal explanation of traditional epistemologies will be hard pressed to defend the assertion that theology is a normative discipline with rational decision procedures. Kaufman's Kantianism precludes the adoption of a criterion of correspondence;[20] his historicism rules out appeal to a single, universal, and thus normative structure of human existence; his conviction that theology is essentially a theoretical constructive activity seeking universal conclusions makes an appeal to normative particular traditions and practices impossible. Given those boundaries and the abstractness of his appeal to pragmatic criteria, it is not at all clear where Kaufman might turn to discover normative rational criteria for evaluation of theological claims.

Despite the importance of Kaufman's attempt to extract theology from its epistemological impasse, his radical rejection of revelation revises but does not repudiate the epistemological paradigm which has dominated modern theology. His failure to separate the question of God's prevenience from the conception of revelation means that he rejects not only God's epistemological priority but any conceivable sense of God's prevenience in relation to theology. Were Kaufman's alternative sufficiently persuasive, it might be possible to argue that the dismissal of that ancient Christian conviction is a bearable price to pay in exchange for a viable conception of theological method. But surely a belief which has been so central to Christian self-understanding should not be jettisoned by default. A belief in God's prevenience is not tied to an epistemological conception of revelation by logical necessity. Whether the former conception can be given coherent formulation independent of the latter notion is still a question open to discussion. But the path to a new conception of God's grace lies not with the reversal of the epistemological paradigm, but with its rejection.

Beyond Epistemology: The Functional View of Authority

"Don't ask for the meaning; look for the use." That Wittgensteinian epigram could easily be the motto of those theologians who have made the most important advance beyond modern theology's epistemological fixation. One problem with foundational epistemologies and their sibling doctrines of revelation is that they conceive of meaning and understanding as singular concepts. If knowing or understanding meaning is a singular process, then the crucial intellectual task is to discover knowing's universal shape. Thus foundationalists launch their philosophical ships on a journey in search of the first cause, the final ground, or the ultimate foundation of all knowledge. But that, the Wittgensteinian theologians argue, is a trip from which there can be no return, because the journey's goal is an illusion created by overactive philosophical minds. There is no single paradigm for all knowing, no single meaning to be discerned in a text. Charles Wood makes the point quite nicely.

> It is commonly asserted that the goal of interpretation is to understand the meaning of the text, as if "meaning" were the object of "understanding." . . . Implicit in the formula is the notion that meaning is a property of a text: the text means. But this is surely misleading. In correct usage, the phrase, "The text means . . ." is always elliptical. What the phrase obscures is the connection between the text and its user or users. . . . There is no escape from the issue of the text's uses, despite the illusory security of "the meaning of the text."[21]

If you ask for use rather than meaning, you find not a singular object of understanding or a singular process but irreducible diversity.

David Kelsey[22] has applied this insight in his criticism of the modern doctrine of revelation. The doctrine is systematically misleading, he argues, because it implicitly denies the variety of ways theologians actually use scripture. An understanding of scripture as "source" of "revealed content" is one possible way to conceive the relation between the Bible and theology, but doctrines of revelation imply that it is the sole normative model for understanding that relationship. God's diverse dealings with humanity through scripture are in doctrines of revelation combined under the single metaphor of "saying" or "telling."

> Although it is logically possible to construe all the different things one might be inclined to say he is "doing" with the Bible as various ways in which God "tells" men something, it is seriously misleading to do so. It makes "revelation" the cardinal theological topic. It implies that scripture's importance rests on its preserving the "content" of "revelation" and requires us to think of "theology" as the translation into an accessible language of *the* "meaning" of what God is "telling" or "revealing" through the Bible's archaic language. (p. 214)

By enshrining a single theological model and by seeking a single determinative meaning in scripture, doctrines of revelation conceal the essential diversity of theological uses of scripture.

The emergence of this "standard model," which defines authority as a quality of the scriptural text and theology as translation of the Bible's revealed content must be overcome and the standard model replaced by a view of authority which allows for theological diversity. Kelsey proposes to define authority functionally. Authority, he argues, is a concept which describes a formal relationship between the biblical text and theology. The precise manner in which scripture functions authoritatively for theology will depend upon the particular way in which the theologian construes the text as a whole, for to call a set of texts "scripture" is "to ascribe some kind of wholeness to it" (p. 89). That wholeness, however, is not simply an uninterpreted given within the text, awaiting translation into contemporary idiom. Rather, the theologian *ascribes* the wholeness through an act of the imagination. The resulting "imaginative construals" of the text are, Kelsey argues, "logically irreducibly diverse" (p. 102). Thus the common view of scripture as a "given" which serves as the foundation of every theological position and as the unchanging standard to which one can appeal to adjudicate disagreements between such positions is severely questioned.

The imaginative image which the theologian creates in order to

make biblical texts usable is formed in the crucible of the common
life of the Christian community. The theologian's task is to propose
reforms in the life of the community through a critical examination
of her speech and action so that the church might "remain faithful
to her task and . . . retain her self-identity" (p. 160). In order to perform this critical function the theologian must possess an image of the
church's true task and identity. In other words, the theologians must
make a decision

> about the *point* of engaging in the activity of doing theology, a deci-
> sion about what is the subject matter of theology. And that is deter-
> mined . . . by the way in which he tries to catch up what Christianity
> is basically all about in a single, synoptic, imaginative judgment. (p.
> 159)

That imaginative judgment concerning Christianity's essence involves
a particular view of "the mode in which God is present among the
faithful" (p. 160). The theologian's imaginative grasp of the mode of
God's presence to the community becomes the logically prior decision
which allows him or her to construe scripture into usable shape and
to develop a *discrimin*, or configuration of criteria, to guide critical
theological activity. Theological positions differ from one another
because theologians construe the mode of God's presence in "logically
irreducible" ways. Thus, their respective visions of God's relation to
his people and of the goal and purpose of Christian belief and action
are functions of their irreducibly diverse imaginative construals. All
positions in which scripture contributes to the formation of the imaginative images are "in accord with scripture," but the particular shape
and content of each theologian's "working canon" will differ in important ways.

Two related aspects of Kelsey's discussion deserve special emphasis.
At one level authority is a purely formal concept describing a relation
between theological interpreter and biblical texts. To say that biblical
texts are authoritative is simply "to say that they ought to be *used* in
the common life of the church in normative ways such that they decisively rule its form of life and forms of speech" (pp. 97-98). That claim
indicates nothing about *how* they should so function or what particular
patterns in scripture should rule Christian life and speech. It is a purely
formal assertion. Kelsey emphasizes that conclusion by saying that the
sentence "scripture is authoritative" functions as a "performative ut-

terance" (p. 109). A theologian uttering the sentence indicates that he or she accepts the rule that scripture ought to norm theological proposals. All who accept that rule are playing the same theological "game," but they hold in common a purely formal understanding of scripture's role in theology.

That formal rule is activated and scripture becomes a *material* norm for theology only when theologians go about the business of applying particular scriptural patterns to the life and speech of the Christian community. The material use of scripture as authority requires an imaginative construal of scripture as a whole, i.e., the shaping of a dominant configural pattern from within the Bible's vast storehouse of images and models. This process yields a diversity of "logically irreducible" patterns, all of which are in accord with scripture and all of which function to authorize diverse theological proposals. At the material level, i.e., at the level of the actual interpretation of biblical content, the authoritative use of scripture is irreducibly diverse. No single interpretation can plead superiority on the basis of an appeal to the scriptural text; all are equally authorized by scripture. Consequently no single interpretation can claim to be the *common* authoritative sense of the Christian community. With regard to the *sense* of the scriptural text, i.e., with regard to a particular interpretation of text or texts, there can be no commonly authorized reading. Readings will be as diverse as scriptural patterns and the imaginative use of those patterns by theologians.

Kelsey's brief for irreducible diversity in theological interpretation implies a major revision of the conception of theology as description or translation of revelation. It does not, however, imply

> that the concept "revelation" should be dropped from Christian theology. On the contrary, it suggests that such claims might be less misleading if they were not all pulled under a conceptual umbrella called *"the* concept of 'revelation' "* and were, instead, scattered out among discussions of other theological *loci.* The proposal in no way denies claims about the cognitive aspect of the life of faith. . . . Locating discussions about the nature and authority of the Bible in the context of discussions of "Christian existence" would not logically invalidate such claims. On the contrary, it would have the advantage of allowing each sense of "revealed" to be discussed on its own terms. (p. 210)

"Revelation" can remain in the Christian lexicon as long as it is not

given a single determinative meaning but is open to a variety of construals, uses, and understandings. Revelation is a distorting category
only when it denies the propriety of theological diversity.

Kelsey's functional account of authority makes two important con-
tributions to current considerations of revelation. First, he removes the
discussion from the context of a general account of how we come to
know and locates it in the particular framework of the use and construal of biblical texts. Whether Kelsey's comments about biblical interpretation have implications for a general theory of understanding,
he simply leaves open. Precision of analysis rather than generality of
theorizing is the good Kelsey seeks. Second, a functional view of authority provides a way of consistently combining normativity and diversity
of interpretation. Such a combination is inconceivable in a position
like Torrance's where normative interpretation is that single meaning
imposed by the object of interpretation. Functionalism moves us beyond
that central conceptual impasse which plagues every foundational
position.

A functional view of authority constitutes a genuine advance
beyond the notion of authority inherent in foundational doctrines of
revelation, but at the same time it raises a new set of problems. While
there is a place for revelation within functionalism, it is not clear that
a functional view of revelation can uphold the conviction which the
foundational doctrine sought to defend, viz., the prevenience of God.
Does the rejection of revelation as a prolegomenal epistemological doctrine imply the rejection of the Christian belief in God's prevenience?
Can the functional view maintain any sense of the priority of God's
grace in its conception of the theological task?

Before we can address those questions to Kelsey's position, we
need to state more clearly the theological implications of a belief in
God's prevenience. Eberhard Jüngel in his remarkable paraphrase of
Barth's doctrine of God has provided a forthright account of the significance of God's prevenience for theology.

> The theological question concerning the being of God *reflects* on the
> being of God. This means, however, that the being of God which is
> the subject of theological inquiry *precedes* the question. The predicate
> is to be taken strictly. God's being *precedes* the theological inquiry [in-
> to] this being. . . . The being of God . . . paves the way for question-
> ing and first of all brings the questioning on the path of thinking. . . .

> The being of God has thus prevenient character. . . . The theological concept with which this special path is properly comprehended is called revelation.[23]

Whether God's prevenience is properly focused on the priority of God's *being* is an issue which can be set aside for the moment. But, as this passage shows with special clarity, belief in God's prevenience manifests itself theologically in the conviction that theology is a *response* to God's *prior* initiative. God's priority can be construed in a variety of ways, but it cannot be eliminated altogether if the centrality of God's grace in the Christian life is to be given theological expression. Epistemological doctrines of revelation, for all their failings, did attempt to preserve the notion that theology is a response to God's prior initiative and is thus enabled by God's grace. Can a functional view of authority maintain that salutary emphasis while relocating revelation under discussions of the Christian life?

At first glance the functionalist position appears to give little support to belief in God's prevenience. The position focuses on theological uses and construals of the scriptural text and speaks of identity formation as the church's act accomplished through theological construals of the text. Thus Kelsey writes " 'Christian scripture' . . . functions to shape persons' identities so decisively as to transform them. . . . [U]se of scripture in [the church's] common life is essentially a way of shaping and preserving identity—both corporate identity as an integral community, and the personal identities of the individuals that make up the community" (91-92). Theologians assist this task by offering proposals for the shaping and reforming of Christian identity based upon their irreducibly diverse construals of the biblical text. Insofar as the church uses the Bible as the means for shaping and transforming Christian identity, it acknowledges scripture's *formal* authority. But the actual shaping of persons' lives takes place only in relation to *particular* construals of the text. Once again we see that authority is a singular notion which is the common possession of the community only as a purely formal concept; as soon as authority functions *materially*, to form actual lives, it is characterized by irreducible diversity. Kelsey's picture then is one of a community which defines its identity in relation to a common set of texts and which seeks to shape the identities of its members in relation to the variety of images derived from the rich storehouse of scripture. But it is a picture which can depict the process of identity formation without explicit reference to God. It does not, therefore, seem to be a position which gives strong support to belief in God's prevenience.

But there is another side of Kelsey's analysis which does require reference to God and may even support some notion of God's priority in the theological task. The church's

> faithfulness to her task depends on God's presence to her. The ends to be achieved through the church's activities are conceived as God's purposes. They are realized only as God makes himself present in and through the activities that are essential to the church's reality. . . . Theologically speaking, such communities say that in and through their use of the texts God also uses the texts to transform men's lives. (p. 93)

Because of the church's conviction that God acts through church and scripture to shape Christian identity, theologians' construals of the text are aptly described as imaginative visions of the presence of God among the faithful. The diversity of theological positions reflects a diversity of theologians' imaginative grasp of the mode of God's presence. Kelsey does not suggest that these organizing images are the pure creations of theological imagination; they are rather *imaginative decisions* to organize theological thinking around certain determinate patterns within scripture itself. These decisions are influenced both by the scriptural patterns and by the ecclesial context within which the theologian lives and works. Kelsey's stress on imagination highlights the fact that these organizing images are not *reducible* to any influencing factor. The theologian's imaginative decision does have logical priority, but that does not deny that theology is in an important sense a response — a response to the common life of the church, to the determinate patterns of scripture, and, most importantly, to the *prior* presence of God in church and scripture. Kelsey's functional account of authority seems to support a view of God's prevenience after all.

It remains puzzling, however, that a factor which is so central to a *theological* account of authority is dispensable in Kelsey's *theologically neutral* account. Does the notion of functional authority, either in its formal or material use, require the assertion of God's prevenience? Is God's use of our uses of the text necessary for scripture to be conceived as authoritative? A careful examination of Kelsey's argument suggests that one must answer "no" to both these questions. Scripture's formal authority is grounded in the church's *decision* to define Christian identity in relation to biblical images and thus in relation to God's prior action. Kelsey admits that "if there are communities that call themselves 'Christian church' and do not understand the use of scriptures as essential to the preservation of their self-identity, then our remarks simply do not apply to them" (p. 113). There is nothing in the notion of church that demands that scripture and God's presence be decisive for Christian identity. So also theologians' material construals of the "presence of God *pro nobis*" results from their *logically prior decisions*.[24] There is nothing inherent in the theological task which demands that theology be oriented toward the presence of God, the Christian community, or its scripture. Both formal and material senses of functional authority can be fully articulated without reference to God's prevenience.

Why then does the notion of God's priority appear to play such an important role in Kelsey's analysis? Simply because the theologians he analyzes not only orient their theologies toward scripture but conceive of theology as a response to God's prior gracious initiative. Why do they so conceive theology? Because in every case they are committed to the centrality of the concept "revelation."[25] The assertion of God's prevenience is natural for these theologians, because they understand their task as a response to God's revelation. Ironically then the source for Kelsey's own account of the importance of God's prior presence for theology is the very doctrine of revelation he seeks to eliminate from contemporary theology. Kelsey emphasizes God's prevenience because his project is descriptive, and the theologians he happens to describe are committed to God's prevenience, because they are committed to doctrines of revelation. Whether that emphasis can be maintained with the relocation of revelation in accounts of Christian existence is unclear. Kelsey has provided no clear *reason* for God's prevenience other than the *decisions* of churches and individual theologians to conceive of theology in relation to God's presence. But whether those decisions are defensible in light of the collapse of the modern doctrine of revelation is certainly open to question.

An appeal to "decision" as the ground of a theological conviction is appropriate as long as that conviction is widely held by the practicing community, i.e., as long as it functions as a background belief. But the collapse of the modern consensus concerning revelation and the end of the so-called "neo-orthodox" era in theology shows that belief in God's prevenience is no longer a deeply held or broadly shared theological conviction. Gordon Kaufman's work is especially important, because he has forthrightly admitted the collapse of the consensus and has set about building a new conception of the theological task. For Kaufman explicitly, and many other theologians implicitly, the categories of "presence" and "prevenience" must be rejected along with the time-worn concept of revelation. In light of such a development the appeal to decision as the ground of a controversial theological conviction seems insufficient. Thus while a functional conception of authority is surely compatible with belief in God's prevenience, it provides no positive support for that belief beyond the decisions of the theologians who hold it to be true.

Are there other resources within a functional view of authority which might provide greater explicit support for a continued theological emphasis on God's prevenience? Charles Wood has argued that a renewed focus on the *sensus literalis* of scripture and on the narrative shape of biblical materials can enable a reaffirmation of scripture as the vehicle for God's self-disclosure. Wood thus implies that a functional view of authority can uphold and encourage a theological accent on God's prevenience and revelation. His argument is important, because it expands upon Kelsey's twofold emphasis on ecclesial and individual decision as the basis for a conception of theology as response to God's prior presence.

To some extent Wood simply reasserts Kelsey's position on the finality of decision. In discussing James Barr's argument that the canon cannot be conceived as a unitary document of a single human author, Wood replies,

> That fact is not fatal to the hermeneutical use of the canon, however, if such use is grounded instead — as was traditionally the case — in the *decision* to regard God, and not some particular human agent, as the "author" of scripture as a whole. . . . We may . . . read scripture *as if it were* a whole, and as if the author of the whole were God. (p. 70, first emphasis added)

If we do so decide to treat the canon as a whole it then becomes possible to understand scripture as the self-disclosing Word of God. The theological decision to consider the canon in a unitary fashion, however, transforms the "Christian canon" (the sixty-six books of the Bible) into a "working canon" (the set of texts to which a theologian actually does appeal in doing theology).[26] That transformation is accomplished by construing the canon under a controlling master image. Wood suggests that the centrality of narrative in the canon, when combined with a decision to treat scripture as Word of God,

> suggests that the canon might plausibly be construed as a story which has God as its "author." It is a story in which real events and persons are depicted in a way that discloses their relationship to God and to God's purposes; a story that finally involves and relates all persons and events, and which, as it is told and heard in the power of God's Spirit, becomes the vehicle of God's own definitive self-disclosure. (pp. 100-101)

A narrative construal of scripture is, as Wood suggests, a powerful way of ascribing wholeness to the canon and of asserting God's prevenience. But as long as Wood insists on grounding that construal simply in theological decision, his defense of a narrative reading of the canon will remain unconvincing, particularly to those critics who have raised serious questions about the entire procedure. An appeal to decision is not *inherently* arbitrary, but when a decision has been challenged by weighty arguments and counterproposals, the refusal to adduce good reasons for that decision can *appear* to be arbitrary. To his credit Wood does attempt to move beyond mere "decisionism" in his account of scripture as self-disclosive narrative. The decision to treat the canon as a narrative whole stems, he argues, from a more basic commitment to the priority of the "literal sense" of the biblical text. To construe the canon as a complex narrative disclosing God's identity is to argue that such a narrative reading constitutes the text's "literal sense."[27]

The move to the literal sense may seem surprising for a Wittgensteinian theologian with a commitment to "multiple uses" rather than "single meaning" of a text. The literal sense has most often been associated with foundational single-meaning theories of interpretation. But Wood does not use the notion of *sensus literalis* in that fashion.

> "Literal sense" is intimately bound up with the conventions of reading, with the capacities and dispositions, linguistic and personal, which the reader brings to the text, by virtue of having been formed in a community with a fairly secure style of interaction with the material. . . . This literal sense . . . which the community of faith has normally

> acknowledged as basic . . . is grounded in the community's own experience with the text . . . it is the sense whose discernment has become second nature to the members of the community. (pp. 41, 43)

The literal sense of the text is the sense determined by the community's conventional use of the text. It is both the *common* and *customary* sense, i.e., the sense which the community shares and the sense to which the community has become accustomed. Wood is arguing that if a narrative construal of the canon does reflect the common and customary sense within the community, then such a reading is grounded not in mere decision but in a deep communal consensus. Not the decision but the consensus is the ultimate ground of the text's literal sense.

> A decision as to what is to count as the literal sense is grounded in what one takes to be the relevant *usus loquendi*. . . . There is a *usus* which has a prior claim to the church's attention, namely, the *usus* which establishes its canonical sense as God's self-disclosive Word. It is this canonical sense which the church has the most reason to acknowledge as the literal sense of scripture. (pp. 117, 119)

Wood's attempt to assert the priority of communal consensus is an important move beyond "decisionism," but its effectiveness is limited by two major factors. First, Wood's own functional view of authority makes an appeal to communal consensus as the ground of scripture's literal sense conceptually implausible. The literal sense is the communally authorized sense. But the functional view of authority Wood shares with Kelsey suggests that there can be no communally authorized sense of a text. Authority is something a community holds in common as a purely formal concept. Formal authority gives neither guidance as to how a text is to be interpreted nor criteria for preferring one interpretation to another. It simply acts as a performative utterance indicating a theologian's decision to play theology by certain rules. When authority becomes a material concept, actually guiding particular readings of texts, it is no longer a concept held in common. Particular interpretations are supported by logically diverse construals of the canon. Wood's invocation of the *sensus literalis* as the common and customary sense of the biblical text cannot be sustained, because his view of authority leads one to expect irreducible diversity at the level of actual textual interpretation. The great advantage of the functional view is that it holds together normativity and diversity of interpretation; it does so, however, at the expense of an authoritative common under-standing of scripture. With regard to the *sense* of the scriptural text there can be no commonly authorized reading. The evident implica-tion of a functional view of authority is that there can be no *sensus literalis* understood as the common and customary sense of the text as used by the Christian community.

Wood rightly states his case in the form of a conditional. If the Christian community customarily uses scripture as a narrative disclosive of God's identity, then a narrative reading of scripture is its literal sense. While a functional view of authority leads one to expect irreducible diversity, it does not demand or create that diversity. If the consensus Wood invokes does in fact exist in the Christian community, then the functional view could be employed to establish a normative canonical sense. But the apparent lack of such a consensus is the second major factor limiting Wood's position. It is certainly *not* the case that there is a *theological consensus* that scripture ought to be used in this way, and one can reasonably doubt that there is any practical *ecclesial con-sensus* on this matter. Anyone who has experienced the "eucharist" at an Anglo-Catholic mass and the "Lord's Supper" at a Baptist ser-vice knows something of the irreducible diversity in Christian prac-tice. Such diversity extends to liturgy, music, prayer, personal piety, virtually every aspect of the Christian life. If commonality cannot be discovered in theological uses of scripture, the prospect for discerning such commonality in Christian practice seems far dimmer. One does not have to know the philosophical criticisms of foundationalism to recognize diversity as an inescapable fact of contemporary life. Such diversity has resulted in part from the breakdown of the realistic reading of scriptural narrative Wood recommends. With the eclipse of biblical narrative, which Hans Frei has documented so thoroughly,[28] comes the shift in the logical status of belief in God's prevenience described in chapter 1. Belief in the priority of God's grace is easily sustained as a background belief when supported by a realistic reading of scrip-tural narrative. But the story of the modern world is one of the pro-gressive demise of that basic belief and its supporting hermeneutic. The predominant evidence thus indicates the absence of the very con-sensus Wood needs to shore up his appeal to theological decision.

The apparent conclusion which emerges from this analysis of Kelsey and Wood is that a functional view of authority does not inherently support belief in God's prevenience and may subtly work to undermine a view of theology as response to God's prior initiative. As a formal descriptive method functionalism is neutral vis-à-vis God's prevenience. If theologians decide to conceive of theology as a response to God's presence, a functional view can give a coherent description of scripture's role in authorizing such theological proposals. But the very neutrality of the view prohibits its advocacy of one conception of theology over another.[29] Functionalism simply reflects theologians' prior decisions about such matters and describes their actual use of authorizing texts. Functionalism does, however, make one normative claim, viz., that a single-meaning theory cannot adequately account for the actual diversity in theological uses of scripture, and thus that the standard view of revelation is radically misleading. That single normative claim does not deny that theology is a response to God's prior initiative, but it does rule out one way of expressing God's priority. Moreover, the formal view of theology implied by functionalism stresses the logical priority of theologians' imaginative decisions and focuses upon the function of text and tradition in forming and reforming Christian character. Thus it encourages a formal view of theology as active imaginative construction and practical character formation. In that respect, if in no other, it resembles the conception of theology proposed by Gordon Kaufman.

Functionalism thus constrains the theological expression of God's prevenience in two ways. First, it tends to subordinate an understanding of theology as response to God's grace to its formal view of theology as imaginative use of text and tradition to form Christian identity. The former material view is justified only insofar as it can be accommodated by the latter formal view. Second, functionalism accommodates the notion of God's prevenience through its emphasis on the priority of theological decision. If theologians decide to conceive of theology as a response to God's presence, then functionalism can describe their imaginative uses of scripture. But the grounding of belief in God's prevenience in *decision* runs counter to the very intention of the belief itself. If theology is a response to God's prior initiative, then our theological "decisions," rightly understood, are not simply our voluntary resolutions but the conformation of our wills and intellects to God's initial bidding. Belief in God's prevenience implies that a view of theology in which logical priority is granted to theological decision is insufficient to capture a sense that theology is a response to God's grace.

Functional views of authority mark an important advance in contemporary discussions of revelation, but their theological neutrality limits their usefulness in mounting a full-scale justification of belief in God's prevenience. In order to make a justificatory argument, a theologian must move beyond analysis to advocacy by offering reasons designed to persuade others that this belief is justified. The reasons offered in support of the theological conviction will not be theologically neutral. Such reasons are always logically related to the master image around which a theology is organized, but it does not follow that the arguments they support are doomed simply to convince the already converted. The diversity of theological positions does not imply their incommensurability.[30] Reasons offered in support of a theological proposition are logically dependent upon the organizing master image, but the scope of their applicability is not limited to those positions which accept the same image. Image-specific reasons may be sufficient to convince theologians of the truth of propositions, even if they do not share all the beliefs and assumptions of the supporting position. In order for rational argument to occur between proponents of theologically diverse positions, one simply needs some set of common beliefs from which to begin the process of persuasion. The more extensive the set of beliefs held in common the broader the range of agreement is likely to be. But persuasion cannot take place at all if the theology-specific reasons for particular beliefs are not explicitly stated. That is to say, the interesting debates about the truth of theological propositions can only begin when theologians move beyond formal methodological studies and once again take up the task of explicating and defending theological positions.

The first three chapters of this book have been concerned with matters of method, but my argument has been designed to show the importance but also the limits of such clarifying analytical activity. If belief in God's prevenience is to be given theological expression, it must be from within a particular theological position, organized around a controlling image. In the next four chapters I will offer a defense of God's prevenience grounded, not in an epistemological account of the origin of Christian beliefs, but in an explication of the internal logic of that Christian conviction in relation to an understanding of scripture as a narrative depicting God's identity. I am not proposing a general theoretical justification for belief in God's prevenience; I am simply offering some good reasons for affirming that belief, reasons which I hope will be convincing even to those who are not committed to the narrative image which lies at the center of my project. I will argue that belief in God's prevenience is implied in faith's conviction that God's promises as depicted in narrative form are true. I will thus defend a modest doctrine of revelation, by which I simply mean an explication of the Christian conviction that the God identified in scriptural narrative truly issues his word of promise to the readers of the text. The doctrine of revelation I seek to defend is not a foundational epistemological theory but an account which traces the internal logic of a set of Christian convictions concerning God's identity and reality. Though my argument emerges from a narrative image of the Christian faith, it strives to express a conviction shared by all those who confess the name of Christ: that all of human life, including our theological thinking, is ultimately dependent on the creating, sustaining, and redeeming grace of God.

CHAPTER FOUR

Toward a Nonfoundational Theology

In their useful little book *The Web of Belief* W. V. Quine and J. S. Ullian designate two strategies for overcoming resistance to an argument: overwhelming and undermining. "To overwhelm we adduce such abundant considerations in favor of our thesis that we end up convincing the man in spite of his conflicting belief. . . . To undermine, on the other hand, we directly challenge his conflicting belief."[1] My argument has thus far been an exercise in undermining. I have tried to demonstrate that the standard defense of God's prevenience, the epistemological doctrine of revelation, is conceptually incoherent and thus cannot uphold the belief it seeks to justify. I have also shown that two recent attempts to replace the standard doctrine fail—one by intention, the other by implication—to preserve an adequate notion of God's prevenience. All three positions fail to account both for God's *priority* and for his *relation* to our human framework of concepts and categories. The standard doctrine conceives of God as external to our conceptual framework and attempts to establish both aspects of revelation by an epistemological argument. While the framers of the doctrine recognize the dual nature of the problem, their causal conception of explanation renders their solution incoherent. The neo-Kantian approach to revelation incorporates "God" within our conceptual framework, thereby establishing the relation at the expense of God's priority. This option willingly rejects the notion of God's prevenience. Functionalism breaks with the epistemological tradition of modern theology and seeks to locate "revelation" in various ecclesial and theological uses of scripture, but its focus on the logical priority of imaginative decision finally undermines its support of God's prevenience. In light of the shortcomings of these attempts the key question now becomes: Can a nonfoundational argument succeed where others have failed, i.e., can it establish both God's relation and priority to our theological framework?

71

In order to answer that question I must leave behind the under-mining strategy and engage in a little "overwhelming." That is to say, I must begin to adduce good reasons in support of the Christian belief in God's prevenience. But to do that I must introduce an alternative to foundational views of theology and theological justification. In the succeeding chapters I am going to employ a form of holist justifica-tion[2] to argue that belief in God's prevenience is both conceptually coherent and theologically indispensable. My argument will rely on a conception of theology as primarily a descriptive activity, a second-order mode of reflection which displays the logic inherent in Chris-tian belief and practice. I use the term *descriptive* in contrast to *ex-planatory*, *not* in contrast to *normative*. A descriptive theology makes normative proposals but does not seek to justify those proposals by developing a foundational explanatory theory. "Description" is an in-terpretive activity which seeks to illuminate the structures embedded in beliefs and practices.[3] Descriptive theology eschews theoretical de-fenses of Christian doctrine, seeking rather to show the intelligibility, aptness, and warranted assertability of Christian beliefs. (For further specification of those criteria see chapter 5, pp. 92–96). Justification requires close attention to the patterns inherent in particular beliefs and practices rather than to a general theory which norms all religious discourse. Since my justificatory argument in defense of God's preve-nience assumes this view of theology, I must begin with a brief sketch of its most important features.

Descriptive Theology: Faith Seeking Understanding

A nonfoundational defense of God's prevenience is characterized by three distinctive emphases which together form the outlines of a nonfoundational or descriptive theology. *First,* justification of Chris-tian belief is specific to the Christian faith, community, and tradition. Nonfoundational justification requires the assumption that there is a Christian conceptual frame supported by specific conventions and prac-tices. I will refer to that complex entity as "the Christian faith," but the use of the singular does not deny the historical and contemporary diversity of the Christian tradition. It simply suggests that for all its variety of expression, its quarrels and disagreements, Christianity *is* a tradition. By tradition I mean that Christianity is "an historically ex-tended, socially embodied argument . . . an argument precisely in part about the goods which constitute that tradition."[4] "The Christian faith" is that set of beliefs and practices which in their social and historical reality provide the context for arguments about which beliefs and practices ought so to function. The Christian tradition is comprised of those voices of the past and present which debate the true nature of the Christian faith. Theology is not intended to provide the universal argument which silences all voices but one; theology is rather the vehicle by which the arguments are voiced. Theologians carry on the conversation not from a privileged position above tradition but from within the polyphony of voices which constitute the Christian community. It follows then that theological positions are to be judged not by a universal criterion beyond tradition or by an imagined consensus within the community but by the content-specific arguments which theologians offer in support of their positions.

Second, this nonfoundational view of theology implies a much closer relation between the direct "first-order" expressions of the church's faith and the reflective "second-order" activity of theology than most foundational views. The most pervasive form of foundationalism in modern theology is that which seeks to ground theological language in a universal religious experience. This foundational theology has a natural suspicion about the reliability of direct expressions of faith.[5] If Christian language is grounded in a universal experience, then, according to this view, the church's first-order speech is a manifestation of that deeper reality. Its meaning and truth is not established by the surface patterns of grammar and logic but by those deep structures which relate that language to its fundamental ground. Theology, the foundationalist argues, ought to follow the form and structure of that deeper reality rather than the penultimate logic of the dependent language of church faith and practice. Theology, a second-order reflective activity, serves the first-order practical language of the church by being both its theoretical defender and its critic. Theology seeks to ground the language of worship and prayer by demonstrating its relation to that deeper reality by means of a prolegomenal and epistemological doctrine of revelation. The belief in God's prevenience, for example, would be justified not in relation to specific Christian beliefs and practices but in relation to that universal experience which the language merely "re-presents."[6]

This expressive or symbolic view of Christian language and the urge toward foundationalism thus usually go hand in hand. Both views seek some fundament beyond the transient diversity of ordinary language on which to base and explain ordinary discourse. Both attempt to penetrate beyond the surface to that *fons et origo* from which all explanation proceeds. While symbolic views of language do not share the same conceptual disorders as their associated foundational epistemologies, their sharp distinction between first- and second-order activities raises a troubling concern. When theology is conceived as a theoretical activity seeking the ultimate ground of church practice, it naturally seeks those goods associated with theoretical activities. Theology takes its place beside other theoretical inquiries ruled by general principles of rationality. Whenever a theoretical inquiry diverges from those general principles, it must justify that divergence by a special apologetic argument. Since Christian claims often appear exceptional when judged by general principles of rationality, theology must regularly undertake to defend its divergent tendencies. If a foundationalist theologian is concerned at all to guard the distinctiveness of the theological subject matter, apologetics inevitably emerges as the *primary* theological task. The two most important theological activities—the development of a universal justificatory argument and the defense of Christian claims before the bar of rationality—are carried on independent of the internal logic of Christian belief and practice and with little reference to criteria of judgment internal to the Christian tradition. As a consequence the foundational view tends to subordinate the characteristic patterns of Christian speech to the patterns of the philosophical and apologetic argument. This position has grave difficulty affirming the irreducible integrity of Christian language. This is especially the case if the primal religious experience which grounds the language of church practice is capable of expression in a universal philosophical language, for then the characteristic patterns of Christian speech are reducible to the structures of the more ultimate basic language.

Since a nonfoundational theology is concerned with justification internal to the Christian framework, its *primary* interests are neither epistemological nor apologetic. In the process of seeking justification it will surely on occasion need to engage in conversation with positions external to the Christian faith. Though the Christian faith has its own internal integrity, it does not exist in a vacuum. The doctrine of God, Christology, anthropology, et al., are all influenced by concepts and categories derived from non-Christian sources. But such borrowings are employed for distinctive Christian uses and sustained by distinctive Christian practices and thus are no longer *systematically* ruled by the original context. They are annexed for Christian purposes and ruled by the new Christian context.[7] The employment of borrowed concepts cannot be equivocal, i.e., a concept cannot be used in a wholly different way in the Christian frame. Thus on certain occasions or when addressing particular audiences the theologian might need to show the analogical connections between Christian and non-Christian uses of particular concepts or beliefs, but that is always a logically secondary and *ad hoc* procedure. The Christian use of such concepts cannot be ruled by the former context of meaning. The primary context is supplied by the concepts' use in Christian community.

Consequently nonfoundational theology seeks its criteria of judgment within the first-order language of church practice. Insofar as it is judge and critic of practice it evaluates and criticizes according to criteria internal to the Christian faith. While some distinction between first- and second-order discourse remains, the distinction is not nearly as sharp as in foundational theologies. Nonfoundational theology is located squarely within Christian tradition and community and seeks to "re-describe" the internal logic of the Christian faith.[8] Theology is a second-order activity precisely because it has no rationale independent of the first-order language of faith. Theology of this kind is a critical reflective activity which seeks the norm for faith and practice not beyond but within the first-order language of the church. Theology seeks to discern the internal logic of Christian belief, i.e., it seeks to uncover the patterns of coherent interrelationships which characterize the beliefs and practices of that complex phenomenon we call the Christian faith. Theology thus presupposes that faith and seeks through critical reflection to understand that faith more fully. Nonfoundational or descriptive theology is in this sense "faith seeking understanding."[9]

Third, nonfoundational or holist justification is not a matter of devising a universal theoretical defense of Christian language-as-such or of discerning the causal relation between our concepts and their external referents. Holist justification consists, rather, in seeking the relation between a disputed belief and the web of interrelated beliefs within which it rests. Holism understands justification as a process of rational persuasion. "We convince someone of something by appealing to beliefs he already holds and by combining these to induce further beliefs in him, step by step, until the belief we wanted finally to inculcate in him is inculcated."[10] Belief in God's prevenience is logically linked to certain other beliefs concerning God's promises, identity and reality in that it serves as an essential presupposition or background belief for them. If those latter beliefs can be shown to be both intelligible and theologically justified, and if the inferential links between those beliefs and belief in prevenience are valid, then that basic Christian conviction is also a justified Christian belief. Holist justification, like the neo-Kantian and functionalist positions, operates within the framework of Christian beliefs. But unlike those options this holist argument seeks to justify belief in the *priority* of God to our theological framework. If this argument is successful, it will establish both God's relation to and his priority to our concepts and categories.

There is, however, one difficulty which must be faced at the outset. Holist justification works most simply when the two parties engaged in discussion share a set of common background beliefs but dispute the propriety of holding a particular dependent belief. For example, two Christians may hold identical beliefs about the sanctity of human life, the sinfulness of human nature, and the role of government in preserving order, but disagree about the moral acceptability of nuclear warfare. In the process of rational persuasion one party might seek to show the other that a defense of nuclear war is inconsistent with the background beliefs they hold in common. Whether or not that approach is successful, the disputants share a fairly stable core of background beliefs as the basis for their discussion. A background belief is thus ordinarily a belief which both parties assume to be true and which serves as a premise for further argument. In our case, however, it is precisely the background conviction, belief in God's prevenience, which is in dispute. Indeed, I have already argued that the modern era has witnessed the breakdown of a cultural consensus concerning that belief and the shift in the belief's function from a background conviction to a dependent belief in need of theoretical defense. How can holist justification work if the belief which ought to serve as the premise of an argument is itself the disputed belief?

Clearly if holist justification is to apply in this case, it must be slightly modified to meet the conditions of our situation. Instead of proceeding from a common background belief to a disputed belief, my argument will begin with a set of accepted dependent beliefs and move by implication to the more general belief upon which they rest. I intend to show the relation of belief in God's prevenience to that cluster of dependent beliefs which it supports. The logical relations among those beliefs are such that rejection of the background belief would entail a radical revision of all the dependent beliefs and rejection of some. But some of the dependent beliefs are both uncontroversial and apparently constitutive of Christian identity. Such beliefs ought to be given up only if there are strong counter reasons, e.g., if an inconsistency among dependent beliefs or between dependent and background beliefs can be shown.[11] Lacking such inconsistency the Christian is justified in assenting both to the dependent beliefs and to their supporting background belief. My argument will thus begin with a group of dependent beliefs concerning God's promises and their narrative fulfillment and concerning the relation of God's identity and reality. I will argue that there are good reasons for assenting to these beliefs as constitutive of Christian identity. If that argument holds, then it follows by implication that the belief upon which they depend, belief in God's prevenience, is also a justified belief constitutive of Christian identity.

The argument will thus be an example of "retrospective justification," an argument which begins with particular Christian beliefs and their supporting practices and seeks to defend the more general Christian belief which they presuppose.[12] The argument moves not from general presuppositions or premises to their implied concrete conclusions (prospective justification) but from actual beliefs and practices to the more general beliefs which they imply (restrospective justification). The point of the argument is to show both the consistency of the implied relation and its importance for defining Christian identity. The argument will thus both describe the connections among those various beliefs and urge their continued acceptance by the contemporary Christian community. In that sense the argument will have both descriptive and normative components.

This retrospective procedure is necessary in part because of the breakdown in both the cultural and theological consensus concerning God's prevenience. The absence of cultural consensus is a fact of modern life, and efforts to regain such consensus are undoubtedly doomed to failure. The breakdown of theological consensus has followed upon the cultural demise. Since belief in human dependence upon God's grace no longer functions as a culturally shared assumption, theologians have taken that fact either as a cue to start the apologetic engines in defense of revelation or as an indication that Christians too must abandon that belief. Both alternatives are wrong-headed, because both allow the cultural situation to determine the logic of Christian belief. Admittedly, if a belief can be shown to be culturally incoherent, then it will be difficult to sustain it as a constitutive Christian conviction. But while some *defenses* of God's prevenience may be conceptually incoherent, the belief itself is not. It may not be widely accepted as true, but that does not make the belief incoherent. I want to argue that theologians ought to re-establish *theological* consensus concerning prevenience, despite the irremediable lack of *cultural* consensus.

Belief in God's prevenience functions logically and theologically as an indispensable background belief within the logic of Christian faith. In this case its background status is not a function of its broad acceptance but of its essential role in the framework of Christian belief. My argument will attempt to reassert the background status of belief in God's prevenience by showing that the logical connections between that now controversial belief and other central theological convictions are sufficiently tight that if one accepts the cluster of related convictions, acceptance of belief in God's prevenience is implied. My argument will further attempt to show that rejection of that background belief will require a radical and unwelcome revision in our understanding of Christian identity.

Descriptive Theology and the Problem of Revelation

Descriptive theology seeks to display the relation between belief in God's prevenience and the supporting and supported beliefs within the Christian faith, or failing in that task, it shows that such a belief cannot be sustained by the logic of Christian belief. The terms of the discussion of revelation within descriptive theology are thus substantially different from the epistemological and causal categories of foundational theology, but the *problem* of revelation, nonetheless, remains strikingly familiar. Descriptive theology must still account for both God's priority and his relation to the framework of Christian belief. How does one argue for God's prevenience from within the context of Christian faith and practice without reducing God's priority to his relation or God's relation to his priority? That problem is not unique to the modern epistemological context but is a perennial aspect of every account of revelation. The tension between priority and relation is evident in the passages quoted from Luther and Barth in chapter 1. Luther argued "that knowledge of Christ and of faith is not a human work but utterly a divine gift." Barth restated that conviction in the following way. "The biblical writers testify that the revelation came to them with a supreme authoritativeness of its own . . . . They *answered* something that came to them, not from them." Revelation involves both a *gift* and a *response*. Revelation as gift emphasizes God's priority as gracious giver; faith as the appropriate response to revelation emphasizes that God's gift is truly related to our concepts and categories, i.e., truly received. But how does one maintain the distinction between divine initiative and human reception so that priority might be granted to the former? How do we identify *God's* initiative from within the framework of *our web of beliefs*?

This problem is particularly pressing for a descriptive theology which presupposes the texts and traditions of the Christian community. That tradition is not itself the revelation but merely the witness to an ostensible divine revelation. If the tradition is itself thoroughly human, then how do we recognize the divine element in the human tradition? James Barr has put the matter well.

> The real problem, as it seems to me, is that we have no access to, and no means of comprehending, a communication or revelation from God which is antecedent to the human tradition about him and which then goes on to generate that very tradition. In attempting to found the status of scripture upon such an antecedent revelation we are explaining what is obscure by what is quite unknown. I am not saying that there was nothing there; only that (a) its status is too obscure for us to base anything upon, and (b) consideration of it thus becomes a speculative exercise in which we are not called to engage.[13]

How can we speak about an antecedent revelation to which the scriptural witness is the response, when that response is itself the source of our knowledge of the antecedent revelation?

The dilemma facing descriptive theology's account of revelation is obvious. Theological inquiry is an interpretation of Christian texts and traditions which are themselves the witness of the Christian community that it has experienced the reality of God. While the community claims a distinction between the divine initiative and the response of faith, the contemporary interpreter has access to God's initiative only in the faith response, i.e., only through the community's interpretation. While the contemporary interpreter need not deny the independence of God's prior action, he or she apparently possesses no tools which would allow the distinguishing of that initiative from the interpretive faith of the community. While a distinction between gift and response, divine initiative and human reception, may be useful for reporting the self-understanding of the ancient community, it appears to have no theological utility for the contemporary religious community. *A fortiori* it would appear to give precious little guidance for the doing of theology. What does it mean to do theology "in accord with revelation" if we cannot distinguish that revelation from the faith of the community? The ostensible purpose of doctrines of revelation is to highlight the peculiarly divine activity in our understanding of God so that theology might be normed by God's action rather than simply the deliberation, choice, or consensus of the human community. But the very distinction the doctrine relies upon is the distinction it appears unable to justify. If God's action cannot be distinguished from human action, nor God's initiative from human response, then a doctrine of revelation appears to be nothing more than a description of the faith of the religious community. But that is to say that it is not a doctrine of *revelation* at all.

The challenge Barr raises to defenses of the priority of God's initiative must be taken seriously, but his particular objection is directed against two aspects of conceptions of revelation which the view I am proposing rejects. First, Barr is concerned about theologians' tendency to identify revelation as an *antecedent* event to which faith is a *subsequent* response.[14] Such theologians assert God's prevenience by arguing for his temporal priority to Christian faith. Barr's quoted response to that defense is devastatingly accurate, but it does not apply with equal force to descriptive theology's account of revelation. Descriptive theology does not rest its argument on a claim either to God's epistemological priority or to God's temporal priority. It seeks rather to establish that God's reality (and thus his "ontological" priority) is implied by a set of concrete Christian beliefs concerning God's identity. Revelation in this view is not simply a temporally prior event to which faith is a response. Revelation is the continuing reality of God's active presence among his people. Since it is a reality "not seen" and not fully experienced, it must be expressed by a confession of faith, i.e., an "assurance of things hoped for, the conviction of things not seen." That conviction is displayed theologically by showing how God's prevenience is retrospectively implied by a cluster of Christian convictions concerning God's promises, identity, and reality. If those latter beliefs are taken to be true, then the belief upon which they rest must also be accepted as true. Descriptive theology seeks God's priority from within the network of current Christian beliefs and practices and defines God's revelation not as an antecedent event but as a present reality awaiting future consummation.

That response to Barr's concern about antecedent revelation could be seen as avoiding the deeper issue implied in his challenge. Barr is asking whether we can speak of God's priority *in any sense* if the only basis for theological claims is the faith and tradition of the Christian community. The original community claimed to have received God's revelation, but the subsequent community has access merely to that self-referential claim and not to the revelation itself. The theologian appears limited to describing what the Christian community believed or believes but can say nothing about the truth or referentiality of those beliefs. That objection relates in part to an understanding of God's temporal priority but, more importantly, it assumes a second characteristic of revelation which the nonfoundationalist rejects. It assumes that the relation between Christian claims and God's reality is *extrinsic*, so that claims about the church's faith *cannot* be claims about an external God who stands outside all human language. On this view self-referential claims cannot imply claims about external reality. Theologians are thus doomed merely to describe the meaning and use of Christian beliefs but are barred access from the domain of truth and reference.

Nonfoundational theology, however, denies that God is *extrinsically* related to Christian belief, because it rejects the common picture of God as external causal agent. Consequently this view also rejects a sharp logical distinction between meaning and truth with regard to claims about God. God's reality is *intrinsically* related to Christian belief and practice, if Christian claims about God are true. For Christians to speak about the gospel is at the same time to speak about the God of the gospel. That is to say, the logically odd category of "gospel" refers both to a human communication and a divine actor, and it must so refer if the gospel is what Christians confess it to be — the good news about God's reconciling action on behalf of his creatures. But the report about God's reconciliation cannot be separated from the good news itself, because the gospel is the *report* of God's reconciliation, the present *gift* of that reconciliation, and the *promise* of the future triumph of God's reconciling action. Meaning and truth are sufficiently linked in the Christian gospel as to preclude a theory of truth and reference logically separable from an account of meaning. On the other hand, nonfoundational theology does not propose an alternative theory of meaning and truth as the external ground of the gospel's claims. It simply says that when the internal logic of Christian claims is examined one discovers that meaning and truth are closely intertwined, because God's reality and Christian language are intrinsically and internally related.[15]

Barr's challenge, insofar as it assumes a doctrine of revelation which views God as extrinsically related to Christian faith and which grounds belief in God's prevenience in his temporal priority, does not apply to the view of revelation I am defending. But insofar as Barr's criticism restates the perennial problem of revelation, the challenge is surely apt. Barr's question to a nonfoundational view of revelation is this: given that you assume the extant faith and tradition of the Christian community, how do you distinguish between divine initiative and communal response? How can God's prevenience be defined from within the logic of Christian faith to assert God's priority and relation to Christian belief? I have tried to show that an account of the intrinsic relation of God's reality to the Christian faith is neither inconceivable nor logically unintelligible. But that defense of its logical possibility is not yet a defense of its theological plausibility. The latter defense cannot be given in general terms but must refer to the specific content of the Christian beliefs which together justify the assertion of God's prevenience. The justification of Christian belief in God's prevenience depends upon the coherent interrelations among Christian convictions concerning God's promises, their narrative enactment and fulfillment, and God's identity. That is to say that God's prevenience is logically linked to the truthfulness of the triune God's narrated promise. That claim will be explicated at length in chapters 5, 6, and 7; but before I move to that discussion I must treat one final preliminary issue.

Descriptive Theology and the Centrality of Narrative

In the succeeding chapters I am going to use the category of narrative in my discussion of God's promises, identity, and reality. Narrative has become a fashionable topic in contemporary theology and is being used by a wide variety of theologians for a range of diverse purposes. Such diversity inevitably breeds imprecision, especially when the category is employed for different or even conflicting ends. Before I embark on my account of God's prevenience, I need to place my understanding of narrative along the spectrum of current practice.

Theologians who are attracted to certain formal qualities of narrative (e.g., centrality of chronological sequence, importance for character description) part company on the question of how the category can best serve theological reflection. Is narrative primarily a transcendental quality of experience, a universal form of consciousness?[16] Or is narrative simply a literary form which demands appropriate interpretive approaches for proper reading?[17] When the *former* conception of narrative predominates, the category becomes useful for theology by providing a deep structure which captures the essential temporality of human being and understanding. Narrative provides the key for a revised philosophical understanding of human selfhood which is applicable to specifically Christian tasks. Narrative as a literary category becomes important for theology because "stories" are the most appropriate form of expression for an essentially temporal self. When the *latter* conception of narrative predominates, the category is most useful as a tool for the interpretation of *biblical* narrative. While speculations about the transcendental temporality of the self may be interesting and occasionally even helpful, they are not directly or primarily relevant for the task of theology. Theology on this view is the description or redescription of biblical narrative into a coherent language which displays the logic of Christian belief. Narrative highlights both a predominant literary category within the Bible and an appropriate theological category for interpreting the canon as a whole.[18] Theology is primarily concerned with the interpretation of text and tradition and only secondarily, if at all, with speculations about the true nature of the self and the deep structures of human understanding.

This division between the predominant uses of narrative is admittedly rough, but it does provide a way of assigning priorities in the use of narrative. It is certainly possible for a single theologian to employ narrative in both of the senses sketched above, but it is unlikely that both tasks could be given equal priority. Inevitably a theologian will prefer one or the other conception of theology which undergirds the two different uses and thus will assign priority to one of the tasks. The first conception of narrative implies a view of theology very much like the foundational theology I have been engaged in criticizing. It

sees the primary theological task to be the construction of a philosophical anthropology—a transcendental view of human being and language—and the correlation of Christian concepts with those transcendental categories. This use of narrative continues the "turn to the
subject" which has dominated theology since Kant. The second conception of narrative implies a view of theology very much like the descriptive theology I have outlined in this chapter. It sees the primary
theological task to be the critical redescription of the Christian faith
in categories consistent with the church's first-order language. It eschews
the systematic correlation of Christian concepts with those of a philosophical anthropology and thus resists theology's "turn to the subject."
Its primary interest in biblical narrative is in discerning God's identity
as agent in the text and in the on-going life of the Christian community.
Anthropological considerations follow from the primary focus on God's
identity and reality.[19]

Obviously I find myself attracted to this second conception of
narrative and its underlying view of theology, but I need to make explicit the primarily theological reasons for that preference. As I explicate
those reasons I will have occasion to show the interrelation of theological, philosophical, and literary considerations in this second understanding of narrative.

Narrative as a theological category provides an organizing image
for a theology concerned to reassert the primacy of God's identity for
the theological task. Narrative is useful to nonfoundational theology's
reassertion of God's prevenience because 1) it provides a coherent theological alternative to those theologies focused on the primacy of philosophical anthropology; 2) it provides a way of construing the canon
as a whole which integrates scripture's first-order language and theology's second-order redescription; 3) it focuses attention on the centrality of God's agency within biblical narrative and Christian community.

1) The breakdown of a "realistic reading" of biblical narrative
is closely linked to the emergence of the modern theological fascina-
tion with the primacy of the human subject.[20] In the reformers' theological reading of biblical narrative the three aspects of interpretation—
explication, meditation, and application[21] —were united under the
guidance of the text's verbal sense. The reformers understand scripture as a narrative whole in which interpretive primacy is to be given
to the verbal or literal sense and to figural interpretation as an extension of literal reading to the whole of the canon. Scripture, when ex-

plicated in this way, depicts a real world, temporally structured, which encompasses both the times and stories of the text and those of the reader. Since the world depicted by the Bible is the only real world, the reader must fit his or her own experience into scripture's cumulative narrative, thus becoming a "figure" of the text. Christian reality claims (meditation) and formation of the Christian life (application) follow from and are normed by the explicative shape of biblical narrative.

That realistic reading breaks down under the pressures of a variety of forces in modern intellectual life. Chief among those factors, however, are the rise of philosophical accounts of reality independent of the Christian faith. Increasingly theologians have come to identify Christian reality claims with referential claims to historical occurrences or ideal essences. Christian reality claims thus become subspecies of more general kinds of referential claims and are thus normed not by the explicative sense of the Christian narrative but by general philosophical rules for reference. Assertions concerning the relevance of scripture for the Christian life are also divorced from scripture's explicative verbal sense. Christian concepts such as sin and redemption are separated from their narrative-specific context and assigned natural universal meanings.

> Redemption in history becomes intelligible from its natural context in our moral and religious experience, so that the wise man readily appreciates that rational, natural religion and morality need to be perfected from beyond themselves by a revealed religion. . . . The religious meaningfulness of historical redemption or revelation . . . depends on there being an antecedent or concomitant religious context, independent of these narratives, within which to interpret them.[22]

Application and meditation are both separated from the narrative shape of explication, and as the independent context becomes in the nineteenth and twentieth centuries an ontology of human being and language, the eclipse of biblical narrative results in the theological turn to the subject.

As I have argued at length, descriptive theology opposes the systematic methodological affirmation of the primacy of anthropology in modern theology. The turn to narrative is one way of providing an alternative to that predominant modern tradition. If a coherent narrative construal of scripture can be given, then that is the first step toward the reunification of the explicative, meditative, and applicative senses under the guidance of the narrative verbal sense.

2) Narrative is one of a number of possible images around which the diverse materials of the canon can be organized, but it has the advantage of integrating a central literary genre in scripture with an organizing theological image. Narrative as a literary category emphasizes the interaction of circumstance and character, incident and identity, in an ordered chronological sequence.[23] The *ordered temporality* of narrative makes it a valuable tool for a theological construal of the canon. Our ability to "follow" a story depends upon the unique combination of succession and configuration within the plot.[24] Narratives move temporally; that is, events succeed one another in a temporal fashion. But mere succession does not enable us to follow the story. The events must be configured into a coherent whole which organizes the events without destroying their temporal succession. Successful narratives pull us along by creating expectations in the reader that the narrated events are moving toward some end or conclusion. To be sure, there is no straight-line progression of events to expected conclusion. Good stories are filled with the unexpected, the sudden turn of plot, the coincidence—what Frank Kermode has called "peripeteia"[25]—as they move toward their endings. And yet when the conclusion has been reached "it all fits," i.e., the configuration of events makes sense from the vantage point of the end.

One major difficulty facing a narrative construal of the canon is the problem of the irreducible diversity of the integral narratives which are found in scripture. The rise of historical criticism has been a major factor in the breakdown of the figural interpretation the reformers used to unify the canon, and historical critics are rightly concerned about the danger of imposing a premature narrative unity on these complex texts. While theologians ought to be aware of this danger, they should, nonetheless, continue to seek the configural narrative unity of the biblical witness. Good narratives are, after all, "discordant-concordant wholes," and the discordance is essential to the plausibility of a story.[26] The biblical narratives depict a world in which God and human beings interact. Often the actions of the human characters seem designed to flout the intention of the creator. At other times the plot takes such bizarre twists that no narrative unity seems apparent. Yet despite (and often because of) "peripeteia" in the development of plot and character, the narratives move toward a discernible conclusion. And as they do, the meaning of the overarching narrative begins to emerge. Occasionally the narrator will offer an explicit interpretation of the action, but more often the meaning is carried through narrated action and dialogue.[27] Like an exceptionally rich novel the biblical narrative provides the structures of plot, characterization, and setting which serve as the clues to the texts' meaning.

This use of narrative as a device for unifying the canon encourages a literary interpretation of the text which seeks clear textual warrants for the description of the overarching biblical narrative. The goal of this endeavor is to seek rational criteria which will guide the intelligent theological interpretation of biblical texts. The failure of interpreters to develop an appropriate "analytical procedure" for explicating realistic narrative has contributed mightily to biblical narrative's modern eclipse.[28] Theologians should be encouraged by the rise of a precise form of literary interpretation of biblical narrative, as exemplified by the work of Robert Alter. Alter argues that the narrative portions of scripture are best interpreted through careful attention to the intricate literary patterns of narration, characterization, and techniques of repetition which constitute the texts' literary unity.

> Attention to such features leads not to a more "imaginative" reading of biblical narrative but to a more precise one; and since all these features are linked to discernible details in the Hebrew text, the literary approach is actually a good deal *less* conjectural than the historical scholarship that asks of a verse whether it contains possible Akkadian loan words, whether it reflects Sumerian kinship practices, whether it may have been corrupted by scribal error.[29]

Precisely in discovering the *literary* art of the biblical narrative the interpreter begins to approach that elusive goal of discerning rational controls for the interpretation of ancient texts. Neither the literary nor the theological uses of narrative are fully refined, but there are ample reasons for literary critics and theologians to believe that a form of narrative unity, governed by the shape of the text itself, can be discovered within the diverse material of the canon.

3) An emphasis on the narrative unity of the canon focuses theological attention on the centrality of God's agency within biblical narrative and Christian community. Characterization is another important element of narrative structure. Through the interweaving of setting and event a narrative depicts the actions of characters. In a realistic narrative characters are caught up in contingent events remarkably similar to those which mark our own lives. As we see the characters

act and suffer within the framework of the plot, we come to know and understand them. Again expectations are created in the reader as we anticipate the reaction of a character to an unexpected twist of plot. The term *character* is intentionally ambiguous, for it can describe both an actor in the narrative and certain traits of that actor which are "characteristically" human. In coming to know George Smiley in John Le Carre's novels we discover something of the traits of patience, persistence, and loyalty. Narratives thus present patterns of characteristic action which depict personal identity. The characteristic unity which allows us to speak of a person's identity in the midst of the diverse actions he or she performs is related to the configural unity of plot. Both plot and character are "concordant-discordant wholes." Despite the variety of action and event, finally a unity is discernible in both. And the unity of character is what we call personal identity.

That same interaction of circumstance and character is present in biblical narrative but in a peculiarly complex way. Scripture's "main character" is God, and yet his direct actions are only rarely described. God's agency is most often depicted through the description of acts of other agents. In Hebrew scripture God is presented both as a character in the narrative drama who is often subject to the contingencies of plot and action and as the one who transcends the narrative, bringing plot and action to their appointed *telos*. This complex characterization is reflected in the way the narratives are structured. The story of David's election as king, for example, is a richly nuanced account in which David is presented both as the instrument of God's directing action and as a free agent who achieves kingship through his own bold exploits.[30] In the first telling of the story (1 Samuel 16) God's direct action predominates, while human deliberations fade into the background and are presented in a distant stylized fashion. Samuel's choice of David is under God's direct guidance as God continually rejects each son of Jesse until the youngest son is finally summoned from the fields. By contrast, in the longer narration of David's rise to kingship (beginning with 1 Samuel 17), accounts of human decision and action predominate, while God remains a silent and indirect presence in the narrative. Yet even when God is not a direct actor in the narrative, he brings the action to its appropriate conclusion. Even as God becomes a hidden force in David's rise to kingship, he remains the decisive force. As the tribes remind David at Hebron, "The Lord said to you, 'You shall be shepherd of my people Israel, and you shall be prince over Israel' " (2 Samuel 5:2). Though in form and content the later narrative is far more subtle and detailed, it reinforces the simple truth of the earlier story—that Israel's destiny is controlled by the actions of Yahweh. Both forms of narration are necessary to depict the identity of Israel's God, a God who brings order from chaos both through his magisterial word and through his careful forming of human shape from the soil. God's complex identity is presented through narrative accounts of his action which stress both his immanence and transcendence, his presence and hiddenness.

In the New Testament narrative God's direct action is almost never depicted. Except for a few key events (e.g., Jesus' baptism and transfiguration) God is not a primary actor in the narrative; rather, he remains hidden behind the actions of Jesus, who now takes center stage in the drama. But God's hiddenness is an essential element of the New Testament message, because the cumulative depiction of Jesus' identity brings an increasing convergence between the activity of Jesus and that of the hidden God of Israel. The connection between Jesus' mission and God's intention is announced explicitly in the baptism and transfiguration stories, but is established more subtly in the narrative sequence itself. In speech and action Jesus appropriates and re-enacts the tradition of God's chosen people of Israel, identifying himself with their mission and destiny. That identification with Israel and the unity between Jesus and God's intention reach their climax in the crucifixion-resurrection sequence of the gospels. Precisely as Jesus is rendered powerless by the apparent contingent events of the plot, he is sustained by the hidden but active power of God.[31] This theme of God's hidden but active power reaches its zenith in the gospel accounts of Jesus' resurrection from the dead. The resurrection itself is not explicitly depicted; thus the narrative modesty witnesses to the hiddenness of God's power in its most effective exercise. The narrative rather focuses on the consequences of that power in the vivid stories of the empty tomb and the post-resurrection appearances.

These brief examples point to the complex pattern of scripture's narrative depiction of God's identity. God's agency is most often depicted through the agency of the people of Israel and of Jesus. If the biblical stories are to function as "identity-descriptions" of God, then this interaction of agencies and the pattern of hiddenness and presence must be reflected in theological redescription of biblical narrative. The theologian is given considerable assistance in this task by the philosophical advances in the application of intention-action language to issues of personal identity.[32] According to this form of philosophical analysis, a person's identity is constituted by the intentions he or she carries into action. Actions are appropriately described as enacted intentions, and intentions are rightly described as implicit actions. Identity-description is nothing more or less than the description of characteristic intention-action patterns across a chronological sequence. Such temporally ordered patterns are given natural description in narratives. "Personal identity is just that identity presupposed by the unity of the character which the unity of a narrative requires. Without such unity there would not be subjects of whom stories could be told."[33] Personal identity, understood as characteristic patterns of intention and action, and narrative description are thus logically intertwined.

Descriptive theology can make good use of these borrowed philosophical categories, for they provide a coherent means of redescribing the complex narrative patterns noted in the biblical stories. The theologian can speak of God's intentions as enacted in the actions of Israel and Jesus. Those acts which occur through human agents are, insofar as they move toward a *telos* retrospectively discerned, the very acts of God. The indirectness of scripture's depiction of God's agency allows an affirmation of God's hiddenness, understood as his sovereign freedom, but the narrative's claim that these actions are the enacted intentions of God maintains a lively sense of God's presence. Thus a set of borrowed philosophical conceptions aids enormously in coherent theological redescription of God's identity as agent. It also allows, as the following chapters will show, an extension of those categories to describe the identity and reality of God within the gathered community of believers.

This account of the theological use of narrative in descriptive theology shows the interaction of theological, philosophical, and literary elements. The reading of scriptural narrative encouraged by this approach is a literary and theological interpretation which seeks clear textual warrants for the interpretation of the overarching biblical narrative. Thus it seeks to bring the literary and theological into much closer proximity than other theological options. In so doing it seeks once again to reintegrate the explicative, meditative, and applicative aspects of interpretation and to allow the explicative verbal sense, the text's narrative shape, to exercise normative influence.

This concluding discussion has attempted to show that a distinctive and coherent sense of narrative is operative in this theological project. But finally the proof of the pudding is in the tasting, and so the time has come to stop talking about descriptive theology and start engaging in it. The concluding three chapters constitute a nonfoundational account of God's prevenience focusing on the notion of "narrated promise."[34] The biblical exegesis and the theological redescription are guided by the principles enunciated in this chapter. I hope to show that a faith which trusts the promises of God and seeks to understand God's identity more fully in the narrative enactment and fulfillment of those promises rightly confesses the lordship of God under a descriptive doctrine of revelation.

CHAPTER FIVE

God's Prevenience:
The Logic of Promise and Agency

"No one is able rightly to love or believe in God," declared the Council of Orange, "except by the prior initiative of the grace of God's mercy."[1] While that dogma has received widespread acceptance in the church, theologians have struggled mightily to find appropriate theological categories for the development and application of that insight. The causal explanation model favored by most modern theologians is, I have argued, conceptually incoherent and cannot provide an adequate defense of God's prevenience. The failure of the modern doctrine of revelation, however, does not leave us bereft of resources as we seek a self-consistent account of God's gracious prior initiative. A revised doctrine of revelation will be a more modest affair, more cautious in its use of borrowed philosophical resources and less attracted to universal explanatory schemes. It will, however, be no less rigorous in its attempts to justify the Christian conviction that we love and believe in God only "by the prior initiative of the grace of God's mercy."

The following three chapters constitute a nonfoundational justification of the Christian belief in God's prevenience. This revised account of revelation will seek to satisfy the following three criteria. 1) "The criterion of intelligibility": Does belief in God's prevenience meet the conditions of intelligible communication? Is it conceptually self-consistent, and can it be coherently integrated with other beliefs in a conviction set?[2] 2) "The criterion of Christian aptness": Is the belief grounded in a coherent construal of scripture?[3] 3) "The criterion of warranted assertability":[4] Are Christians warranted in assenting to this belief as true? While these criteria are in accord with the principles of descriptive theology as developed in chapter 4, it may be helpful to address some possible objections to the final criterion before undertaking the actual process of justification.

The notion of warranted assertability may raise opposing objections among contemporary theologians. To some the criterion may appear to be an invitation to the kind of foundational theorizing I have so vigorously criticized in the preceding chapters. Obviously I do not intend my inquiry into the warrants for Christian truth-claims concerning God's prevenience to be a return to foundationalism. My justificatory argument will be neither a theoretical demonstration of the universal religiousness of the human species nor a causal explanation of the origin of theological knowledge. It will involve nothing more highfalutin than displaying the warrants of the Christian confession that God's promises are trustworthy. The grounds for that confession have little or nothing to do with the innate capacity of human feeling, reason, or language, but everything to do with the identity of God, the form and content of the promises he makes, and the character of that form of life called Christian discipleship. To ask for "warranted assertability" is not to move back toward philosophical foundationalism but is simply an attempt to show that the Christian has resources for responding to the question, "Why do you believe God's promises to be true?" The grounds in support of that belief may be Christian-specific, but they are not for that reason any less capable of detailed and careful description. The task of Christian theology, and particularly of a Christian doctrine of revelation, is (if possible) to give a coherent and intelligible theological account of the grounds of Christian faith and hope.

Other theologians may fear that "warranted assertability" says too little about Christian claims to truth. John Dewey coined the term in order to stress that "the attainment of settled beliefs is a progressive matter; there is no belief so settled as not to be exposed to further inquiry."[5] If that is the case, an epistemological realist might ask, can we make historical and ontological truth-claims? Do our theological claims actually correspond to reality as it truly is? As Julian Hartt has recently reminded us, "When we are seriously and affirmatively engaged with the Christian faith we not only *believe* the Gospel is true, we *claim* it is true, and we assert its truth."[6]

I cannot hope to solve the tangled issues of truth-claiming in religion in the scope of this project, but I do want to suggest that it is important to distinguish between the logic of our truth-claims and the logic of the justification of those claims. The collapse of epistemological foundationalism may mean that we cannot justify our truth-claims by noninferential self-evident arguments. But it does not follow that we can no longer make historical or ontological claims to truth.

The "dogma of divided truths" falls along with epistemological foundationalism; consequently, believing something to be true (for good
reasons) and asserting its truth may not be as logically distinct as the
above quotation implies. Though justification of belief is always a "progressive matter," still beliefs can be settled and truth-claims justified.
Those who fear that progressive justification undermines truth-claiming
altogether may be victims of what Richard Bernstein has called "the
Cartesian anxiety," that "grand and seductive Either/Or. *Either* there
is some support for our being, a fixed foundation for our knowledge,
or we cannot escape the forces of darkness that envelop us with madness,
with intellectual and moral chaos."[7]

My inquiry into warranted assertability will ask whether Christians are warranted in believing God's promises to be true. Since these
truth-claims take the form of promises, their justification has an inevitable prospective or eschatological dimension. The justifiability of
one's trust in the truthfulness of a promise is never fully confirmed
(or disconfirmed) until the promiser actually fulfills (or fails to fulfill)
his/her promise. Until the time of fulfillment the promisee must justify
trust on the basis of a judgment concerning the character of the promiser. It is justifiable to trust a promiser if his/her behavior on balance
warrants that trust. Thus investigation into warranted assertability must
examine the identity of the promiser, the nature and context of the
promises, and the demands made of those who await their fulfillment.
It is only in the context of that relationship that Christian claims to
truth can be justified. I am in full agreement with George Lindbeck
when he argues that "Christian ontological truth-claims" are made "in
the activities of adoration, proclamation, obedience, promise-hearing,
and promise-keeping which shape individuals and communities into
conformity with the mind of Christ. . . . Truth and falsity characterize
ordinary religious language when it is used to mold lives through prayer,
praise, preaching, and exhortation. It is only on this level that human
beings linguistically exhibit their truth or falsity, their correspondence
or lack of correspondence to the Ultimate Mystery."[8]

Finally, some theologians may object to this entire approach to
theological justification, arguing that it threatens to compromise God's
absolute sovereignty. Karl Barth has argued forcefully that there can
be no linguistic or logical connection between God's revelation and
human language.[9] While revelation assumes linguistic form, the struc-

ture of language, he argues, contributes nothing to the content of revelation.

> The form of God's Word, then, is in fact the form of the cosmos which stands in contradiction to God. It has as little ability to reveal God to us as we have to see God in it. If God's Word is revealed in it, it is revealed "through it," but in such a way that this "through it" means "in spite of it."[10]

Barth is so insistent that God's revelation takes place only when and where the sovereign God chooses that he sunders every connection between human speech and divine revelation other than that which God creates in the very act of revelation. Consequently there can be no grounds for Christian truth-claiming other than God's gracious electing will. From Barth's point of view theological justification of God's prevenience demands not an intellectual *inquiry* but simply a faithful *acknowledgment* of God's gracious revelation when and where it occurs.

While I share Barth's worry that a systematic correlation between the category "Word of God" and some innate human capacity for transcendence threatens the integrity of Christian discourse, I cannot follow his radical disjunction between human speech and divine reality. That approach "solves" the problem of revelation, viz., the relation of God to human concepts and categories, by severing all relations between the two and taking refuge in the miracle of grace to bring them together. Theological reflection is surely no substitute for the miracle of grace, but neither should the appeal to miracle be invoked prematurely. The art of theology is knowing where an appeal to miracle and mystery is rightly placed. Barth is the twentieth-century master of the art, but in this case his aim is faulty. Surely there is no *natural* or *innate* connection between human language and God's reality, but Christian faith demands that once God has claimed a piece of creaturely reality as his own and bound himself to it, then we are warranted in accepting the God-forged link between the human and divine. God's claim that the man Jesus is his "beloved Son" makes it possible for Christians to speak of the actions of Jesus as the enacted intentions of God. "You must know that there is no other God than this man, Jesus Christ."[11] In like manner if God has annexed some form of human language, e.g., the promise, as the vehicle for his communication, then that form contributes to our understanding of that communication. "God does not deal, nor has he ever dealt, with man otherwise than through faith in the Word of his promise. . . . These two, promise and faith, must necessarily go together."[12] In seeking theological justification for belief in God's prevenience theology is simply analyzing the form and content of God's promises, which serve as the ground of Christian faith and hope.

An Historical Precedent

I am proposing that a doctrine of revelation, i.e., a defense of God's prevenience, can be given self-consistent formulation if it is organized around the notion of "narrated promise." The challenge to a doctrine of revelation is to account for both God's priority and his relation to the framework of Christian belief. Such a doctrine must maintain a distinction between divine initiative and human reception, while granting priority to the former. The standard modern doctrine fails in part because it conceived of the divine-human relation in causal terms. When God is granted ultimate causal efficacy, the human recipient of revelation becomes the wholly passive effect of the wholly other God's prior action. In such a conception the relation between God and the human framework of belief is jeopardized. On the other hand, when human agents are granted a role in the causal process it becomes difficult, if not impossible, to maintain God's ultimate causal priority. While the modern doctrine of revelation has developed under the peculiar pressures of post-Enlightenment culture, the problems which plague the doctrine are not without parallel in the history of theology. A brief look at a previous crisis in the Christian doctrine of grace will provide a helpful orientation as we begin to reconceptualize the doctrine of revelation.

Pre-Reformation Western theology commonly conceived of the divine-human relation in causal terms.[13] St. Augustine, for example, spoke of grace both as God's saving causal action, i.e., his love directed to us, and as the effects of that action among us, i.e., our love for God which God creates in us. In like manner, Thomas Aquinas defined grace both as God's action in moving our wills to the good and as the divinely bestowed disposition within us. In this way God's causal priority is maintained without denying the involvement of our wills in the process of salvation. Thus Thomas speaks of God's prior action in moving the will to believe as "operating grace" and of our secondary but necessary involvement in that willing as "cooperating grace." Robert Jenson has clearly analyzed the consequences of this cooperative causal process.

> [W]hen the saving relation between God and believers is understood as the causality of one substance on another, salvation is necessarily understood as a *process*. . . . Whatever may be the virtues of such descriptions as phenomenology of religion, they are theological catastrophes. . . . For if salvation is thus understood as a stepped process between two agents, then unless I am to be a mere spectator of my own life, there must be points in the process when the move is up to me and where the next stage will not occur unless I make the move . . . [T]he traditional doctrine of "grace" is a works-righteous *structure* lodged at the heart of the chief theological concern and achievement of the Western church.[14]

The Lutheran reformers responded to this incipient works-righteous structure by reconceptualizing the doctrine of grace. The *locus classicus* for this revised conception is Article IV of *The Apology to the Augsburg Confession*, authored by Philip Melanchthon.[15] The term which Melanchthon uses in order to stress God's absolute gracious priority is "promise."

> All Scripture should be divided into these two chief doctrines, the law and the promises. In some places it presents the law. In others it presents the promise of Christ; this it does either when it promises that the Messiah will come and promises forgiveness of sins, justification, and eternal life for his sake, or when, in the New Testament, the Christ who came promises forgiveness of sins, justification, and eternal life.[16]

The use of the word *promise* here is both broad and complex and deserves our careful attention. Melanchthon continually relates promise to the tripartite blessing of forgiveness, justification, and eternal life. It is clear that promise is not solely concerned with the pledge of some future benefit, though that is certainly included under the blessing of eternal life. But additionally Melanchthon asserts that Christ's promise is the granting of the very blessings it pledges. Christ's promise *bestows* the forgiveness and justification in the act of promising. Thus the promise is simultaneously a pardon and a declaration of righteousness. Furthermore, Christ not only issues the promise but is himself the content of the promise. "The Gospel is, strictly speaking, the promise of forgiveness of sins and justification because of Christ."[17] In his greater Galatians commentary Luther makes the point more directly. "The Gospel is the revelation of the Son of God. . . . Christ is the subject of the Gospel."[18] In the words of Robert Jenson, "The biblical promise has a narrative content; it is 'about Christ.' "[19]

The foregoing discussion shows quite clearly that Melanchthon uses the word *promise* as a synonym for *gospel*. Why does he insist on emphasizing the notion of promise, even to the point of stretching its meaning beyond ordinary usage, when he has another term like *gospel* available? He does so because the notion of promise highlights the *unconditional* offer of salvation which comes through God's grace. Promise offers Melanchthon a way of breaking the causal conception of the divine-human relation with its works-righteous structure and asserting the absolute gracious prevenience of God.

> This promise is not conditional upon our merits but offers the forgiveness of sins and justification freely. . . . [I]f the promise were conditional upon our merits and the law, which we never keep, it would follow that the promise is useless. Since we obtain justification through a free promise, however, it follows that we cannot justify ourselves. Otherwise, why would a promise be necessary?[20]

Melanchthon includes a breathtaking variety of concepts in his discussion of promise. Promise is the unconditional offer of salvation, the forgiveness of sins, the justification of the sinner, the narrative concerning Christ, the pledge of eternal life, and the key to a noncausal view of God's grace. He does not adequately explain how promise can incorporate so many different aspects, and at times his discussion seems loose and imprecise. He fails to explain, for example, how a promise can function as a pardon, or how a narrative can proclaim a promise. While his theological argument depends on the equation of promise with an unconditional pledge, he never fully justifies that equation. And finally he never makes completely explicit just how promise serves to safeguard the absolute prevenience of God.

Despite the evident shortcomings of Melanchthon's discussion, I am convinced that his focus on the notion of promise offers an alternative not just to the causal conceptions of medieval Western Christianity but to the foundational epistemologies of post-Enlightenment doctrines of revelation as well. In the remainder of this chapter I will seek to offer an account of the logic of the category "narrated promise" in order to show the intelligibility of a defense of God's prevenience organized under that rubric.

The Intelligibility of God's Narrated Promise

In order to test the intelligibility of the concept of God's prevenience we need first to locate that belief within the web of supporting Christian beliefs and practices. While the status of the belief has been uncertain in recent Christian theology, it has remained a relatively stable background belief within Christian practice. Consider the words of the eucharistic prayer, or great thanksgiving, spoken during the service of Holy Communion.

> Holy God, mighty Lord, gracious Father: Endless is your mercy and eternal your reign. You have filled all creation with light and life; heaven and earth are full of your glory. Through Abraham you promised to bless all nations. You rescued Israel your chosen people. Through the prophets you renewed your promise; and, at this end of all the ages, you sent your Son, who in words and deed proclaimed your kingdom and was obedient to your will, even to giving his life. . . . Therefore, gracious Father, with this bread and cup we remember the life our Lord offered for us. And believing the witness of his resurrection we await his coming in power to share with us the great and promised feast. . . . Send now, we pray, your Holy Spirit, the spirit of our Lord and of his resurrection, that we who receive the Lord's body and blood may live to the praise of your glory and receive our inheritance with all your saints in light.[21]

Liturgical language illustrates with particular clarity the complex nature of all speech-acts. In the act of speaking we communicate both through the propositional content of our speech and through the "force" which that speech possesses in a particular linguistic context. For example, if I say "shut the door" that utterance could function either as a request or a warning. If I have been talking to my daughter in my study and wish to return to my work as she leaves, I might request her to close the door to provide a quieter atmosphere in which to write. If, however, I were to utter those very same words just as a mad dog began to rush into our living room, the words would possess a very different force. J. L. Austin has distinguished the "locutionary act" *of* uttering a particular sentence from the "illocutionary act" which we perform *in* uttering that sentence.[22] The locutionary act can be identified by a sentence's propositional content, but the illocutionary act can be identified only in the particular context within which the speech-act is performed. That distinction will be important throughout our discussion of the logic of narrated promise.

Analysis of the force and propositional content of the eucharistic prayer shows that this liturgical act presupposes the prevenience of God. Indeed, this act is unintelligible if God's prior gracious reality is not presupposed. The prayer incorporates doxology, narration of salvation history, and eschatological invocation in an utterance addressed simultaneously to God and the congregation.[23] As doxology and invocation its primary function is to address God. As narration it reminds the congregation of the great acts God has performed on behalf of his people. But both the address to God and the recital of his actions require the prior assumption of God's reality. Neither the prayer nor the liturgy of which it is a part make sense without the presupposition of God's prevenience. The activities of worship—adoration, confession, thanksgiving, and supplication—are the church's response to God's initiative and action. If God's prevenience is not assumed, then these activities are either pointless or function in a way not specified by the primary liturgical context. The language of church practice, placed in its natural setting of worship, necessarily presupposes belief in God's prior reality and action. Belief in God's prevenience thus serves as an essential background conviction for Christian worship.

The propositional content of the eucharistic prayer further specifies the web of beliefs within which belief in God's prevenience rests. The prayer exemplifies three patterns of speech which characterize the language of Christian practice, patterns which function to identify God and the worshipping community. God is identified primarily as the *God of promise* whose promises receive *narrative enactment and fulfillment* in the history of Israel and the life, death, and resurrection of Jesus. God's identity is further specified by the *triune structure* of the eucharistic prayer. It is addressed to the Father, God of creation and promise; it narrates the actions of the Son which extend and fulfill the Father's promises; and it invokes the gift of the Spirit, the presence of God among the gathered faithful and the pledge of God's consummate fulfillment of all his promises. That triune structure is replicated in the prayer's description of the church as that community which remembers the story of God's saving acts, trusts in God's continued faithfulness to his promises, and hopes for his final return in power. The event which unifies the church's memory, faith, and hope is Christ's resurrection, for in that act the saving history reaches its culmination, Christian faith is created and sustained, and Christian hope engendered.

The eucharistic prayer with its mutually reinforcing themes of promise, narrative, and trinity specifies the particular identities of God and that community which worships him. Both identity descriptions require the logically prior belief in God's prevenience. God's identity as the one who creates, promises, and fulfills and the church's identity as a community which remembers, trusts, and hopes necessarily imply a relationship in which God is the primary actor and initiator and the church the primary recipient. If God is as he is described by the eucharistic prayer, then God cannot be conceived as other than prevenient. God's prevenience is a necessary "pragmatic implication"[24] of the force and content of the language of Christian practice. The logic of Christian worship implies belief in God's prior reality, and the worshipper who would authentically participate in these rites cannot do so consistently while denying God's prevenience.

Christian identity is shaped by the stories, traditions, and practices of the community. The preceding analysis shows that belief in God's prevenience is a belief constitutive of Christian identity as formed by the church's worship life. Belief in God's prevenience continues to operate as an essential background belief for Christian worship, whatever its uncertain status in theology. The denial of God's prevenience then not only disrupts the traditional configuration of Christian beliefs, but it also requires a radical revision of the form and content of Christian worship, a revision which would strikingly alter Christian self-understanding. There are, I believe, good reasons for resisting such a revision, reasons having to do with the logical integrity of Christian belief and the importance of continuity with the self-understanding and self-description of earlier generations of Christians. But the invocation of integrity and continuity can appear both illusory and nostalgic unless backed with sound theological reasoning in support of belief in God's prevenience. While such belief may be required for consistent and authentic participation in Christian worship, it is not thereby theologically justified. The analysis of the logic of worship shows the essential background status of belief in God's prevenience and the relation of that belief to the categories of promise, narrative, and trinity, but it does not yet provide the full theological argumentation for sustaining that belief. This analysis does, however, show that the belief is a deeply held Christian conviction, i.e., "a persistent belief such that if X (a person or community) has a conviction, it will not easily be relinquished and it cannot be relinquished without making X a significantly different person (or community) than before."[25] The theological justification of such a conviction requires additional arguments, but this analysis has shown that belief in God's prevenience belongs to a conviction set which includes the themes of promise, narrative, and God's triune identity. If this conviction is to be theologically justified, it must be returned to a theological context in which these themes are prominent. Consequently a doctrine of revelation should be placed, not within theological prolegomena, but within the material claims of Christian theology.

Though I have placed belief in God's prevenience in its appropriate context within Christian practice, I have not yet tackled the difficult challenges to the belief's intelligibility. In particular I have not yet shown how the notion of "narrated promise" addresses the central problem of revelation, i.e., the difficulty of affirming both God's priority and his relation to our theological framework. Nor have I undertaken a clarification of the puzzles generated by Melanchthon's account of promise, e.g., how does a narrative proclaim a promise or what is the relation between promise and pardon?

The criterion of intelligibility inquires after the consistency and coherence of theological claims. The following discussion of the logic of narrated promise will address these four issues: 1) Can one intelligibly speak of a narrative functioning as a promise? 2) Can one intelligibly identify a pardon, e.g., the forgiving of sin, as a promise? 3) Is it conceptually coherent to speak of a scriptural or liturgical promise as God's speech-act? Is it possible to identify God as the agent of such promises? 4) Is the God who is identified as the agent who promises rightly understood as prevenient? What is it about our identification of him which leads us to affirm his prevenience?

1) Our analysis of the locutionary and illocutionary components of speech-acts is useful in addressing this issue. Ordinarily we communicate both through the propositional content and the force of our language. As our previous example showed, the same sentence can take on different forces, depending on the linguistic context in which it is uttered. Take, for example, a simple sentence like "it is raining."

If no linguistic context is specified we are most likely to analyze this sentence as a proposition describing a state of affairs. And if I had just glanced out the window and informed my wife of the state of the weather, then the sentence would have the force of "describing or reporting." But suppose the sentence is uttered by someone who has just hung out the wash to dry. Then the utterance could be an expression of dismay or an instruction to the children to bring in the clothes. Or suppose two people had wagered on the possibility of rain before deciding to attend a baseball game. Then the utterance could be both a triumphant cry and the calling in of the bet. The point is obvious. A sentence which appears to be a simple description of a state of affairs can take on a variety of different forces within different linguistic contexts.

Narratives, too, can have a variety of illocutionary forces. Ordinarily we think of a story's primary force as that of "narrating," and often we are correct in that assessment. But like the apparent "descriptive" sentence, narratives can perform other functions than simply "narration." Fairy tales like "Little Red Riding Hood" function not just to "narrate" but also to "warn" children not to wander into the woods in defiance of their parents' instructions. More complex stories involve a great variety of illocutionary forces and generate a broader range of possible interpretations. In addition written narratives, or texts, in contrast to direct speech, possess "semantic autonomy;"[26] their meaning is fixed in a written form which is distanced from both its author's intention and from any particular reader or audience. Consequently their illocutionary forces remain ambiguous and must be discerned through the art of interpretation. Any attempt to discern a narrative's illocutionary force requires careful analysis of the text's content and its specific interpretive context.

It is clear from the above discussion that one can intelligibly assert that the New Testament narratives function as promise. That claim raises no particular *logical* difficulties. The more complex problem is to show that the texts are *plausibly* interpreted in that fashion. But that issue cannot be addressed until we undertake a detailed analysis of the content and context of those stories in the following chapter.

2) Melanchthon's tendency to classify the forgiveness of sin and justification under the rubric of promise is puzzling. Forgiving and justifying would seem more appropriately classified as pardons. Promises and pardons appear to be distinct speech-acts, and there is the

danger that Melanchthon, and those who would follow his lead, are simply conflating two separate actions. Pardons are distinctive in that they are effective upon acceptance; they immediately restore broken relations between the parties. Promises, on the other hand, seem to require some future act to which the promiser is committed. Only when that future act is accomplished, i.e., only when the promise is fulfilled, has the action become fully effective. Can one intelligibly equate pardons and promises?

Melanchthon's claim, though odd, is not, I would argue, illicit. Note again his initial definition of promise. Scripture, he says, "presents the promise of Christ; this it does either when it promises that the Messiah will come and promises forgiveness of sins, justification, and eternal life for his sake, or when, in the New Testament, the Christ who came promises forgiveness of sins, justification, and eternal life." The biblical promise, though it is always "the promise of Christ," has a complex temporal structure. In the context of Israel's story "the promise of Christ" (here the genitive is objective) manifests the ordinary structure of promise. The promiser, in this case God, specifies a future act to which he commits himself.[27] The "representative or descriptive conditions"[28] of that promise are fourfold: the coming of the Messiah, forgiveness of sins, justification, and eternal life. But as the syntax of Melanchthon's sentence indicates, those conditions have a particular internal relation. The promised Messiah will bring with him the promised blessings of pardon, righteousness, and eternal life. Those blessings are contingent upon the Messiah's arrival.

Thus far Melanchthon has used the term *promise* in a perfectly straightforward and ordinary way; however, when he moves to describe the promise in its New Testament context, his analysis becomes more complicated. The new covenant is inaugurated by the Messiah's arrival ("the Christ who came"). Christ now plays the dual role of the fulfiller of God's initial promise and the agent of his new promise. In the New Testament context the phrase "the promise of Christ" must be construed as a subjective genitive, for the promise is now the one which Christ issues. The representative conditions of the promise are the threefold blessing of forgiveness, justification, and eternal life. Christ as the agent of promise commits himself to share those blessings with the Christian community. Pardon is thus one of those conditions which, when satisfied, marks the fulfillment of the promise; it is a component of the complex speech-act of promising.

Promise, as Melanchthon uses the term, has a complex narrative structure. It evokes the remembrance of God's promises to Israel, the fulfillment of those promises in Messiah's coming, the bestowing of the promised blessing and the renewal of the promise in forgiveness and justification, and the further promise of a final consummation in eternal life. Whenever words of pardon and absolution are spoken in Christ's name, believers recall the narrative scope of God's promises in Christ and become participants in the world that narrative depicts. Forgiveness and justification are the present benefits of the reconciliation accomplished through the history of Israel and the life, death, and resurrection of Jesus the Christ. To call God's pardon a promise is to place forgiveness within the temporal flow of God's reconciling action begun in Israel, secured through Christ, and to be consummated in eternal life. The restoration of the relation between God and sinners through the act of pardon is one essential stage in the ongoing drama of God's narrated promise. While Melanchthon's account stretches the ordinary meaning of promise to enrich it with theological significance, the notion surely remains within the realm of intelligible discourse.

3) The question of God's agency in the issuance of scriptural or liturgical promises emerges directly out of the preceding analysis. Melanchthon claims that the promises and pardons spoken in the Christian community are those of Christ and God, yet he does not specify the procedures by which we identify God as the agent of promises uttered by human speakers. Is it logically self-consistent to designate as *God's* speech-act a pardon or promise uttered by a human speaker?

We will take as our example a liturgical pardon, the declaration of grace spoken immediately following the congregation's confession of sins.

> In the mercy of almighty God, Jesus Christ was given to die for you, and for his sake God forgives you all your sins. To those who believe in Jesus Christ he gives the power to become the children of God and bestows on them the Holy Spirit.[29]

Once again the complex narrative pattern is evident. The declaration combines a report of a past state of affairs ("Jesus Christ was given to die for you"), a declaration of the present consequences of that act ("for his sake God forgives you all your sins"), and a pledge of present and future benefits to those who respond appropriately ("to those who believe in Jesus Christ he gives the power to become children of God and bestows on them the Holy Spirit"). The final phrase is particularly interesting, because it uses the present tense in order to speak of blessings which are fully realized only eschatologically. Thus the future element of promise, though minimized in this explicit pardon, is still evident. A similar emphasis is found in the absolution of the Episcopalian rite. "Almighty God have mercy on you, forgive you all your sins through our Lord Jesus Christ, strengthen you in all goodness, and by the power of the Holy Spirit keep you in eternal life."[30] The pardon restores that relationship between Father and children which culminates in the eschatological blessing of eternal life.

In both forms of absolution a complex form of "double agency" is operative. Though the speaker in the liturgical act is the presiding minister, the speaker who is committed to action is *God*. That the minister speaks *for* and not only *of* God is made explicit in an alternate form of absolution in which the pastor says, "As a called and ordained minister of the church of God, and by his authority, I therefore declare to you the entire forgiveness of all your sins, in the name of the Father, and of the Son, and of the Holy Spirit."[31] These words are to be taken as the speech of God every time they are spoken. Is this notion of double agency intelligible?

That the utterance of one speaker should be taken as the enacted intention of another presents no particular logical problem. Such complex speech-acts are a common occurrence in ordinary experience. Consider the following examples: A sister calls to her brother, "Mom says, 'it's time for dinner!' "; a town crier reads a royal decree in the public square; a minister reads a Presidential proclamation from the pulpit on Thanksgiving morning. In every case one speaker speaks on behalf of another agent and enacts the agent's intention to "call," "decree," or "proclaim." All that is required for intelligibility is that the context and/or content of the address make clear the situation of double agency. The liturgical pardon does that in its content-references to the primary agency of Father, Son, and Spirit or in its representative mode of speech ("by [Christ's] authority I declare to you . . ."). The liturgical context reinforces the intelligibility of the pardon by providing the congregation with ample opportunities for correlative responses which show their acknowledgement of these promises as God's, e.g., confession of faith, prayer, doxology.

The notion of double agency is intelligible provided there are available procedures for identifying and distinguishing the acts and intentions of the two agents. The liturgical context specifies that the promises and pardons of worship are to be heard as God's speech-acts. In addition the liturgy identifies God as the one whose promises are effective in the history of Israel and Jesus of Nazareth (see, for example, the eucharistic prayer). The issue of God's identifiability is crucial for a doctrine of revelation, because previous attempts to formulate the doctrine have often failed to distinguish sufficiently divine and human agency.[32] Thus we need to ask whether this narrative identification is sufficient to provide a uniquely identifying description of God. The final evaluation of the success of the narrative identifying description must await completion of the exegetical analysis of the next chapter. For now we simply want to test the intelligibility of the suggestion that a narrative identification can uniquely identify God.

Christians have traditionally spoken of God as a person who is capable of love, righteous anger, mercy, etc., and who acts in ways consistent with those personal attributes. Talk of God as a promising subject, who undertakes obligations and intends to perform future acts, identifies God as an intentional agent, the bearer of a personal identity. A narrative which purports to provide an identifying description of God must specify certain characteristic patterns of behavior which designate God's distinctive personal identity. God's activity must be described in such a way that the narrative "1) calls attention to the agent's purpose or aim, in his movements, utterances, and so forth, and 2) credits him with regulating his behavior in accord with that purpose."[33] The narrative must provide a sufficiently detailed account of the agent's patterns of action so that we can assign "traits of character"[34] by which we can characterize and appraise the person's behavior. These traits of character will then serve to describe the agent's "dispositional properties,"[35] i.e., the propensity of the person to act in certain ways in particular situations. Such character traits and dispositional properties are rightly assigned only to those individuals capable of undertaking purposive action over a sufficiently broad span of time to allow us to specify his or her behavior as both personal and characteristic. There is, as Thomas Tracy has shown, "a necessary logical relation"[36] between trait of character predicates and intentional action. "In using our language of character traits to describe a person's distinctive identity we are calling attention to patterns in the way he conducts his life as an agent of intentional actions."[37] The implication for our talk of God as promising subject is obvious. "If God is to be a *personal* being, [i.e., a subject of traits of character], then he must be an agent of intentional actions."[38] The biblical narrative must describe God with sufficient precision to allow us to identify him as an agent of intentional actions.

Further, God as the logical subject of such actions must be a uniquely identifiable referent of human speech.[39] The biblical narratives offer the indispensable identity descriptions of God, i.e., they provide the description of God's characteristic intention-action patterns across a chronological sequence. Consequently, a uniquely identifying description of God will inevitably be bound to scripture's narrative depiction of God's actions.[40] In the next chapter I will show that biblical narratives do provide a sufficiently precise depiction of God's activity to allow the construction of a uniquely identifying description. That description locates God as an agent of intentional action both within the scriptural text and within our common world of experience. The central identifying claim of the biblical narrative is that Yahweh, God of Israel, is "the one who raised Jesus from the dead." In making that claim Christians are asserting that God's actions, though uniquely depicted in the biblical stories, are, nonetheless, real happenings in the human world of experience. Though God is a character in the Bible's realistic narrative, he is also the creator of the universe, the redeemer of a sinful humanity, and the reconciler of a broken world. The warrants for these assertions, though grounded in the narrative depiction of God, apply to our real world of experience. A uniquely identifying narrative description is complete only as it moves beyond the level of sense to the level of reference.

Thus the three criteria of justification are inevitably intertwined. In displaying the conditions of intelligibility this first criterion anticipates the narrative account which will satisfy the criterion of Christian aptness. That account in turn raises issues of truth and reference which are addressed under the criterion of warranted assertability. These final three chapters together serve as the justification of the Christian belief in God's prevenience and so function as a descriptive doctrine of revelation.

4) How does the identification of God as the agent of promise establish his prevenience? How can a doctrine of revelation focused on the notion of narrated promise provide a viable alternative to the standard foundational doctrine?

I have argued that the standard modern doctrine of revelation, organized around the paradigm of knowledge and conceiving of justification as a matter of causal explanation, cannot consistently affirm both God's relation and his priority to our human conceptual framework. If the paradigm of narrated promise is to provide the basis for an intelligible account of God's prevenience, it must succeed where previous doctrines have failed.

The foundational doctrine of revelation conceives of humanity's relation to God as parallel to the knowing subject's relation to an ontologically distinct object. Subject and object stand over-against one another as ontologically distinct entities. The problem of revelation is understood to be the problem of overcoming the ontological distance which separates God from humanity. Theologians have sought therefore to describe the process of knowing by which these separated entities can be successfully related. Following the lead of modern philosophical epistemology, most modern theologians have conceived of that process in causal terms. But, as I have shown in chapter 2, the conceptual difficulties associated with this causal view of knowing are so great that epistemological doctrines inevitably collapse into self-contradiction. Consequently modern theologians have failed to devise an account of revelation which consistently incorporates both God's relation and his priority to our framework of belief.

The great advantage of the paradigm of narrated promise is that it conceives of God and humanity as essentially in relation and seeks to generate the distinctions between the two from within that relation. A doctrine of revelation organized around the theme of promise begins from the basic Christian conviction that "God was in Christ reconciling the world to himself, not counting their trespasses against them, and entrusting to us the message of reconciliation" (2 Corinthians 5:19). That "message of reconciliation" is God's narrated promise, which binds God and humanity together while granting absolute priority to God's initiating action.

A promise is an intentional speech-act by which the speaker assumes an obligation to perform some specified future act on behalf of the hearer.[41] Such a speech-act, made in accord with the conventions of promising, announces the speaker's stance of commitment and obligation (primary conditions) and describes the future act with appropriate specificity (representative or descriptive conditions). In addition, the speaker must exhibit the requisite sincerity so that the speaker's intention to fulfill his/her obligation is communicated to the hearer in such a way that both speaker and hearer recognize that the specified future act would not come about in "the ordinary course of events," i.e., without the speaker's intentional action (affective or psychological conditions). Note that the primary and descriptive conditions rely solely on the action of the promiser. The affective conditions, on the other hand, require an act of recognition on the part of the hearer in addition to the speaker's exhibition of sincerity of intention. That act (Austin calls it "uptake")[42] simply reflects the fact that every utterance requires a receiver as well as a sender and is limited to the hearer's mere grasp of the speaker's intention. It should not be confused with the consequential effects which the promise produces in the hearer, e.g., trust, suspicion, a feeling of dependence.[43]

This logical analysis demonstrates that the speech-act of promising provides a category which will allow a consistent conception of God's relation and priority to our framework of belief. Promise is a relational category which requires both a speaker and a hearer but grants primacy in that relation solely to the one who promises. The structure, content, and fulfillment of a promise depend solely on the initiative of the promiser. The promiser specifies the future act, expresses the intention to perform that act, undertakes the obligation implied in the promise, exhibits the requisite trustworthy behavior, and alone can perform the action which will fulfill the promise. The hearer, on the other hand, though he or she would "prefer" that the promiser fulfill his obligation, cannot, if the act is to remain a promise, compel the promiser so to act. To understand God's relation to humanity under the rubric of promise is thereby to understand that relation as one in which God alone is the gracious initiator, actor, and fulfiller of his own promises, i.e., to understand God as prevenient.

The notion of promise breaks the "cooperating framework" inherent in all causal conceptions of the divine-human relation. In order for a promise to be "nondefective" the hearer must merely acknowledge that this speech-act fulfills the conditions of promising. But that acknowledgment does not in any sense constitute the promise. Nor should that act of recognition be equated with faith. Faith requires a further movement of the heart and spirit in response to the proffered promise; it is not an implicit work which I must perform in order to make the promise effective. The logic of promise as applied to God demands that unconditional priority be given to the one who promises. "This promise is not conditional upon our merits but offers the forgiveness of sins and justification freely."[44] The logic of promise implies God's unconditional prevenience.

In the following narrative analysis that conclusion will be expanded and sharpened in the following way. When God's identity as the one who promises is uniquely specified by scripture's narrative description, then it will follow that if Yahweh, Israel's God, is the one who raised Jesus from the dead, then he cannot not be prevenient. God's prevenience is necessarily implied by this uniquely identifying description of God.

CHAPTER SIX

The Promising God:
The Gospel as Narrated Promise

My rather formal defense of the intelligibility of belief in God's prevenience must now be supplemented by a more detailed account of the biblical basis for the belief. In this chapter I will attempt to show that the biblical narrative does provide an individuating description of God as prevenient God of promise. "Narrated promise" not only provides a coherent and thus intelligible basis for asserting God's prevenience, it is also a notion deeply embedded in the biblical tradition and thus satisfies the criterion of "Christian aptness." I argued previously that the category of narrative is useful for theology because it integrates a central literary genre in scripture with an organizing theological image. But narrative has the further significance of providing the language by which we specify personal identity. A theology which seeks an individuating identification of God is a theology naturally attracted to narrative.

In order to answer questions which inquire after a person's identity, e.g., "Who is Jane? What is she like?" we relate a story which identifies a pattern of behavior as "characteristically hers" and which allows us to attribute to her certain traits of character. Narrative identification thus entails the description of *patterns of behavior* which because of their persistence over time we identify as *characteristic*. These characteristic patterns then warrant the *ascription of character traits* to a persisting subject or self. Narrative identification thereby accounts both for the variety and change of behavior patterns and for the persistence of a subject throughout such changes. If an intelligible narrative account, inclusive of those diverse patterns, can be given, then we can speak of Jane or of God as a persisting identifiable personal subject.[1]

The following narrative account will focus on a single New Testament book, the Gospel of Matthew. Ideally a narrative description of

God's identity would range over a wider variety of biblical narratives to show how they cumulatively render God as a distinctive personal agent.[2] An account of such breadth would, of course, require book-length treatment and is clearly beyond the limits of this project. What my more modest approach sacrifices in scope, it should regain in precision. Theologians have often been criticized for imposing upon scripture grand interpretive schemes which ignore or violate the structures of biblical texts. Theological interpretation of narrative, if it is to avoid that danger, must be characterized by close textual analysis guided by clear textual warrants. Such analysis requires in turn a limitation of the material to be discussed.

I will undertake a literary and theological analysis of the book of Matthew which seeks a uniquely identifying description of God. I will treat the Gospel as a consciously constructed narrative in which the author uses various literary devices for theological purposes. Relying upon the literary structures Matthew employs and the formal philosophical tools of identity description I will redescribe Matthew's narrative depiction of Jesus and the implications of that depiction for the identification of God. Such an analysis is congenial to the Gospel, because the theological goal of the book of Matthew is to identify Jesus of Nazareth as Emmanuel, the Son of God,[3] the one who enacts God's intention to save his people from sin through death and resurrection. God is thereby identified as the one whose promises are fulfilled in the mission of the Son of God and who enacts his intention to save in raising Jesus from the dead.

The Identity of Jesus Christ

> Now when Jesus came into the district of Caesarea Philippi, he asked his disciples, "Who do men say that the Son of man is?" And they said, "Some say John the Baptist, others say Elijah, and others Jeremiah or one of the prophets." He said to them, "But who do you say that I am?" Simon Peter replied, "You are the Christ, the Son of the living God." (16:13–16)

This pericope, long recognized as a turning point in the Gospel of Matthew, poses the question which Matthew's narrative depiction of Jesus seeks to answer. The writer of the Gospel skillfully develops three patterns of identifying discourse which cumulatively display Jesus' personal identity. These narrative patterns, which correspond to the three major sections of Matthew's Gospel, begin with the most general and stylized depictions of Jesus and progress toward greater specificity until Jesus' identity as a particular individual who uniquely fulfills the role of Son of God becomes clear in the crucifixion and resurrection sequence. Jesus is related first to the people of Israel and Israel's God, then to the coming Kingdom of God, and finally to those events of death and resurrection which bestow his unsubstitutable identity. Throughout this narrative progression Jesus' relation to God is subtly but unmistakably indicated.

Matthew deftly controls two types of individuating descriptions. The title "Son of God" specifies Jesus' *formal* identity. The first section of the Gospel (1:1–4:16) establishes the crucial connection between that title and Jesus' unique God-given mission of saving "his people from their sins" (1:21). Through Matthew's careful narrative construction a general title applicable to Israel's kings becomes a specific messianic title applicable only to the one God has chosen for the mission of salvation, i.e., to "the Christ, the Son of the living God." The Son of God is the one who uniquely enacts his Father's intention to save.

The subsequent sections of the Gospel provide the narrative identifications which specify Jesus' *individual personal* identity. In the second section of the Gospel (4:18–20:34) Matthew stresses the ambiguity which characterizes Jesus' personal identity, particularly his identity as Son of God. The narrative operates on two levels, which correspond to the disjunctive reactions of Jesus' hearers to his healing and teaching ministry. On the one hand, Matthew surveys the responses of the Jewish leaders, the crowds, and the disciples, all of whom are either confused about his identity or misidentify him as "teacher," "the carpenter's son," "the blasphemer," etc. On the other hand, Matthew recounts the confession of those who see through the ambiguity to recognize Jesus as the Son of God, e.g., the Gadarene demoniacs, the Roman centurian, and, most importantly, the disciples. Because in this section Matthew portrays Jesus as an agent enacting his own intentions, the relation of his actions to *God's* intentions, and thus his role as Son of God, becomes obscured. Nonetheless, Matthew emphasizes, Jesus remains recognizable as the Son of God by those who have faith.

The final section of the Gospel (21:1–28:20) completes Jesus' personal identification and decisively connects it to the initial formal individuating identification. In the passion narrative Jesus is most sharply individuated as a personal agent. Precisely as Jesus acts and suffers in his passion and crucifixion he is also most clearly identified as the unique Son of God who obediently enacts the intentions of his Father. In an artful literary and theological conclusion Matthew shows the unity between the intentions of God and Jesus as manifested in the events of crucifixion and resurrection. In obediently submitting to his crucifixion Jesus of Nazareth shows himself most clearly to be God's Son, an identification which is confirmed and completed in the resurrection. At the Gospel's ending the careful reader will have discovered the identity not only of the Son of God but also of the one he calls "Abba, Father."

1:1–4:16

In the first four chapters of the Gospel Jesus is identified solely by his relation to the people of Israel and Israel's God. Matthew's descriptions of Jesus function not to individuate him as a particular person but to specify his unique role as Son of God. Matthew avoids all techniques of verisimilitude[4] when describing Jesus in order to focus attention solely upon his mission and the formal identity which God bestows on him through that mission. Jesus is initially identified through his genealogy, which designates him as "the son of David, the son of Abraham" (1:1), thereby linking him to the two great covenantal promises of Israel, the promise of a nation and the promise of eternal Kingship. The inclusion of Tamar, the seductress of her father-in-law, Judah (Gen. 38); Rahab, the prostitute of Jericho (Jos. 2); Ruth, the Moabite; and Bathsheba, the partner in David's adultery (2 Sam. 11) may foreshadow Jesus' mission to sinners and outcasts,[5] but the major function of the genealogy is to show that Jesus is the inheritor of God's promises to Israel.

The nativity stories which follow the genealogy do include realistic elements but none of them contributes to the personal identification of Jesus. The story of Joseph's dream functions to link Jesus' divine origin with his mission of salvation. Joseph is told that the child which Mary carries "is conceived in her of the Holy Spirit" (1:20) and that his name should be called "Jesus, for he will save his people from their sins" (1:21). All this is accomplished, Matthew informs his reader, to fulfill Isaiah's prophecy concerning the one whose "name shall be called 'Emmanuel' (which means God with us)" (1:23). Matthew moves so swiftly here that the reader may miss the full significance of this com-

plex pattern of identification. Indeed its *full* significance cannot be
appreciated without the subsequent narrative development. Matthew
anticipates the assignment of the title Son of God to Jesus by connecting his divine origin, his name, his role as fulfiller of prophecy, and
his mission. As the one conceived by God's spirit, this Jesus, born of
Mary, inherits and fulfills the great convenantal promises of Israel by
being the one designated to save his people from sin. Consequently
he is to be called Emmanuel, a name which anticipates his formal
designation as Son of God. Thus the name Jesus is associated with a
rich and complex pattern of identification. Yet these designations remain general and formal. We are told nothing of Jesus' particular identity, not even the conditions of his birth.

This distant perspective on Jesus is maintained in the first lengthy
narrative which describes the arrival of "wise men from the East" (2:1).
While the story contains elements of verisimilitude, particularly in its
description of Herod's frantic efforts to ascertain the location of the
child, they in no way contribute to the reader's grasp of Jesus' personal identity. He is merely "the child" whom the magi worship. Indeed, this marvelously crafted story with its bitter conclusion of the
slaughter of the innocents functions primarily to occasion the flight
to Egypt so that Jesus might be further identified with the people of
Israel. As God in his great saving act brought Israel out of Egypt, so
now he calls out the son of Abraham and David, who is for the first
time associated with the implied designation "Son of God." "Out of
Egypt have I called my son" (2:15). If we were to ask at this point
in the narrative "Who is Jesus?" we could only answer with the formal
designations Matthew has provided us. The narrative is constructed
in such a way as to focus solely on Jesus' formal identity.

That emphasis is particularly apparent in Matthew's construction
of the pivotal baptism and temptation scenes. These stories describe
the first actions Jesus undertakes as an independent agent and provide an opportunity for a personal individuating description of Jesus.
Though Matthew describes John in vivid detail (3:4–11), he offers no
such description of Jesus' behavior or character. He simply states that
Jesus appears at the Jordan to be baptized in order "to fulfill all
righteousness" (3:15).[6] By recounting Jesus' baptism with such spare
narrative prose Matthew continues to identify him solely in terms of
the formal designations he bears. Jesus—the representative of Israel,
conceived by God's spirit, and assigned a mission of salvation—

undertakes in his first narrated act to associate himself with those in need of repentance. By focusing so single-mindedly on Jesus' formal identity Matthew is able to weave those various designations into a single individuating identification, Son of God. That title specifies both the unique relation to God and the unique mission of the title-bearer. The Son of God is the one who enacts God's intention to save by virtue of his identification with sinners. In the act of baptism Jesus shows his willingness to undertake the mission implied by that title. Jesus' identity as Son of God, a designation implied in the angel's message to Joseph, is made explicit both by Jesus' act and by God's declaration, "This is my beloved Son, with whom I am well pleased" (3:17). That title, which is so prominent in these early chapters, will appear only four times (8:29, 14:33, 16:16, 17:1) in the large middle section of the Gospel, but will re-emerge as the predominant title in the passion narrative. Jesus' sonship is for Matthew associated with his saving mission on behalf of God's sinful people. With his acceptance of that mission the Son of God's first step toward Jerusalem is taken here in the waters of the Jordan.

Matthew will begin, in the next section of the Gospel, to describe Jesus as a particular individual, an agent who enacts his own intentions. That description will inevitably obscure the relation of Jesus' actions to God's intentions. Thus in this first section Matthew establishes Jesus' unique formal identity as Son of God. By rigorously refusing to individuate his description of Jesus, Matthew guides his readers to connect the name Jesus with the title Son of God. As he moves toward a more personal identification, however, Matthew needs a category which will allow him to maintain the link between Jesus' emerging intentional actions and God's intentions. Thus in the final stories of this initial section Matthew begins to depict Jesus as the *obedient* Son of God, i.e., the one who purposefully enacts his own intentions in conformity with the intentions of the Father.

The importance of Jesus' obedient sonship is stressed in the story which concludes the first section of Matthew's Gospel, the account of Jesus' temptation. Stylized elements once again dominate the Matthean narrative. Jesus is led by the Spirit into the wilderness to be tempted by Satan, who identifies him as Son of God and seeks to have him deny his sonship. Three times the tempter requests an action of Jesus which will demonstrate that the Messianic age has dawned. In each case Jesus' refusal takes the stylized form of a quotation from Hebrew scripture. The final temptation is set on "a very high mountain" (4:8) where Satan displays the glory of the kingdoms of the world. "All these I will give you. . . . " Jesus rejects Satan's offer and banishes him from his presence with a quote from Deuteronomy concerning true worship of God.

This story is best understood if it is seen as foreshadowing the concluding scene of the Gospel where Jesus, once again on a mountain, receives the worship of the disciples (28:17) and announces "all authority in heaven and on earth has been given to me" (28:18). Jesus' ultimate authority is granted in the aftermath of his death and resurrection. Matthew shows in this earlier story that the obedient Son of God cannot accept such authority prematurely. The true exercise of sonship, Matthew asserts, consists in obedience to God's will and the fulfillment of righteousness by the identification with sinners. To accept that mission is, as the subsequent narrative will show, to follow a path to the cross.

Matthew has in this initial section skillfully constructed the framework within which the Gospel is to be read. By avoiding the techniques of verisimilitude in his description of Jesus, Matthew focuses attention not upon the individual identity of Jesus of Nazareth but on the unique saving mission of the Son of God. Jesus is the inheritor and fulfiller of Israel's promises, the designated savior of a sinful people, the obedient servant who is baptized as an act of identification with those in need of repentance, and who by virtue of acceptance of his God-bestowed mission is Emmanuel, Son of God, who enacts the intentions of his Father. Having clearly defined Jesus' mission and thereby designated Jesus' formal identity, Matthew moves in the subsequent chapters to provide a narrative-based specification of his personal identity.

4:18–20:34

This middle section of the Gospel is a collection of sayings, miracle stories, and parables and does not exhibit the tight structure of the first and last sections. Matthew, nonetheless, provides narrative unity by focusing on the question of Jesus' authority. Jesus' identity is defined in these chapters primarily by his authoritative teaching and healing ministry, but since Jesus now begins to act as an agent in his own right, the source and nature of his authority are not readily apparent to his hearers. Matthew surveys the reactions of the Jewish leaders, the crowds, and the disciples to Jesus' ministry and constructs a narrative which constantly moves on two levels, stressing both the ambiguity of Jesus' identity and the continuing possibility of recognizing him as Son of God. That explicit title virtually disappears from this section as Jesus' identity must be discovered in his words and actions. While the crowds and Jewish leaders represent those who either remain confused or reject Jesus as Son of God, the disciples represent those who move from confusion to confession, from "little faith" to true faith.

From the outset of this section Jesus is depicted as an agent enacting his own intentions. "From that time Jesus began to preach saying 'Repent for the kingdom of heaven is at hand' " (4:17). But even as Jesus begins to emerge as a particular individual, his message is characterized by a crucial ambiguity. "From that time" refers to the arrest of John the Baptist, and Matthew attributes to Jesus the identical message which John had proclaimed. Indeed, many take him to be John *redivivus* (14:2, 16:14). Jesus often speaks in his own right ("But I say unto you"), but at other times he speaks on behalf of an obscure eschatological figure ("Son of Man"). He acts with authority and manifests the signs of the kingdom, but regularly attributes healing to the faith of the recipient. His teaching often takes the form of parables which create confusion in his hearers, "because seeing they do not see, and hearing they do not hear, nor do they understand" (13:13). By stressing the ambiguity which surrounds Jesus' person and message Matthew is able to demonstrate the essential role faith plays in recognizing Jesus as Son of God. To confess Jesus as Son of God in face of the ambiguity which surrounds him is, Matthew argues, to commit oneself to a life of faith and discipleship.

Throughout the first section of the Gospel Jesus is portrayed as a solitary figure, the representative Son of God who speaks in formulaic quotations from Hebrew scripture. As he begins the exercise of his public ministry, however, Jesus speaks in the first-person singular. (First-person locutions occur twenty-three times between 4:19 and 7:29.) In addition he calls to himself disciples who will share his mission with him (4:18–22). These disciples do not seek out Jesus and present themselves for instruction in the usual rabbinic fashion. Rather Jesus takes the initiative and creates disciples for his kingdom. "And he said to them, 'Follow me, and I will make you fishers of men.' *Immediately* they left their nets and followed him. . . . *Immediately* they left the boat and their father, and followed him" (4:19–20,22).[7] These brief call narratives give us our first glimpse of Jesus' authority. Matthew's stresss on "immediately" emphasizes the powerful effect of Jesus' call, but the brevity of his account maintains the sense of ambiguity about the nature and source of his authority.

The theme of Jesus' ambiguous authority also dominates Matthew's description of his teaching. Jesus is portrayed as the reinterpreter and transformer of the Israelite tradition of which he is the heir. Though he radically reinterprets the law, apparently by his own authority ("but I say unto you . . . truly, I say to you . . . yet I tell you"), he insists that he remains in continuity with the previous tradition, "Think not that I have come to abolish the law and the prophets; I have come not to abolish them but to fulfill them" (5:17). While maintaining the authority of the law, Jesus exercises his own authority by radicalizing its demands. "You have heard that it was said to the men of old, 'You shall not kill.' . . . But I say unto you that every one who is angry with his brother shall be liable to judgment" (5:21,22). The whole of chapter five is dominated by the formula "you have heard that it was said. . . . But I say unto you." Despite his evident authority, Jesus' identity remains cloaked in ambiguity. Who is able to interpret the law by his own authority? Does Jesus speak on his own behalf or on behalf of another? When he speaks of God, he refers to him as "the Father" or "our Father" but only once as "my Father" (7:21). The reaction of the crowds exhibits both their wonder and their uncertainty in response to his message. "The crowds were astonished at his teaching, for he taught them as one who had authority" (7:28). Jesus is recognizable to the crowds as a teacher with authority, but his authority is not recognized as the God-given power of the Son of God. Even his disciples do not confess him as Son of God, for when they experience his authority in the stilling of the storm, they ask, "What sort of man is this, that even winds and sea obey him?" (8:27). The answer is delivered in the very next story when the Gadarene demoniacs ironically provide the identification which the disciples cannot give (8:29).

Matthew brings his discussion of Jesus' authority to a climax in the masterfully formed story of the healing of the paralytic (9:1–8). The theme of Jesus' ambiguous authority is given its most powerful expression in a story which, like the entire middle section of the Gospel, operates on two distinct levels. A paralytic is brought to Jesus for healing. "And when Jesus saw their faith, he said to the paralytic, 'Take heart, my son; your sins are forgiven' " (9:2). The scribes observing the scene recognize this as an act of blasphemy, for Jesus had taken to himself the divine prerogative to forgive sin. Jesus' reply apparently clarifies the nature of his authority.

> But Jesus, knowing their thoughts, said, "Why do you think evil in your hearts? For which is easier, to say, 'Your sins are forgiven,' or to say, 'Rise and walk'? But that you may know that the Son of man has authority on earth to forgive sins" — he then said to the paralytic — "Rise, take up your bed and go home." And he rose and went home. (9:4–7)

The meaning of Jesus' reply depends on one's answer to Jesus' rhetorical question. If the answer is "your sins are forgiven," then Jesus has presented a straightforward *a fortiori* argument. "It is easier to forgive sins than to heal paralytics. If I can heal this paralytic, then surely I have the power to forgive sins." Matthew certainly intends his readers to grasp this level of Jesus' answer, for it is a direct reply to the scribes' accusation. It is, however, also an argument which the scribes (i.e., those without faith) can understand. In addition it produces the kind of "sign" which Jesus adamantly refuses to provide in the subsequent narrative (16:1–4). How would the logic of the argument proceed if one answered the rhetorical question in the opposite fashion? Matthew's readers know on the basis of the first section of the Gospel that the power to forgive sins is granted to a single human being, the Son of God. Since forgiving sins is a unique action which can be performed only by the Son of God, it becomes the far more difficult action. Thus for Matthew's readers (i.e., those with faith) the logic of Jesus' argument runs in the opposite direction. The healing of the paralytic pales in significance when compared to the forgiving of sins, but that truth can be grasped only by those who in faith recognize Jesus as Son of God. Jesus has thus only apparently provided a "sign" to his accusers. In fact this ironic reply only confirms their faithlessness. Jesus' unique authority is that which he has received from the Father and which he exercises in forgiveness on behalf of his sinful people. But the true nature and source of his authority cannot be known by those who refuse to confess him as Son of God. Matthew concludes this artfully constructed story by attributing to the crowd a middling reaction. While they recognize the God-given authority in Jesus' healing, they do not yet recognize Jesus as Son of God. "When the crowds saw it, they were afraid, and they glorified God, who had given such authority to men" (9:8).

While Jesus' authority is manifested in his reinterpretation of the law, and in his power over disease, the most radical expression of his authority is manifested in his claim to be able to forgive sins. At this crucial point in the narrative Jesus affirms publicly, though ironically, the essential character of his mission on behalf of sinners. Jesus' identification with sinners is reiterated in the verses immediately following this pericope. The special relationship between Jesus and the outcasts of Israelite society is signified by his call to discipleship of Matthew the tax collector (9:9) and his table fellowship with "tax collectors and sinners" (9:10). Again the defenders of the Israelite tradition are appalled at this defiling violation of the law. But Jesus' response is an unequivocal pronouncement of the gracious character of his mission. "Those who are well have no need of a physician, but those who are sick. Go and learn what this means, 'I desire mercy and not sacrifice.' For I came not to call the righteous but sinners" (9:12–13). Jesus once again appeals to the Israelite tradition against its contemporary interpreters. His reinterpretation of the law, his power over demons and disease, his association with sinners and forgiveness of their sins derives from the gracious and merciful God who has bestowed this mission upon him. His divine authority is a merciful authority to receive where the law would reject, to love where the law would demand, to forgive where the law would condemn. Jesus' transformation of the law brings to the center of God's relation with sinners mercy, forgiveness, and love. This becomes clear in Jesus' response to the Pharisees' inquiry about the great commandment in the law (22:36). Jesus answers by quoting from the Israelite tradition, first from the *Shema* (cf. Deut. 6:4f.) and then from Leviticus 19:18. "You shall love the Lord your God with all your heart, and with all your soul, and with all your mind. . . . You shall love your neighbor as yourself. On these two commandments depend all the law and the prophets" (22:37–40). Jesus' gracious authority reiterates the very heart of the Jewish faith, thus establishing his continuity with that tradition. But by summarizing the whole of the law and prophets under these great commandments, he also reinterprets the tradition. For this authority allows the doing of good on the Sabbath (12:1–13) in apparent opposition to the law. Such reinterpretation can only lead to conflict with the defenders of the Israelite tradition. Following the miracle of healing on the Sabbath, Matthew writes, "But the Pharisees went out and took counsel against him, how to destroy him" (12:14).

Following the crucial discussion of authority, Matthew focuses attention on the disciples and their transformation from confusion to true faith. Jesus shares with them his mission and authority (10:1) and begins to instruct them in the "secrets of the kingdom" (13:11). Matthew's description of Jesus becomes increasingly clear as he explicitly assigns him traits of character based on his narrative descriptions. Four times he characterizes Jesus as "compassionate" (9:36, 14:14, 15:32, 20:34) when confronted by the needs of those in the crowds. He portrays Jesus as speaking openly to his Father in prayer and explicitly defining his divine sonship. "All things have been delivered to me by my Father; and no one knows the Son except the Father, and no one knows the Father except the Son and any one to whom the Son chooses to reveal him" (11:17). Precisely as the disciples are instructed in the secrets of the Kingdom and the identity of its proclaimer, those who refuse to see or hear "take offense at him" (13:57) because he is merely "the carpenter's son" (13:55).

Matthew constructs his narrative in such a way that his readers are gradually led to identify the distant figure of the early chapters, the stylized Son of God, with the concrete person Jesus of Nazareth. While for some the identification of a particular personal agent, the carpenter's son, with the Son of God is both offensive and blasphemous, Matthew's cumulative narrative depiction argues precisely for that identification. His case is surely not self-evident, for then the response of offense would be logically impossible, but, Matthew argues, it is nonetheless true. To affirm that this particular man is Son of God requires an act of faith and discipleship. Jesus' disciples have been throughout these chapters as confused as the crowds about Jesus' identity. Twice he calls them "men of little faith" (8:26, 14:31) when they express fear during storms on the sea. But on the second occasion, after Jesus has walked on the water and rescued Peter from drowning, they exclaim, "Truly you are the Son of God" (14:33). Such recognition is possible only by those who possess faith, and with that confession the disciples have made the initial movement of faith.

The disciples' confession on the sea anticipates Peter's great confession in chapter 16. Matthew builds toward that confession by interweaving themes from the Gospel's middle portion. Chapter 16 opens with the Pharisees and Sadducees demanding "a sign from heaven." Though Jesus had apparently provided such a sign earlier (9:1–9), he now refuses, saying that they are unable to "interpret the signs of the times" (16:3). Jesus thereupon warns the disciples about "the leaven of the Pharisees and Sadducees," (16:6) which leads to a misunderstanding concerning bread, emphasizing the disciples' inability to perceive. Once again Jesus calls them "men of little faith," a reference which recalls the stories of storm stilling and the disciples' recent confession of faith. In collecting this disparate material Matthew has reintroduced the problem of the ambiguity surrounding Jesus' identity. The Jewish leaders refuse to recognize who Jesus is, and the disciples, despite their confession, seem once again confused. In this context of ambiguity, rejection, and confusion Jesus poses the crucial question of his identity, using the obscure eschatological title he used in controversy concerning forgiveness. "Who do *men* say that the *Son of Man* is?" But he asks the disciples, "Who do you say that *I* am?" and Peter makes explicit the identification between Jesus of Nazareth and Son of God which has been implied by the dramatic actions of the preceding chapters. With this "blessed" confession, revealed by the Father, the second major portion of the Gospel reaches its climax. Matthew thus assures his readers that though ambiguity surrounds the person of Jesus, the Father does reveal his true identity to those who follow him.

But Matthew introduces one crucial modification into his depiction of discipleship. Peter's confession indicates his apparent grasp of the identity and mission of Jesus. But when Jesus begins to share with his disciples the final secret of the Kingdom, which until this time he alone had borne, Peter cannot bear the full implications of Jesus' sonship.

> From that time Jesus began to show his disciples that he must go to Jerusalem and suffer many things from the elders and chief priests and scribes, and be killed, and on the third day be raised. And Peter took him and began to rebuke him, saying, "God forbid, Lord! This shall never happen to you."

The previously bold confessor objects to any such fate for his Son of God. Jesus' response makes a striking connection with the satanic temptation with which his mission was inaugurated. "Get behind me, Satan! You are a hindrance to me; for you are not on the side of God, but of men" (16:23). If the mission for which he was born, the salvation of sinners, is to be accomplished, the Son of God *must* suffer and die. Anything less is a false notion of sonship which must be rejected. The validity of Jesus' suffering exercise of his sonship is once again con-

firmed by God in the transfiguration scene in chapter 17, as he repeats
the words with which he had inaugurated Jesus' ministry. "This is my
beloved Son, with whom I am well pleased" (17:5).

Matthew's message to his reader is clear. Faith entails discipleship.
The correlative action asked of those who would follow the Son of God
is that they prepare to share in his destiny. "If any man would come
after me, let him deny himself and take up his cross and follow me"
(16:24). With this climactic revelation of the true nature of Jesus' sonship and the correlative quality of Christian discipleship, Matthew has
set the stage for the final and decisive portion of his Gospel narrative.
By the end of this second section Jesus has become an individuated
agent, and he has been identified as the suffering Son of God. Nonetheless, he has not yet begun to enact that suffering sonship fully. At
the end of the Gospel's first section the title Son of God was linked
to the bare name of Jesus. By the end of this section that title is linked
to an identifiable person, Jesus of Nazareth—the carpenter's son, the
compassionate healer and proclaimer of the Kingdom, the one who
associates with sinners and tax collectors. And yet the key aspect of
sonship, suffering and death on behalf of a sinful people, is present
only by anticipation. The events surrounding Peter's confession set a
mood of expectation as Jesus begins his trek to Jerusalem (20:17) to
fulfill his mission of salvation.

21:1–28:20

The major motifs of Matthew's Gospel reach their culmination
in the passion, crucifixion, and resurrection sequence, as Jesus' identity as Son of God is confirmed in a remarkably constructed realistic
narrative. Jesus' unsubstitutable personal identity is constituted by these
final events, and the reader recognizes that precisely in his individuated
personal identity Jesus is Son of God. Thus Matthew's two types of
identifications merge in a definitive specification of the identity of Jesus
Christ.

Throughout the Matthean narrative we have witnessed a gradual
development of the theme in which Jesus is first identified as heir of
the Israelite tradition and then increasingly as its radical transformer.
Whereas in the early stages of the story Jesus' identity is bestowed by
the Israelite tradition, in the final portion the tradition is fully transformed so that the true nature of God's covenant can be seen only
in light of Jesus' identity. A continuity between old and new remains,
but it is a continuity established in Jesus Christ.

Throughout chapters 17 to 20 Matthew portrays Jesus as advancing inexorably toward Jerusalem and his final destiny. As he enters the city of Israel's king and messianic expectation, he is acclaimed with "hosannas" by "the crowds that went before him and that followed him" (21:9). These crowds, gathered from outside the holy city, recognize him as "Son of David" who "comes in the name of the Lord." But Matthew carefully indicates that with the exception of the children (a common symbol of the Kingdom) no one in Jerusalem recognizes the identity of this Messiah. "And when he entered Jerusalem, all the city was stirred, saying, 'Who is this?' " (21:10). The expected heirs of the Israelite tradition, the inhabitants of Jerusalem, are for the most part blind to the one who has come as the Son of God.[8] Matthew thus depicts Jesus from this point on in the narrative as the unyielding judge of Jerusalem and the leaders of contemporary Judaism. Immediately upon entering the city he drives out the buyers and sellers in the Temple, dramatically signifying the advent of the Messianic age,[9] thereby purifying and reclaiming the Temple for the transformed Israelite tradition. This process of transforming the Temple is symbolically concluded by the tearing of the "curtain of the Temple" upon Jesus' death (27:51). Much of the remaining material of chapters 21 to 25 consists of the denunciation and condemnation of the contemporary representatives of the ancient tradition for their lack of repentance and faith.[10]

But what is the nature of this radically transformed Messiah which should make Jerusalem so blind to his identity? Matthew leaves little doubt that the lowliness and humility of the Messiah-king occasions his rejection. His entrance into Jerusalem is linked with a prophecy from Zechariah 9:9. "Tell the daughter of Zion, behold, your king is coming to you, humble, and mounted on an ass, and on a colt, the foal of an ass" (21:5). The king in whom the tradition of Israel finds its culmination is one whose majesty is manifested in humility. The refusal of Jerusalem to accept this lowly Messiah leads to its ultimate rejection and the bestowal of the Kingdom upon those whom Matthew calls "sinners." "Truly, I say unto you, the tax collectors and the harlots go into the kingdom of God before you" (21:31). Thus Jesus' lowliness applies not primarily to his personal style or demeanor but to his identification with those sinners and outcasts for whose sake he humbly and obediently goes to his death. His lowliness is a function of the service he renders in giving "his life as a ransom for many" (21:28).

The identification of Jesus with sinners is made on two other crucial occasions in this concluding section. Jesus' passion is inaugurated in the home of an outcast, Simon the leper, through his annointing by an unnamed woman. Though the disciples object to this waste of oil, Jesus accepts her act as preparation for burial (26:12). Moreover, she receives a word of highest praise. "Truly, I say to you, wherever this gospel is preached in the whole world, what she has done will be told in memory of her" (26:13).[11] Although this is a difficult passage to interpret, one possible explanation is that this anonymous woman, one of the least in the Kingdom, becomes the greatest because through her act she draws attention not to herself but to her Lord. She is the epitome of Jesus' charge to his disciples, "Whoever would be great among you must be your servant, and whoever would be first among you must be your slave" (21:26–27).

Following this act of inauguration Jesus celebrates the Passover meal with his disciples, and once again identifies himself and his mission with sinners. The institution of the meal of the new Kingdom takes place in the context of the Jewish passover feast. As he passes the cup of wine to his disciples, Jesus says, "This is my blood of the covenant, which is poured out for many for the forgiveness of sins" (26:28). A continuity remains between God's covenant and the Kingdom inaugurated by Jesus Christ, but the point of continuity is established in the person of Jesus Christ and in his forgiving mission on behalf of sinners.

Throughout my discussion of the identity of Jesus Christ I have emphasized the importance of the title Son of God as the most appropriate designation of the one who enacts this saving mission on behalf of sinners. Significantly that title reappears in the final scenes of the passion narrative. The definitive identification of Jesus as the obedient son of his Father, going to his death on behalf of sinners, is offered in these closing scenes of Matthew's Gospel.

The prayer in Gethsemane portrays for one of the few times in the Gospel the interior life of Jesus and serves as an important source of the claim that he is the obedient Son of God. Jesus, who began his mission as a solitary figure, now faces his final destiny in an even more painful solitude. He asks that three of those disciples with whom he had shared his mission and authority share with him the burden of these final hours. His agonized prayer shows that Jesus must face one final temptation to his sonship before his mission is completed. He pleads with his Father that this mission be accomplished some other way than through his death. "My Father, if it be possible, let this cup pass from me" (26:39). "Nevertheless, not as I will, but as thou wilt." Matthew depicts Jesus as offering his prayer three times,[12] and each time the obedient Son of God becomes more accepting of the necessity of his own death. "My Father, if this cannot pass unless I drink it, thy will be done" (26:42). Finally at the completion of his solitary striving with God, Jesus recognizes that "it must be so" (26:54). In that moment when Jesus affirms for the final time his obedient sonship, he once again becomes a solitary figure. Those disciples who sleep during his agonized prayer forsake him and flee when his captors arrive. The Son of God faces his final destiny alone.

The identity of Jesus Christ as Son of God is fully enacted and established in the crucifixion and resurrection. The trial and crucifixion scenes are dominated by questions and claims about the identity of Jesus of Nazareth. After Jesus is silent in face of the charge of the false witnesses that he would destroy the Temple, Caiaphas, the high priest, demands in words strikingly similar to Peter's confession that Jesus identify himself. "I adjure you by the living God, tell us if you are the Christ, the Son of God" (26:63). Jesus' reply is a simple, "You have said so." Thus the symbol of those elements of the Jewish tradition which reject Jesus unwittingly confesses the true identity of the suffering Son of God. So too the inhabitants of Jerusalem who stand at the foot of the cross taunt Jesus in words which ironically acknowledge his true identity. "If you are the Son of God, come down from the cross. . . . He trusts in God; let God deliver him now, if he desires him; for he said, 'I am the Son of God' " (27:39,43). Even in their blindness those who most clearly reject Jesus make confession to him. Though they do not recognize what they have said, they acknowledge that the true Son of God must be a crucified Messiah. Nowhere is that truth more evident than in the climactic moment of the entire narrative, when Jesus cries again to his Father, "My God, my God, why hast thou forsaken me?" Jesus' identification with sinners, his obedience to his mission, is so complete that he suffers their fate—God-forsakenness. As he yields up his spirit the ultimate identification is made by one who stands outside the people of Israel, a Roman centurian, who articulates the theme of the entire Gospel of Matthew. "Truly, this was the son of God" (27:54).

Though in his crucifixion Jesus has been unmistakably identified, the narrative does not end at Jesus' death. Though his death was necessary, it is not the last event in the divine drama. The claim of the Matthean narrative that Jesus of Nazareth is "the Christ, the Son of the living God" remains unconfirmed despite Jesus' obedient enactment of that claim in his ministry and crucifixion. As long as Jesus remained in the grave one could only assert that he willingly died for the sake of his own principles, that he died in accord with his claim about himself. The absolute powerlessness of Jesus at this point in the narrative is the culmination of the development we have witnessed in this final section. The one who was conceived through the power of God's spirit, who enacted his divine authority in his ministry, has in this final stage willingly given up the exercise of that authority (see especially 26:53–54). Beginning with his entrance into Jerusalem and especially following the prayer in Gethsemane, Jesus becomes a passive subject whose destiny is determined by others. Clearly Jesus chooses this passive stance as an act of obedience to his Father, but the possibility that this is a hollow tragic act is raised by his God-forsaken cry on the cross. If Jesus is to be more than a tragic figure victimized by his enemies, then God must act decisively in the face of his son's powerlessness. The message of the angel at the open tomb announces that God has indeed acted on behalf of his obedient son. "He is not here, for he has risen, as he said" (28:6). God himself completes Jesus' mission by raising him from the dead, thereby vindicating Jesus' claim and confirming his status as Son of God. With the resurrection Jesus' mission of salvation for sinners is completed and his identity fully enacted. Thus he receives with unmistakable finality the divine authority due him. "All authority in heaven and earth has been given to me" (28:18). The one who was designated Emmanuel at his birth, who enacted that identity through a humble identification with sinners, triumphantly affirms that he is the very presence of God in the concluding words of the Gospel. "And lo, I am with you always, to the close of the age" (28:20).

In this concluding integral narrative Matthew brings together his personal and formal individuating identifications. Jesus of Nazareth,

who suffered and was crucified, is by virtue of his resurrection unmistakably identified as Son of God. Jesus is most clearly individuated
in his passion and death. Matthew's depiction is vividly realistic and
the elements of verisimilitude function to define Jesus' identity. Ironically, Jesus' character becomes most sharply articulated when he no
longer controls his own action. His purposive and obedient exercise
of mission bring him to Jerusalem, where external circumstances determine his destiny. The Jewish leaders plot against him; one of his
disciples betrays him; the Romans execute him. He exercises control
over his behavior until the moment in Gethsemane when he submits
to his Father's will. The events which then overtake him become the
vehicle of the enactment of God's intention to save his people. In order
for those sinners with whom Jesus identified himself to be saved, Jesus
had to offer his life as a "ransom." Jesus' intentional action once again
gives way to the primacy of the Father's intention. But Jesus does not
retreat into a stylized representative figure, but is most unmistakably
himself in his passion and crucifixion. By maintaining the realism of
his depiction Matthew brings his narrative to its appropriate conclusion. The Son of God who enacts his Father's intentions is this very
man Jesus of Nazareth who endures the mockings, the beatings, the
crucifixion, and God-forsakenness and so does the Father's will. The
unmistakable coincidence of the formal and personal identifications
is established in the resurrection, as God alone acts to raise the crucified
Jesus from the dead. Jesus, having accomplished his mission, receives
his authority and sends his followers out to baptize in the name of
the Father who sent him, the spirit who conceived him, and the Son
who, having accomplished their salvation, will be with them to the
close of the age.

God's Identity as Prevenient God of Promise

1) God, the Father of Jesus Christ

Just as the title *Son of God* serves as Matthew's central identifying term for Jesus, so the term *Father* is his most prevalent designation for God. In contrast to one prominent tendency in the Old Testament narratives, Matthew does not often portray God as a character
acting directly within the Gospel stories. Only twice is God explicitly

portrayed as an actor, and in each case he is limited to a single speech. "This is my beloved Son, with whom I am well pleased" (3:17) and "This is my beloved Son, with whom I am well pleased; listen to him" (17:5). Matthew's strict limitation of God's direct participation in the narrative action has a double purpose. On the one hand, it focuses attention on the actions of Jesus, who as God's Son is cumulatively identified as the one who acts on behalf of God. To know what God intends, Matthew argues, one must refer to the actions of Jesus narrated in the Gospel. On the other hand, when God does appear in the narrative the dramatic effect of his speech is enormously heightened. God first speaks following Jesus' baptism. God's declaration functions as a definitive identification of Jesus and as the authorization of his mission. God thus identifies himself with this particular man and his mission on behalf of sinners. God's second speech occurs in the aftermath of Peter's confession and immediately following Jesus' revelation that both his sonship and true discipleship entail suffering and death. In the context of the transfiguration, where Jesus is identified both with the Sinaitic covenant (Moses) and with Israel's messianic expectation (Elijah), God again declares his unity with the person and mission of his Son and urges the disciples (and by implication Matthew's readers) to heed him.[13]

The term *Father*, as Matthew uses it, specifies God's unity with the person and mission of Jesus. While Father and Son remain distinct persons (one important consequence of Matthew's direct portrayal of God's speech), God's will or intention is rightly expressed in the actions of Jesus. God's definitive identification and authorization of Jesus and his mission warrant the conclusion that Jesus' obedient actions enact not only his own intentions but also God's. Matthew explicates that unity of intention and action through a careful manipulation of Jesus' speech concerning the Father. Prior to Jesus' sharing of authority with the twelve disciples (10:1), he refers to God almost exclusively as "your Father" (fifteen times). Only once does he call God "our Father" (6:9) or "my Father" (7:21). Following the commissioning of the twelve, however, virtually every reference to God identifies him as "my Father" (eighteen times, eleven of which occur after Peter's confession). Other references to "(the) Father" (11:26, 24:36, 28:19), "his Father" (16:27) or "their Father" (13:43) in every case imply a primary identification of God as the Father of Jesus. Many of these passages cast Jesus in the role of judge who clearly acts as the agent of his father's will. But those passages which are most central to the narrative action of the Gospel are Jesus' two prayers to the Father (11:25-29 and 26:36-46).

These two prayers, when interpreted together, specify the relation of Father and Son as one of self-differentiated unity. The first prayer emphasizes the unity shared by Father and Son. "All things have been delivered to me by my Father, and no one knows the Son except the Father; and no one knows the Father except the Son and any one to whom the Son chooses to reveal him" (11:27). Father and Son are differentiated in that the Father is the one who delivers all things (including "all authority" 28:18) to the Son. And yet that differentiation is set in the context of a unity of mutual identification. The Father alone knows the Son, and those who in faith come to identify Jesus as the Father's Son do so by the Father's gracious revelation (16:17). The Son in turn has exclusive knowledge of the Father, and those who learn to identify God as Father do so only through the Son's revelation. Father and Son are thus reciprocally identifiable both to themselves and to those with whom they graciously share their identities.[14] Jesus then proceeds to specify his own identity and that of the Father whose "gracious will" (11:26) he enacts.

> Come to me, all who labor and are heavy laden, and I will give you rest. Take my yoke upon you, and learn from me; for I am gentle and lowly in heart, and you will find rest for your souls. For my yoke is easy, and my burden is light. (11:28-29)

The prayer at Gethsemane completes this complex pattern of relation by stressing the differentiation within the paternal and filial unity. Jesus enacts the Father's will as the obedient Son. That obedience, born of Jesus' intention to act in accord with the Father's will, is most severely tested in the hours before the passion. Thus Jesus pleads that "this cup pass from me," while still submitting to his gracious Father: "nevertheless, not as I will, but as thou wilt." His second prayer indicates Jesus' recognition that the Father's intention must be enacted by his death and that his own intention must conform to the Father's. "My Father, if this cannot pass unless I drink it, thy will be done." For all their unity Son and Father remain distinct persons with distinguishable intentions. Completion of the Father's intention to save his people from their sins requires the conformation of Jesus' intention to that will. Though unified in mutual identification through mutual action, the identity of neither Father nor Son is absorbed in the other. Theirs remains a relation of true mutuality.

These two prayers make explicit the pattern of relation manifest in the narrative action of the Gospel. God is depicted in the first section of the Gospel as Yahweh, God of Israel, who conceives a son of the virgin Mary in order to enact his intention to "save his people from their sins." He calls his son "out of Egypt" to inaugurate his saving mission through submission to baptism. Having authorized Jesus' mission by declaring him to be his "beloved Son," the Father fades into the narrative background in the middle section of the Gospel. Jesus now takes center stage, as he first ambiguously and then with increasing clarity enacts his identity as the Father's Son. As the readers recognize that Jesus of Nazareth is Son of God, so they also recognize that in Jesus they may know God as Father (5:9,45). At the crucial turning point of the narrative, as Jesus prepares to go to Jerusalem, the Father reiterates his unity with his beloved Son. In the culminating section of the Gospel, God is identified by this complex relation of unity and distinction. The differentiation of Father and Son is stressed by the fact that Jesus undergoes the events of passion and crucifixion as a solitary individual. The God who appeared at the Jordan and on the mount of transfiguration is conspicuously absent as Jesus suffers and is crucified. Though Jesus implores the Father at Gethsemane, there is no dramatic narrative answer. The disciples continue to sleep as Jesus' betrayer approaches, and the sense of Jesus' isolation is heightened. God's absence from the narrative is most profound when Jesus cries out not "my Father" but "my God, my God, why have you forsaken me?"

If the narrative had ended with the words "And Jesus cried again with a loud voice and yielded up his spirit" (27:50), then Matthew's story would have been as Albert Schweitzer described it.

> There is silence all around. The Baptist appears, and cries: "Repent, for the Kingdom of Heaven is at hand." Soon after that comes Jesus, and in the knowledge that He is the coming Son of Man lays hold of the wheel of the world to set it moving on that last revolution which is to bring all ordinary history to a close. It refuses to turn, and He throws Himself upon it. Then it does turn; and crushes Him. Instead of bringing in the eschatological conditions, He has destroyed them.

The wheel rolls onward, and the mangled body of the one immeasurably great Man, who was strong enough to think of Himself as the spiritual ruler of mankind and to bend history to His purpose, is hanging upon it still. That is His victory and His reign.[15]

But the narrative continues and describes the descent of an angel whose message defines Matthew's story as "gospel." "He is not here; for he has risen, as he said" (28:6). That message casts the reader back to Caesarea Philippi where Jesus concludes his passion prediction with the words "and on the third day be raised" (ἐγερθῆναι). The aorist passive verb points to the one who, though apparently absent from the narrative, has acted to raise his Son from death and to grant him his ultimate authority (28:18). By that act the Father not only completes his intention to save but also unmistakably binds himself in differentiated union with his Son. In the resurrection Jesus is definitively identified as Son of God, and God is definitively identified as his Father. Just as the formal identification Son of God is given its personal content in the narrated events of crucifixion and resurrection, so also God's identity as Father is specified by those same events. To call God "Father" is to identify him as the one who raised Jesus from the dead.

2) God as Yahweh, the God of Gospel and Promise

The word *promise* (ἐπαγγελία) never appears in the Gospel of Matthew. Yet the notion of promise hovers like an enormous parenthesis surrounding the entire narrative. More than any other evangelist Matthew depicts Jesus as enacting the will of the Father by fulfilling prophecy. Fifteen times Matthew explicitly designates a narrative occurrence as fulfilling a prophecy of Hebrew scripture. Such references are especially prominent in the Gospel's first section, where Matthew painstakingly identifies Jesus as the inheritor of Israel's tradition. The stylized use of the fulfillment motif (e.g., "all this took place to fulfill what the Lord had spoken by the prophet") occurs infrequently within the realistic passion narrative, but Matthew's more subtle use of quotations from and allusions to Hebrew scripture is striking.[16] There are at least twenty such instances in chapters 26 and 27 alone.

Matthew achieves a number of purposes by employing the prophecy-fulfillment motif. First, he associates Jesus, Son of God, with the Israelite heritage, thus identifying him as Son of Abraham and

David, i.e., as inheritor of the two great covenantal promises. Second, he establishes Jesus' continuity with his tradition precisely as he depicts him as its transformer. Jesus and not the contemporary Jewish leadership is the true interpreter and fulfiller of the law and prophets. Third, and for our purposes most importantly, Matthew uses the prophecy-fulfillment motif to specify further the identity of the God Jesus calls Father. Jesus' Father is Yahweh, the God of Abraham, Isaac and Jacob, the God whose promises the prophets declared and Jesus now fulfills. The God of Israel is the Father of Jesus Christ. Thus to call God "Father" is, Matthew argues, to identify him as Yahweh, the one who raised Jesus from the dead.

There is one final way in which God can be identified on the basis of Matthew's Gospel. Jesus' death and resurrection, which provide the final identification of both Father and Son, also accomplish the salvation of sinners. Because Jesus successfully completed his mission, the disciples' confession "You are the Christ, the Son of the living God," has been confirmed. Matthew constructs his narrative in such a way that his readers are led to identify with the disciples in their transition from confusion to faith. The narrative thus functions not only as a description of past events but as an invitation to the reader to share in the disciples' confession of faith. That is to say, the narrative serves as both report and proclamation. If Jesus is Son of God, then he has accomplished the salvation of all sinners who in faith confess his name and undertake the life of discipleship. Matthew's narrative is thus "gospel," the proclamation of the good news concerning Jesus Christ.

The word *gospel* (εὐαγγέλιον) appears only four times in Matthew. The first two times it appears in the formulaic sentence "And he [Jesus] went about . . . teaching in their synagogues and preaching the gospel of the kingdom and healing every disease and every infirmity among the people" (4:23, 9:35). This phrase first occurs at the outset of Jesus' own ministry in chapter 4 and is repeated in chapter 9 immediately prior to the commissioning of the twelve. Matthew does not use the word *gospel* again until chapter 24 when, shortly before the passion narrative, Jesus warns of the signs which will accompany "the close of the age" (συντελείας τοῦ αἰῶνος) (24:3). "And this gospel of the kingdom will be preached throughout the whole world, as a testimony to all nations [πᾶσιν τοῖς ἔθνεσιν); and then the end will come" (24:14). The word *gospel* appears for the final time in the

enigmatic story which introduces the passion account, Jesus' annointing with oil by an unnamed woman. After indicating that she has an-
nointed him for burial, Jesus says, "Truly, I say to you, wherever this
gospel is preached in the whole world what she has done will be told
in her memory" (26:13). These broadly separated uses of the word
gospel capture the progression inherent in Matthew's narrative. The
"good news" is originally that authoritative message which Jesus
preached and enacted in his teaching and healing ministry. Then it
is that message which the disciples proclaim when they are given
"authority . . . to heal every disease and every infirmity" (10:1). Gradually the scope of the good news widens to include "the whole world"
and "every nation." Finally the content of the gospel itself shifts subtly
but importantly at the point of the passion narrative. Jesus refers simply
to "this gospel" which "when preached to the whole world" will serve
as a memorial to this unnamed woman. That memorial is accomplished
when the gospel becomes *this narrative* concerning Jesus of Nazareth,
the Son of God. When the narrative which identifies Jesus as Son of
God is proclaimed as gospel to all nations, this woman, whose act in-
augurates Jesus' passion, will be forever remembered. The "gospel"
within Matthew's narrative shifts from the message Jesus proclaimed
to the message proclaimed about Jesus. That important shift is cul-
minated when, in the final verses of the Gospel, the resurrected Jesus
again shares his authority with his disciples, sends them to make
disciples "of all nations" (πάντα τὰ ἔθνη cf. 24:14) and to baptize
them "in the name of the Father, and of the Son, and of the Holy
Spirit," and finally promises to be with them until "the close of the
age" (συντελείας τοῦ αἰῶνος cf. 24:3). As they now baptize in his
name, so when they proclaim the "gospel" they proclaim his story.
Matthew's story appropriately ends with Jesus' *promise*, for this narrative, seen from the perspective of its own ending, functions for its
readers as gospel, i.e., as the *narrated promise* of Jesus of Nazareth,
Son of God.

3) God's Prevenience

The Gospel of Matthew provides the requisite individuating
description of God. God is identified as Yahweh, the God of promise,
the Father of Jesus Christ, who by raising Jesus from the dead accomplished his intention to save his sinful people. *A God so described
cannot be other than prevenient.* In part that conclusion follows from

the way this description of God fulfills the conditions of authentic promising.[17] As God of promise Yahweh is the one who specified his intention to save through his prophets, who designated Jesus' death and resurrection as the acts whereby he would enact his intention, who in his declared unity with Jesus identified himself as Father and undertook the obligation implied in his promise, and who, when he raised Jesus from the dead, uniquely fulfilled the conditions of his own promise. God as identified in Matthew's narrative is alone the gracious initiator, actor, and fulfiller of his own promises. The central act in this complex intentional action is the raising of Jesus from the dead, for in that deed both Father and Son are definitively identified, and God's promise is fulfilled. Yahweh, who called forth creation from the void and formed Adam from the dust of the ground, now raises his Son from death in a second uniquely creative act. The God who raised Jesus from the dead is necessarily prevenient.

Matthew's narrative portrayal of God demonstrates that God's prevenience is a necessary implication of his identity as God of promise. Theology would be well advised to follow the logic of Matthew's identifying description by locating its justificatory account of God's prevenience neither in the *prolegomena* to theology nor in a separate doctrine of "God's Word" but within its account of God's identity. *The doctrine of revelation ought to be a subtheme within the doctrine of God.* When the justification of God's prevenience is internally related to God's identity, then the significance of God's *triune* identity begins to emerge. Precisely as God is described in his intertrinitarian relations his essential graciousness becomes evident. To designate God as triune is to assert that his utter graciousness, i.e., his prevenience, is a necessary implication of his identity. I am going to argue, by way of conclusion, that Matthew's narrative description of God and the belief in prevenience it implies receive their most precise theological redescription in certain trinitarian categories. I cannot in this brief space articulate a full doctrine of the trinity,[18] but I do want to indicate how Matthew's identifying description of God has a characteristically trinitarian character which theology ought to enhance and develop.

The concluding verses of Matthew provide the trinitarian baptismal formula which becomes the basis for the triune shape of Christian liturgy. Matthew certainly does not develop a complete account of the identities of Father, Son, and Spirit, nor of their unified interrelation. His depiction of the Spirit is particularly lean. The Spirit is one who conceives Jesus and leads him into the wilderness following his baptism. The Spirit is further present in the form of a dove as God declares Jesus to be his Son. Other than these two events, the Spirit is absent from the narrative flow of the Gospel. Yet these stories, when bolstered by Jesus' references to the Spirit, allow the construction of a minimal identity. The Spirit is described as being "of God" (3:16, 12:18,28) or "of the Father" (1:16). The Spirit, moreover, is the one who will empower the disciples to speak in the persecutions of the end-time (10:20). These few references show the Spirit to be the means of God's relation to his Son and the source of power for the disciples' witness.

When this spare description is added to the much richer depiction of Father and Son one can see the emergence of an incipient conception of God as triune. The mysterious relation of three to one is surely present. The Father is clearly identified with Yahweh, and both Jesus and the Spirit are said to be "of God." When Jesus is granted final authority his disciples worship him, an indication of his equality with God. In the baptismal formula all three persons are assigned equal status, implying a coequal relation as God. But whether Matthew actually teaches a doctrine of three in one is neither particularly important nor interesting. That the elements for the subsequent development of the doctrine are present is unquestionable.

Much more important for our purposes is the way Matthew conceives God in a relation of differentiated unity. Both the distinctions and the unity in the relation among Father, Son, and Spirit are narrative-based. Each person is given a particular name and an unsubstitutable role in the narrative action. The Father promises, enacts his intention to save, and fulfills his promise by raising Jesus from the dead. The Son is conceived, receives a mission of salvation, and obediently accomplishes that mission through crucifixion. The Spirit conceives Jesus, confirms his Sonship, and empowers the disciples' witness. Despite their irreducible particular identities, all three "persons" are mutually and necessarily related. In declaring Jesus to be his Son, the Father ties both his identity and action to the Son. Jesus is obedient Son only in relation to the Father who designated his mission. The Spirit establishes the relation between Father and Son in the act of conception. Though distinguishably identifiable, the identities of all three persons are mutually and necessarily related. They live in a self-differentiated unity.

One final element of Matthew's narrative identification deserves mention. The Father and Spirit (most particularly the Father) are hidden but active during the crucial events of crucifixion and resurrection.[19] Jesus alone is present, and yet he is powerless and unable to act. The power which is exercised in the resurrection is that of the Father, who is never depicted in these concluding events. The theme of God's hidden but active power has a long history in biblical narrative (see chapter 4, pp. 88–90) and suggests the complex patterns theologians must devise if their redescription of God is to be grounded in such a narrative depiction. God must be conceived in such a way that both his hiddenness and presence in human history are accounted for. That pattern cannot simply be correlated with the pattern of Father and Son, for though the Son does enact the Father's intentions, the very fact that we can identify those intentions as the *Father's* curbs any attempt to conceive of the Father as eternally hidden. The distinction between hiddenness and presence must rather cut across the entire conception of God as Father, Son, and Spirit. That is, of course, what the Cappadocian fathers attempted to do in devising the distinction between the "immanent" and "economic" trinity.[20] That distinction guards both the hiddenness and the presence of God's identity, because it asserts that the self-differentiated unity we observe in God's narrative relations is a reiteration of God's inner but hidden identity. The narrative description of God is reliable, because it shows us God's "immanent" identity though in "economic" depiction. God's hiddenness is not some elusive self lurking behind or beyond the narrative depiction. God's hiddenness is simply a quality of God which the shape of the narrative itself indicates. God is the perfection of agency, the one whose activity is not limited by anything beyond the reach of his intentional control.[21] That is to say, God is a self-constituting agent who exercises sovereign control over his own identity. If he should intend that his identity be shared with that which is external to him that sharing is grounded solely in his sovereign intention.[22] Or to put the matter differently: if we come to know God's identity, we do so by grace alone.

A triune conception of God's identity, grounded in a biblical narrative description, is a natural and appropriate vehicle for the expression of God's gracious prevenience. The promising God deigns to share his identity with us and thereby establishes a relation with our human concepts and categories, enabling them to be the vehicle of his communication. But that relation is established in such a way that God's prior gracious initiative is necessarily implied. If it is this God—Father, Son and Spirit—whom we are able to identify, then that identification has been enabled by his gracious action. God, conceived as triune, is a God necessarily prevenient.

CHAPTER SEVEN

Promise and Prevenience: Revelation as the Doctrine of God's Identifiability

Matthias von Grünewald's well-known depiction of the crucifix-ion on the centerpiece of the Isenheimer Altar provides a powerful example of the way the "narrative content" of a work of art can engage the world of the viewer. Grünewald's painting is starkly realistic. The crucified Jesus dominates the center of the picture, his head slumped in the posture of death, his beaten body stretched upon the cross. His fingers point grotesquely toward the blackened sky, a reminder of his earlier God-forsaken cry. To the viewer's left Mary begins to collapse into the arms of the beloved disciple, her pale face and wringing hands attesting to her sorrow. Nearer the cross the darker figure of Mary Magdalene kneels in agonized prayer.

The stunning realism of the depiction, however, extends only in part to the figures on the viewer's right, and Grünewald uses that modified realism to shift the flow of the painting's narrative content. To Jesus' left stands John the Baptist; a lamb, standing at his feet, embracing a small cross and a chalice, gazes toward the crucified Christ. John is clothed in the crude apparel of a wilderness preacher, but in his left arm he holds an open Bible. His long slender index finger points dramatically toward Jesus, and from his mouth proceed the words, "Behold the lamb of God who takes away the sin of the world." John's presence not only disrupts the temporal realism of the painting, but his gaze is directed not toward the cross but outward toward the viewer. He thus "breaks" the narrative frame and extends the depiction beyond the altar's wooden surface and toward the world of the viewer. As he announces the identity of this crucified man, he invites the viewer to enter into the world of those who stand and kneel beside the cross. And between the three mourning figures and the picture's frame,

Grünewald provides an open space, large enough for a full human figure, as if awaiting the viewer's presence.

A similar shift in narrative flow is also present in Matthew's Gospel. As the Gospel reaches its climax in the passion narrative, the role of the disciples undergoes a subtle but important transformation. Prior to chapter 26 the disciples are confused but active participants in Jesus' ministry. They had shared in his authority and proclaimed the message of the coming Kingdom. But following Jesus' anointing by the unnamed woman, the disciples take on a much more passive role. As the narrative focuses on Jesus' unsubstitutable identity, the disciples function more to disrupt than to enhance Jesus' obedient sonship. They fall asleep in Gethsemane; one of them betrays him; another denies he even knows him; all of them forsake him and flee at the moment of his arrest. None of them are numbered among those who witness the crucifixion. "There were also many women there, looking on from afar, who had followed Jesus from Galilee, ministering to him; among them were Mary Magdalene, and Mary the mother of James and Joseph, and the other Mary, mother of the sons of Zebedee" (27:55–56).

The only actions of the twelve which Matthew describes during the passion narrative are Peter's denial and Judas' betrayal. Indeed, the final response of the disciples to Jesus' resurrection is left indeterminate. "Now the eleven disciples went to Galilee, to the mountain to which Jesus had directed them. And when they saw him they worshiped him; but some doubted" (28:16–17). The Gospel concludes with Jesus, identified for the reader as Son of God and savior, but surrounded by his uncertain disciples, issuing a final promise. "And lo, I am with you always, to the close of the age" (28:20).

This artfully constructed conclusion, which juxtaposes the promise of the one who claims that "all authority in heaven and on earth has been given to me" to the doubting response of his disciples, functions to carry the world of the Gospel narrative into that of the reader. Matthew devises no dramatic confession of faith to conclude his story, nor does he introduce an explicit narrator to proclaim the Gospel's message. Rather, he uses Jesus' final act of promising to extend the Gospel's promise "to the whole world." Jesus, whose identity is depicted in the Gospel's narrative, now becomes the agent of promise as this story becomes a proclamation addressed to the reader.[1] It is as if in this final episode Jesus directs his gaze for the first time outside the frame of the story and issues his promise directly to the reading audience. Thus the reader is invited to respond to this narrated promise by entering the world of the narrative and joining with those on the mountain who worship him.

Matthew creates "narrative space" for his readers within the Gospel story by explicitly reminding them that the fellowship of the disciples has been reduced in number. Only eleven of those originally called to follow still remain, and some of them continue to doubt. In addition, some not originally numbered among the twelve have taken on the responsibilities of discipleship. The women alone continue to follow him during the events of the passion and are the recipients of the angel's proclamation of his resurrection. Joseph of Arimathea, though not previously identified as one of the twelve, is called "a disciple of Jesus" when he asks for the body. Thus the opportunity remains for the reader to join the company of disciples by responding in faith and undertaking the journey of discipleship.

By refusing to provide premature closure for his story Matthew allows the narrative discourse to flow from the text to the reader. The reader who responds in faith is incorporated into the world of the narrative, and the story continues through the community created by this narrated promise. Precisely as the narrative provides its definitive identification of God and Jesus, it also functions as a promise of direct address. In narrating the story of God's promise, the Gospel identifies Jesus as the one in whom God's intentions are enacted, and so addresses that narrated promise to the reader. Thus the discourse which functions within the text to identify the story's chief characters also functions between the text and the reader as an invitation to enter the world of the text.

That extension of the narrative's textuality into the world of common human reality provides the crucial context for the final formulation of a revised doctrine of revelation. I have argued throughout this project that an adequate justification of belief in God's prevenience must account both for God's relation and his priority to our framework of belief. God's prior initiative must be distinguished from the response of the community of faith. God's prevenience must be established not only as an intelligible category within the discourse of the text but also as a reality which confronts the reader *through* the text. In that transition from narrative identification to narrative address the Gospel story announces that it seeks to embrace the whole of human reality within its purview. The God identified within this narrative now addresses his promise of salvation through this narrative to those who read the text and hear his promise. The promises of God depicted within the text now become his promises to those who stand outside the text.

Thus the narrative itself provides the structures by which we can interpret the Christian claim concerning God's prevenience. The sense of the biblical narrative, i.e., its patterns of identification and predication, provides the structure for the narrative's referential claims, i.e., its way of tying language to the world.[2] The narrative's propositional content suggests its primary illocutionary force, which in turn invites the response which will complete the "interlocutionary act" between speaker and hearer. By "interlocutionary act" I mean a successful act of communication which elicits an appropriate response from the addressee.[3] When a sergeant issues the command "About face!" and the private reverses his direction an act of communication has been successful. The sign of its success is the appropriate correlative action performed by the addressee. So also a promise elicits an appropriate correlative response from the recipient which signals that a successful communication has taken place. That correlative act does not establish or constitute the promise. The promise *is* a promise solely by virtue of the promiser's locutionary and illocutionary acts. But an appropriate response by the recipient does indicate that a successful interlocutionary act has taken place, i.e., that the promise has been heard as promise, its propositional content believed to be true, and the promiser believed to be trustworthy.

In order for a successful interlocutionary act to occur both the propositional content and the force of discourse must be communicated. The hearer must comprehend the patterns of identification and predication within an utterance or text (sense) and the relation of those patterns to the world (reference). In addition the discourse must successfully transmit its illocutionary force. In the case of scripture's narrated promise, both the story's identification of God through narrative description and its force as promise addressed to the reader must be evident in the communicative situation.

Stated in terms of our analysis of the Gospel of Matthew: the biblical narrative's identification of God as the one who fulfills and renews his promise in raising Jesus from the dead suggests that the story's primary illocutionary force is that of promising. That promise serves further as an address to the Gospel's readers, inviting the response of faith and discipleship. In that interlocutionary situation of address and response the reader is offered the opportunity to make a judgment concerning the reality of the God who invites and the truth of the promises he issues. Thus questions of truth and reference arise in the interlocutionary context. In order to respond to this invitation the reader must recognize this narrative as God's personal promising address. To recognize the gospel as God's personal address the reader must further acknowledge that God is an existent promising agent in actual communication with the human recipient. A correlative response of faith and discipleship indicates that the hearer recognizes both the *extra nos* and *pro me* character of God's narrated promise.

While the structure and content of biblical narratives invite a recognition of the gospel's claims to truth, those claims are hardly *self-evident* implications of the text. Thus the text does not *compel* the reader to acknowledge the narrative as God's personal address. The ambiguity which surrounds the text's reference is a function of three factors. First, reference is primarily a matter of the context within which a text is used. "Language has a reference only when it is used. . . . The same sentence, i.e., the same sense, may or may not refer depending on the circumstances or situation of an act of discourse. . . . To refer is what the sentence does in a certain situation and according to a certain use."[4] While a text's sense can and does provide the essential clues to its own referential claims, those clues remain open to diverse (but not necessarily equally plausible) interpretations. The biblical text functions as God's promising address only in the context of a successful interlocutionary act, i.e., only when the recipient responds with the appropriate correlative action.[5]

Second, biblical narratives, as literary texts, inevitably disrupt the evident dialogical relation which characterizes direct speech. The illocutionary force of an utterance in direct discourse is usually clear because of the presence of a dialogical context. When in a situation of direct verbal address I say to you, "I'll save you a seat at tonight's concert," the illocutionary force of my utterance is evident, and you would undoubtedly respond appropriately by saying something like, "All right, I'll see you there at eight o'clock." But a text, unlike direct speech, possesses "semantic autonomy";[6] its meaning is fixed in a written form which is distanced from both its author's intention and from any particular reader or audience. Thus the illocutionary forces of a text's content are inevitably ambiguous.

Finally, the biblical texts themselves depict God's actions in an indirect and hidden manner. Thus the misidentification of God and Jesus remains as much a possibility for the contemporary reader as for those within the text who refuse to acknowledge Jesus as Son of God. That the reader may refuse to accept this story as God's personal promise of salvation is a possibility the text itself reckons with. Moreover, the event which establishes both God's identity and the narrative's promissory function is Jesus' resurrection. To acknowledge this narrative as God's promise is to confess that Jesus, the crucified, now lives. That confession requires an act of faith which contradicts ordinary experience concerning the finality of death. The gospel narrative can be God's promise to me if, and only if, he has raised Jesus from the dead. The gospel's claim to truth thus demands acceptance of a deeply paradoxical claim which lies at the heart of the narrative's meaning.

Though the biblical narratives do not compel acceptance of their truth-claims, the content of those narratives provides the interpretive structures by which the reader moves from sense to reference, i.e., from the narrated promise within the text to the narrated promise addressed to the reader. I have argued that the Gospel of Matthew is understood in a manner most consonant with its own content when it is read and heard as God's address of promise. Sense not only precedes but also anticipates reference, because of the primacy of the narrative's identifying discourse. The narrative shape of the text and the content of its identifying discourse concerning Jesus and God serve as reliable criteria of denotation.[7] It is not that sense determines reference independent of the context of interpretation, but in one important way the text does create its own context. When God is identified as God of promise, and the biblical narrative as his promissory address, then the reader is invited to respond in faith and discipleship. If the reader does so respond, a context of interpretation is created in which the content and force of the text are logically prior to the correlative response. Thus the context for the interlocutionary act can rightly be said to flow *from* the text *to* the reader. Promise and promiser must precede the faithful or doubting response of the recipient.

Once a context is created by the biblical narrative it takes on a life of its own and cannot be coerced by the text. Indeed, a dialectical situation is created in which text and context are mutually interdependent, and, as modern hermeneutical theories have taught us, context most often functions to control our interpretations and construals of text. I do not deny that such theories are descriptively accurate, but I do want to argue that the biblical narratives ask to be excepted from this general rule — not because of any luminous self-evident quality of the text or because these texts mediate an experience of the numinous, but simply because the structure and content of these texts suggest a reverse hermeneutical procedure for their interpretation. If these texts do indeed describe an existent God who offers his promise of salvation, then their narrative content, i.e., their identification of God, becomes decisive for the correlative response. Indeed, the Christian can claim that God in his grace creates the responding faith and thus creates the interlocutionary situation.

The Christian possesses no *theory* to *explain how* this reverse procedure occurs. All theology can do is describe the characteristics of biblical narrative and the correlative qualities of Christian discipleship which together constitute an interlocutionary relation in which priority is given to the promiser and his promise. The notion that a promise creates its own context of interpretation follows in part from the very logic of promise. The promiser alone can specify both the nature of the obligation he or she willingly undertakes and the conditions of its fulfillment. While a nondefective promise requires the recipient's recognition of those conditions, the recipient does not and cannot establish them. Promises thus ordinarily suggest a context for their interpretation, and so the theological suggestion I am making is not unique.

That a reader who takes the biblical narrative as God's personal promissory address has performed an intelligible act based on a coherent reading of the text has surely been established. *How* the reader comes to such a decision is a complex matter not easily subject to theological analysis. The act of coming to believe is a person-specific act with both reasons and causes related to that person's individual history. Theology ought not seek to devise an explanatory theory for the subjective conditions for the possibility of faith, for such theories obscure both the diversity and the mystery of human response to the gospel. To acknowledge the biblical narrative as God's promise is to believe that the crucified Jesus lives. Theology can explain neither why nor how persons come to believe such a paradoxical claim. Theology can only show that the sense of the biblical text implies that referential claim. If a reader does hear the biblical narrative as God's promise, theology can indicate that such a response is warranted given the content, force, and context of scripture. But the ultimate explanation of that mysterious movement from unbelief to faith lies beyond theology's descriptive competence. If a reader comes to believe the gospel's promises, the theologian, as member of the Christian community, can simply join the chorus of witnesses in glorifying God for his miracle of grace.

The content of the biblical narrative thus gives rise to a distinctive hermeneutical situation within the Christian community. The text's content gives rise to its illocutionary force, and content and force together invite the correlative response of faith which will provide the context for faithful interpretation. Text and context thus stand in *dialectical but asymmetrical relation*. The biblical narrative functions as God's promise only in relation to a believing community, but that function further depends upon an assertion of God's priority as the sole initiator, guarantor, and fulfiller of his promise. The Christian community, created in response to God's narrated promise, provides the essential context for the on-going interpretation of biblical narrative. But the community discovers its essential role precisely as it sees itself as the grateful recipient of God's gracious promise. The community's contextual function is inextricably tied to its recognition of God as prevenient God of promise. The church's identity as a community of faith, love, and hope is thus shaped in accord with its acknowledgment of God's prevenience. As the community of promise it trusts that God will faithfully fulfill his pledge of salvation, and so responds with a life of discipleship which reflects God's sacrificial and self-giving love. As it awaits God's consummate fulfillment of his promise, the community manifests its hope in mission and ministry to the world.

Theology, too, participates in that dialectical but asymmetrical relation between God and the community. Theology is a critical and reforming activity which assists the church in its understanding of God's narrated promise. Christian understanding involves the development of the requisite skills for the interpretation (*explicatio, meditatio, applicatio*) of the Christian tradition. Such interpretation brings text, tradition, and context into a critical interplay within which Christian identity is shaped and formed. Precisely as the Christian comes to understand God's identity in Jesus Christ, he or she begins to learn the appropriate responsive patterns of belief and behavior which constitute Christian identity. Theology assists this process by articulating the rules which guide the interpretation of text and tradition and the correlative formation of Christian character. Those specific rules which regulate the development of doctrine and virtue are themselves governed by an overarching "meta-rule." *Let all Christian interpretation proceed in a manner which recognizes the absolute primacy of God's promising grace.*

The theologian thus seeks to clarify the gospel's complex nature as narrative and promise and to identify God and the Christian community in their mutual but asymmetrical relation. Theology, like all activities within the Christian community, is appropriately conceived as a response to God's prevenience, for it depends not only upon God's promise but also upon the correlative response of faith for its *raison d'être*. Theology's descriptive and proclamatory roles presuppose both the narrative designation of God's identity and the communal recognition of the narrative's promissory force. Though it is a critical and formative activity, theology, as an act of Christian discipleship, remains first and foremost an act of trust and gratitude in response to God's narrated promise. It is a response which involves faith and intellect, imagination and reason, in the process of explicating and justifying Christian belief. One aspect of that justifying responsibility involves a defense of the warranted assertability of belief in God's prevenience. Such a defense seeks neither to establish the subjective possibility of Christian faith nor to provide an explanation of the mystery of grace. It is rather an exercise of the believing intellect which seeks to fulfill the Petrine injunction, "Always be prepared to make a defense to any one who calls you to account for the hope that is in you" (1 Peter 3:15).

The Continuing Significance of a Doctrine of Revelation

The category of "narrated promise" does provide a way of justifying Christian belief in God's prevenience, because it allows for the coherent assertion of both God's relation and priority to our framework of interpretation. While this revised account of revelation operates from within the context of Christian tradition and community, it provides a way to distinguish God's initiative from faith's response. Within the Gospel of Matthew, narrative and promise work together to specify God's identity as Yahweh, God of Israel and father of Jesus, who accomplishes his intention to save (and thus fulfills his promise) by raising Jesus from the dead. God's identity is thus inextricably linked to the actions of Jesus which are God's enacted intentions on behalf of sinners. God is identified as God of promise only as he relates to sinners through Jesus, but his identity-in-relation designates him as the one who cannot not be prevenient. God is most clearly established as *extra nos* when he is identified as the one who is *pro nobis*. Thus the notion of revelation as God's narrated promise is shown to be intelligible and Christianly apt discourse which establishes God's relation and priority to faith.

God's priority is not, however, solely a matter of semiotic relations within the biblical narrative. Christians are warranted in asserting that the biblical narrative serves as God's promising address to those who stand outside of the text as well. Matthew's text claims that to discern God's identity in the narrated actions of Jesus is to recognize that narrative as God's promise. The text's narrative content has the illocutionary force of issuing the promise of salvation precisely as it describes God's identity in Jesus Christ. Peter's confession at Caesarea Philippi functions both to indicate a successful interlocutionary act within the text and to signal the possibility of a parallel interlocutionary act between the text and its reader. The pattern of narrative discourse functioning as promise within the text can be reduplicated if the text is heard by the reader as God's personal address. Biblical narrative does in fact function as promise in our common world of experience if the reader acknowledges the text's central claim to be true — that Jesus the crucified, now lives. That the text makes that claim is clear. That the text urges the reader to accept that claim and so anticipates its own interlocutionary context is also clear. But how the reader makes the actual transition from unbelief to faith and thus how the text does in fact tie its language to the world of a believer in any particular communicative situation cannot be explained within theology's descriptive competence. All theology can say is that if the reader does accept the text's central claim, then narrated promise brings the reader's world into the world of the text. The promising God is then understood not simply as a character within the narrative but as the transcendent God who through the narrative issues his promise to the believer. Though the act of faith is necessary for the success of this interlocutionary act, it does not constitute the act. Faith is a response to the God who issues the promise and who alone establishes the possibility of the act of communication. Faith is a necessary though secondary element in God's act of promise. Thus we see again the same pattern of relation and priority. God's *extra nos* reality as the existent God who issues his promise to the reader through the text is recognized precisely as the *pro nobis* character of his reality is acknowledged. God's priority and relation to human faith and intellect are appropriately conceived when revelation is understood as God's narrated promise.

The success of this defense of God's prevenience depends on the primacy it grants to the paradigm of promise rather than knowledge in conceiving of God's relation to humanity. Promise provides a category within which the notions of relation and priority can be held in dialectical balance. The standard epistemological doctrine fails to provide an adequate defense of God's prevenience because it borrows a set of dichotomous categories from philosophical theories of knowledge and thus creates for itself an insoluble problem. By conceiving of humanity's relation to God as parallel to the knowing subject's relation to an ontologically distinct object, the standard doctrine portrays the problem of revelation as the difficulty of overcoming the "infinite qualitative distinction" between God and humanity. Thus the problem of revelation is understood to be the general dilemma of knowledge writ large. How can the human subject grasp an object which is infinitely and qualitatively distinct? How can the ontological gap between God and humanity be bridged? That way of posing the question assumes that the creature/Creator distinction can be restated as the distinction between the schematizing consciousness of the human subject and the unschematized reality of the independent object. It also assumes that if these ontologically separated realities are to be brought together their relation must be causally understood. To know, modern epistemology has assumed, is to have the subject's inner representations of the object correspond with that which is given to the subject.[8] But the correspondence can be guaranteed only if the mechanism by which we know is causally determined and thus reliable. To know is thus to be compelled either by the reality of the object or by the invariant structure of the subject's consciousness. The ontological gap is then bridged either by the imposition of the object's nature upon the knowing subject or by the imposition of the subject's consciousness upon the unschematized object. In both cases knowing is a matter of causation. But when this model is applied to theology, it results either in the denial of the integrity of human subjectivity (Torrance) or the denial of the independent reality of the divine object (Kaufman). Thus the

problem of revelation — the problem of accounting for both God's relation and priority to our framework of belief — is not solved by the
modern doctrine of revelation because it postulates a gap which it is
finally unable to bridge.[9]

My argument in the first three chapters attempted to show that
these borrowed epistemological assumptions are philosophically suspect,
because they are internally inconsistent. Bad coinage transferred to a
new realm is no less false currency. Thus the dichotomous categories
of epistemology need not and ought not provide the conceptual base
for Christian thinking about the relation of God and his creatures.
To construe the creature/Creator distinction under the epistemological
categories of subject and object is to begin theological thinking with
an insoluble problem created by the borrowed philosophical categories
themselves. The problem of ontological distance is in part a problem
which theology inherited when it adopted the assumptions of modern
epistemology. To reject that inheritance is also to reject the problem
of ontological distance as the inevitable starting point for all thinking
about matters of knowledge.[10] The theologians who devised the modern
doctrine of revelation made a fateful mistake in their epistemological
borrowings, and contemporary theology would be ill-advised to per-
petuate that error.

Given the natural affinity between the concepts of revelation and
knowledge of God, it may appear misleading to call my defense of
God's prevenience under the category of narrated promise a doctrine
of revelation. My criticism of epistemology combined with my preference for promise over knowledge may constitute a *prima facie* case for
elimination of "revelation" from the theological lexicon. I am not,
however, advocating such an excision of the language of revelation from
our theological vocabulary. Talk of revelation need not be pernicious.
The problem with much modern speech about revelation is that it is
wedded to a foundational epistemology. It is modern epistemological
foundationalism and its associated metaphors which ought to be ex-
cised from the theological lexicon, not talk of revelation *per se*. When
Luther speaks of Jesus as the revelation of God he means that Christians recognize God's identity as God of promise in Jesus Christ. That
use of the term *revelation* ought to be encouraged. In addition, the
language of revelation is deeply rooted in both Protestant and Catholic
traditions[11] and will continue to be used in doctrinal and theological
formulations. Descriptive theology ought to seek reform of such dis-

course rather than its elimination. Finally, the goal of the modern doctrine of revelation to offer justification for Christian belief in God's prevenience under the changed cultural and intellectual conditions of modernity is surely worth pursuing. However, that goal is more realistically, but no less rigorously, sought under a nonfoundational or holist view of justification.

Ordinarily a doctrine of revelation is understood as an investigation of God's knowability. That definition encourages a conception of the doctrine as an inquiry into the conditions of the possibility that God can be known, i.e., as a foundational transcendental inquiry. In order to guard against that view but to maintain some sense of continuity with a traditional understanding of revelation I suggest the following alternate formulation. *A doctrine of revelation is an account of God's identifiability*. That definition locates the doctrine within reflection on God's identity, i.e., within the doctrine of God, rather than in prolegomenal or methodological reflection. The Christian claim to revelation asserts that God is identifiable 1) within the narrative as Yahweh who raised Jesus from the dead, 2) through the narrative as the God of promise who in addressing his promise to the reader is recognized as *pro nobis* and *extra nos*, and 3) beyond the narrative as the one who, faithful to his promises, will fulfill his pledge to those whom he loves.

Is it appropriate within this reconceptualized doctrine of revelation to speak of "knowledge of God?" Insofar as the notion of knowledge relies primarily on metaphors of sight, i.e., on a notion of knowing as seeing, it remains a problematical notion for theology. Not only does that conception participate in the images of a worrisome epistemological tradition, but, more importantly, it seems particularly inappropriate as a description of our relation to God this side of the *parousia*. "For *now* we see through a glass darkly; but *then* face to face." Knowledge of God as a kind of seeing may well describe that eschatological moment when "we know even as we are known," but, Paul's talk of obscure sight and partial knowing notwithstanding, our current situation would be better described with non-ocular images. The metaphor of sight is appropriately applied to a non-eschatological knowledge of God only if we are justified in asserting that our present situation contains anticipatory experiences of that which is to come but is as yet unknown (the *eschaton*). But how does one recognize a foretaste of that which is unknown? Our present knowledge of God is a form of seeing only if 1) the eschatological knowing is rightly described as a seeing and if 2) our present knowledge somehow participates in that future knowing. But if 1) is unknown, then 2) appears unknowable. This conundrum is resolvable only if there is a form of present knowing which is an indubitable guide to eschatological knowing. But that requires in turn an appeal to a form of intuitive knowing, which places us squarely in the grip of the very modern epistemological problem which we have sought so strenuously to overcome.

We can, however, continue to speak of our current situation under the category "knowledge of God," without employing the troublesome images of sight. As Christians we can claim to "know God" in the sense that: 1) We can give a narrative-based individuating description of God which identifies him as Yahweh who raised Jesus from the dead. 2) We can give an intelligible account of the way the readers of the biblical narrative recognize the Yahweh of the narrative as the really existent God (*extra nos*) who issues his personal promise to them (*pro nobis*). 3) We can assert, because we take the biblical promises to be God's, that, given God's identity, we must acknowledge those promises to be true. But that is nothing more than to say that the God identified in biblical narrative is trustworthy, i.e., that those to whom he issues his promises trust him and wait in the expectant hope of fulfillment.

But are Christians justified in believing these not yet fulfilled promises to be true? The justifiability of one's faith and hope in the trustworthiness of a promiser is never fully confirmed (or disconfirmed) until the promiser actually fulfills (or fails to fulfill) his/her promises. Until the moment of fulfillment the recipient must justify faith and hope on the basis of a judgment concerning the character of the promiser. It is justifiable to trust a promiser if his/her behavior on balance warrants that trust. Insofar as the biblical narrative functions as the discourse which identifies God's "characteristic behavior," and insofar as that discourse depicts a God who continually keeps his promises despite situations which threaten to contravene them (cf. Abraham, Joseph, and Jesus, among others), then Christians are provided a *prima facie* plausible case for continuing to wait in hope. But since the narrative purports to describe the real world which we all inhabit, God's characteristic behavior must be sufficiently exemplified in this world in order for that hope to be justifiably sustained. Surely there are some who find the waiting increasingly difficult and finally conclude that these promises are no longer believable. That this movement from faith to unbelief is intelligible cannot be doubted, but that does not make the continued hope of those who wait unintelligible. Because we live between the time of the making of the promise and its fulfillment, we live not by sight but by faith. Consequently we live in a situation in which there can be no indubitable foundation for knowledge and thus in which both belief and refusal to believe can appear to be justified. That does not mean, however, that both positions are equally plausible or that the disagreement can never be adjudicated. It does mean, however, that there is no position-neutral point of view from which one can evaluate the competing positions. All "good reasons" will be reasons which are part of a textured web of beliefs which each party brings to the discussion. The complexity of such disputes suggests that no single argument from either side — neither a disproof of God's existence nor a demonstration of the essential religiousness of human nature — will suffice to settle the disagreement. Such arguments may well be part of an overall apologetic strategy, but they ought not be given systematic and thus foundational priority in the strategy. For the dispute concerning God's prevenience is ultimately about the kind of life one ought to live in a world which has (or has not) been created, redeemed, and reconciled through God's grace. The world of "common human experience" will simply be different depending on one's belief concerning God's prevenience, and thus disputes of this generality and inclusiveness will not readily be solved by single "knock-down" arguments.

The fact that we are *in via* and thus cannot clearly discern the end of our journey does not mean that therefore we can know nothing of our destination or of the God who awaits us there. The inability of the Christian to convince a skeptical questioner by displaying the Christian-specific grounds in support of belief in God's prevenience does not mean that the belief is therefore not justified. It simply means that the disputants have not yet reached sufficient common ground to allow adjudication of their disagreement. The difficulty of finding a set of such common beliefs is an inescapable part of our pluralistic culture and does not as such undermine the case of either party in the dispute. The failure as yet to have reached such common ground should not lead either party to give up the disputed belief. The search for a real common basis for discussion can continue only as long as the parties continue to affirm their conflicting beliefs. The pluralistic situation of modern culture requires both parties "to achieve a frame of mind in which [they] may hold firmly to what [they] believe to be true, even though [they] know it might conceivably be false."[12] That, it seems to me, is an appropriate way of recasting Paul's conviction that, though our sight remains clouded and our knowledge partial, we can affirm that the God identified in and through biblical narrative is a God Christians "know," i.e., a God whose gracious reality they can justifiably affirm.

A doctrine of revelation, understood as an account of God's identifiability and recast under the category of narrated promise, provides an appropriate rationale for the Christian belief that the universe is God's, created, redeemed and reconciled by his grace, i.e., for belief in God's prevenience. For that reason, if for no other, the attempt to formulate the doctrine coherently is "worth the trouble." But a doctrine of revelation does not provide an indubitable foundation for the adjudication of disputes between Christians and non-Christians. At best it provides the framework within which the Christian believes, reasons, argues, and lives. It thus provides not the end of the debate between believer and nonbeliever, or between the believer and nonbeliever in every Christian, but simply makes it possible for the debate to continue. For finally the doctrine of revelation is an articulation of a profound Christian conviction concerning the triumph of God's grace within a world characterized by deep and contradictory experiences of good and evil. In that respect a doctrine of revelation is simply an expression of Christian hope grounded in the gospel of Jesus Christ. "The Gospel is the revelation of the Son of God. . . . Christ is the subject of the Gospel. What the Gospel teaches and shows me is a divine work given to me by sheer grace. . . . And I accept this gift by faith alone."[13]

Notes

Introduction: A Doctrine of Revelation: Worth the Trouble

1. Stanley Hauerwas, *A Community of Character* (Notre Dame, Ind.: University of Notre Dame Press, 1981), 57.

2. Two very early attacks on the notion of revelation come from European Lutherans who were reacting against the Calvinist categories which predominate in the modern theological discussion. Werner Elert, *Der Christliche Glaube* (Hamburg: Furche Verlag, 1956) writes: "Nowhere [in the New Testament] is it said that God has revealed, reveals, or will reveal himself" (pp. 134-135). Gustaf Wingren, *Theology in Conflict* (Philadelphia: Muhlenberg, 1958) offers a sustained polemic against Barth's "unbiblical" employment of the notion of revelation, esp. pp. 23–44 and 108–128.

3. F. Gerald Downing, *Has Christianity a Revelation?* (London: SCM Press, 1964), 274, 284, 238.

4. James Barr, *Old and New in Interpretation* (London: SCM Press, 1966), 65–102 and *The Bible in the Modern World* (New York: Harper & Row, 1973), 120–132.

5. David Kelsey, *Uses of Scripture in Recent Theology* (Philadelphia: Fortress Press, 1975).

6. Gordon Kaufman, *An Essay on Theological Method*, 2nd ed., (Missoula, Mont.: Scholars Press, 1979) and "Constructing the Concept of God," *The Theological Imagination* (Philadelphia: Westminster Press, 1981), 21–57.

7. Despite the prominence of this conviction, doctrines of revelation have rarely given a clear account of the precise relation between divine gift and human response. A doctrine of revelation requires a sharp distinction between divine initiative and human reception, precisely so that the origin of revelatory content might be located in God. But such an account is not easily accomplished, because every act of knowing appears to be *our* act, *our* knowing, and the exact nature of the divine contribution to that act is not readily apparent. Yet clearly such a distinction is crucial to the claim that our knowledge is *God's* revelation. The failure of the representatives of the "biblical theology" movement sufficiently to maintain the divine-human

distinction led to the criticisms which ultimately brought about the demise of the movement and its central doctrine of revelation. Langdon Gilkey's now classic article "Ontology, Cosmology and the Travail of Biblical Language," *Journal of Religion* 41 (1961), 194–205, demonstrated the logical confusion surrounding the concept "revelation" in the biblical theology movement. See also James Barr, *The Bible in the Modern World*, 120-121.

8. *Lectures on Galatians*, vol. 26 of *Luther's Works*, ed. Jaroslav Pelikan (St. Louis: Concordia, 1963), 64, 72.

9. Karl Barth, "The Christian Understanding of Revelation," *Against the Stream* (London: SCM Press, 1954), 207, 224.

10. Downing, *Has Christianity a Revelation?*, 275.

11. David Tracy, *Blessed Rage for Order* (New York: Seabury, 1978), 106.

12. Ibid., 108–109.

13. For an especially powerful argument of this sort see, Thomas F. Tracy, "Enacting History: Ogden and Kaufman on God's Mighty Acts," *Journal of Religion*, 64/1 (January 1984), 20-36.

14. Ludwig Feuerbach, *The Essence of Christianity* (New York: Harper & Row, 1957), 206-207.

15. Blaise Pascal, *Pensées* (London: Penguin, 1966), 152.

16. Schubert Ogden, *The Reality of God* (New York: Harper & Row, 1963), 23.

17. Ibid., 37.

18. For an extended discussion of the problems which pluralism presents to theology see Ronald F. Thiemann, "From Twilight to Darkness: Theology and the New Pluralism," *Trinity Seminary Review*, 6/2 (Fall, 1984), 12–24. This essay was first presented as The Fendt Lecture at Trinity Lutheran Seminary, Columbus, Ohio in February 1984.

19. Tracy, *Blessed Rage for Order*, 186.

20. Foundationalism in epistemology is represented by philosophers as diverse as Plato, Descartes, and Locke, among many others, and is the most common model employed by theologians for formulating doctrines of revelation. However different their ideas may be in the actual content of their theories of knowledge, foundationalists all agree that knowledge is grounded in a set of non-inferential, self-evident beliefs which, because their intelligibility is not constituted by a relationship with other beliefs, can serve as the source of intelligibility for all beliefs in a conceptual framework. These non-inferential beliefs function as the givens or foundations of a linguistic system because the mode of their justification is direct and immediate. The mental act by means of which direct justification is bestowed is usually termed *intuition*. Through intuition the knower grasps with absolute certainty "clear and distinct ideas" (Descartes), "impressions" (Locke), or "sensations" (Russell).

A necessary structural characteristic of foundationalism is that a relationship of representation or correspondence is established between the incorrigible belief and that to which it refers, whether ideas or sense impressions. Foundational propositions are then true by correspondence with (in the example of modern empiricism) states of affairs in the concept-independent world. All other propositions are true by virtue of their inferential relation to these foundational beliefs.

21. For a careful analysis and critique of the ontological argument upon which Tracy relies see Alvin Plantinga, ed., *The Ontological Argument* (Garden City, N.Y.: Doubleday, 1965) and John Hick and Arthur McGill, *The Many-Faced Argument* (New York: Macmillan, 1967).

22. Most critics of revelation fail to see this issue clearly. The one exception to this rule is Gordon Kaufman, who has consistently been willing to face the radical implications of his polemic against revelation. For Kaufman theology is not properly conceived as a response to God's prior act of grace. Kaufman, the most thorough-going critic of revelation, appears to reject completely the notion of the prevenience of God's grace. Kaufman views "revelation" and "imaginative construction" as opposing, incommensurable concepts. Since theology is an imaginative constructive activity, it cannot be a response to God's prior initiative. (For an analysis and criticism of this argument see Ronald F. Thiemann, "Revelation and Imaginative Construction," *Journal of Religion* 61/3 [July 1981], 242–263). According to Kaufman, the concept "grace" can be used within a theological framework in order to symbolize the humanizing function of the concept "God;" however, "grace" cannot designate the prior action of God to which theology itself is a response. (See the more detailed treatment of Kaufman's position in chapter 3.)

1. The Modern Doctrine of Revelation: Faith Seeking Foundation

1. When Luther speaks of God as *deus revelatus* he consistently means "the God who is clothed in his promises—God as he is present in Christ" *Selected Psalms I* (vol. 12 in *Luther's Works*), ed. Jaroslav Pelikan (St. Louis: Concordia, 1955), 312. The revealed God is the God of the gospel, proclaimed through word and sacrament. The relation between God's revelation and his hiddenness is, however, quite a complex matter. Prior to 1525 Luther defines God's hiddenness as the medium through which he is revealed. God's hiddenness is "the humility and shame of the cross" *Career of the Reformer I* (vol. 31 in *Luther's Works*), ed. Harold J. Grimm (Philadelphia: Concordia, 1957), 52. Hiddenness in this sense designates the marks and means of God's revelation. In contrast to the God revealed in hiddenness Luther speaks of the "naked God" of majesty, whose brilliance we cannot bear to view. But in *De Servo Arbitrio* Luther *contrasts* God's revelation to his hiddenness and

identifies the God beyond revelation as the *deus absconditus*. Thus the term "hidden God" can sometimes mean the God clothed in his promises and revealed to faith; other times it can mean the unknown and unknowable God beyond his revelation. Luther is consistent, however, in his equation of revelation and gospel. For a careful study of the problem of hiddenness in the thought of the reformers see B. A. Gerrish " 'To the Unknown God': Luther and Calvin on the Hiddenness of God," *Journal of Religion* 53/3 (July 1973), 263–292.

2. In *Calvin: Institutes of the Christian Religion*, vol. 20 in *The Library of Christian Classics* (Philadelphia: Westminster Press, 1960) the editor speaks of "Calvin's epistemology" although he means by the term "the meaning of knowledge in faith," p. 35. The best secondary treatment of Calvin on knowledge of God is E. A. Dowey, Jr., *The Knowledge of God in Calvin's Theology* (New York: Columbia University Press, 1952).

3. John Locke, *An Essay Concerning Human Understanding* (New York: Dover, 1959).

4. Richard Rorty, *Philosophy and the Mirror of Nature* (Princeton; N.J.: Princeton University Press, 1979) writes, "We owe the notion of a 'theory of knowledge' based on an understanding of 'mental processes' to the seventeenth century, and especially to Locke," p. 3.

5. Calvin, *Institutes*, 43–44.

6. Ibid., 43.

7. The notion of background belief is derived from various "holist" treatments of the justification of beliefs. See especially Clark Glymour, *Theory and Evidence* (Princeton: Princeton University Press, 1980); Gilbert Harman, *Thought* (Princeton: Princeton University Press, 1973); W. V. O. Quine and J. S. Ullian, *The Web of Belief* (New York: Random House, 1970); and W. V. O. Quine, *Word and Object* (Cambridge, Mass.: M.I.T. Press, 1960). The idea of background belief is put to good use in two projects in the field of religion. See Nicholas Wolterstorff, *Reason within the Bounds of Religion* (Grand Rapids, Mich.: Eerdmans, 1976) and William Werpehowski, "Social Justice, Social Selves," (Ph.D. diss., Yale University, 1981), 109–135.

8. Immanuel Kant, *Religion within the Limits of Reason Alone* (New York: Harper & Row, 1960).

9. René Descartes, *Discourse of Method and Meditations* (Indianapolis: The Library of Liberal Arts, 1960).

10. Ibid., 61.

11. Ibid.

12. Ibid.

13. *Discourse on Method*, 29.

14. *Meditations*, 84.

15. Ibid., 91–108.

16. "I feel as though I were suddenly thrown into deep water, being so disconcerted that I can neither plant my feet on the bottom nor swim to the surface." Ibid., 81.

17. Ibid., 92. In the Third Meditation Descartes clearly asserts that the principle of clarity and distinctness is grounded in the formal characteristics of his argument for the necessary existence of the ego. The argument for God's existence is designed to remove the hypothesis that God is a deceiver who "might perhaps have given me such a nature that I would be mistaken even about those things that seemed most obvious to me," p. 93. Regarding the principle of clarity and distinctness, the argument for God's existence serves as a rebuttal to the hypothesis of the deceiving God. As such it bears only indirectly on the establishment of the conclusion itself. (For this use of the term *rebuttal*, see Stephen Toulmin, *The Uses of Argument* [Cambridge: Cambridge University Press, 1964].) Descartes's argument in the *Meditations* thus undercuts the stronger statement he makes in the earlier *Discourse*. "The very principle which I took as a rule to start with, namely, that all those things which we conceived very clearly and very distinctly are true, is known to be true only because God exists," p. 29. While Descartes consistently asserts ontological dependence upon God, he does not in the *Meditations* assert such a direct epistemological dependence.

18. I have chosen these three thinkers for analysis because they represent three distinct historical periods and three different theological options. Locke's seventeenth-century laditudinarianism, Schleiermacher's nineteenth-century liberalism, and Torrance's twentieth-century neo-orthodoxy present sharply divergent theological alternatives; nonetheless, each position exemplifies the formal characteristics of the muddled modern doctrine of revelation.

2. Revelation and Reasonableness: Three Case Studies

1. John Locke, *An Essay Concerning Human Understanding*, vol. II (New York: Dover, 1959), 416. All subsequent page citations from this volume will be included in the text.

2. Locke discusses miracles in only two places in the *Essay*. In the chapter "Of the Degrees of Assent" Locke includes one brief paragraph concerning the role of miracles in guiding reason's assent, p. 382. At the end of chapter 19, "Of Enthusiasm," Locke contrasts the warranted assent of reason to the unbridled consent of enthusiasm by pointing to the "visible signs" which confirm the true claim to divine authority and guide faith's reasonable assent, pp. 438–441.

3. I am here following an observation made by Ian T. Ramsey in his

introduction to John Locke, *The Reasonableness of Christianity* with *A Discourse of Miracles* and part of *A Third Letter Concerning Toleration* (Stanford, Calif.: Stanford University Press, 1958), 9–20.

4. Ibid., 92 (emphasis added). Cf. Ramsey's introductory notes, pp. 78–79 and 88–90.

5. In this regard it is quite similar to Schleiermacher, *On Religion: Speeches to Its Cultured Despisers* (New York: Harper & Row, 1958).

6. The feebleness of Locke's defense of revelation made his position easy prey for the Deists, who sought to deny all claims to particularistic revelation. See especially Matthew Tindal, *Christianity as Old as the Creation* (London, 1732).

7. Immanuel Kant, *The Critique of Pure Reason*, trans. Norman Kemp Smith (New York: St. Martin's Press, 1929).

8. "But however great a difference we make between this supra-rational and the common human reason, it can never, without falling into self-contradiction, be set up as an *absolutely* supra-rational element." Friedrich Schleiermacher, *The Christian Faith* (New York: Harper & Row, 1963), 65. All subsequent page citations from this volume will be included in the text.

9. "Unless the Reformation from which our church first emerged endeavors to establish an eternal covenant between the living Christian faith and completely free, independent scientific inquiry, so that faith does not hinder science and science does not exclude faith, it fails to meet adequately the needs of our time. . . . Precisely this position, my dear friend, represents that of my *Glaubenslehre*." "The Second Letter to Dr. Lücke," *On the Glaubenslehre* (Chico, Calif.: Scholars Press, 1981), 64.

10. Schleiermacher qualifies even this modest claim so as not to assert uniqueness for the Christian revelation. "Christian dogmas . . are supra-rational in the respect in which everything experiential is supra-rational." *The Christian Faith*, 67.

11. Note the similarity to Locke's argument in *The Reasonableness of Christianity*: " 'Tis no diminishing to revelation, that reason gives its suffrage too, to the truths revelation has discovered. But 'tis our mistake to think, that because reason confirms them to us we had first certain knowledge of them from thence, and in that clear evidence we now possess them," p. 66.

12. "If a system of propositions can be understood from their connexion with others, then nothing supernatural was required for their production." *The Christian Faith*, 50.

13. Ibid., 12–18.

14. Schleiermacher vigorously defends himself against each of these charges in the two letters to Dr. Lücke. See *On the Glaubenslehre*, 52, 56, 70.

15. "Second Letter to Dr. Lücke," ibid., 76.

16. Schleiermacher discusses the role of philosophical theology in *Brief*

Outline on the Study of Theology (Richmond: John Knox Press, 1970), 29–40. For an analysis of how Schleiermacher's view of theology as a science undermines his claim that "practical theology is the crown of theological study" see Ronald F. Thiemann, "Piety, Narrative, and Christian Identity," *Word & World* 3/2 (Spring 1983), 148–159.

17. Richard R. Niebuhr has commented: "The self in question here is the self that is not qualified by or determined by specific objects and energies located in its world. It is the self in its original identity, in its being-in-such-and-such-a-way *(Sosein)*. . . . Piety or religion is the name of the level of self-consciousness that is most decisive of all. . . . It is a consciousness of the self prior to all of its specific social and practical relations." Richard R. Niebuhr, *Schleiermacher on Christ and Religion* (New York: Scribner's, 1964), 183–184.

18. "Belief must be something different from a mixture of opinions about God and the world, and of precepts for one life or two. Piety cannot be an instinct craving for a mess of metaphysical and ethical crumbs. . . . Wherefore, it follows that ideas and principles are all foreign to religion. . . . If ideas and principles are to be anything, they must belong to knowledge which is a different department of life from religion. . . . Nothing is of less importance to religion, for it knows nothing of deducing and connecting. . . . All is immediately true in religion, for except immediately how could anything arise? But that only is immediate which has not yet passed through the state of idea, but has grown up purely in the feeling. . . . Those dogmas and opinions that would join themselves more closely to religion than is fitting, are only designations and descriptions of feeling. In short, they are a knowledge about feeling, and in no way an immediate knowledge about the operations of the Universe, that gave rise to feeling." Friedrich Schleiermacher, *On Religion: Speeches to Its Cultured Despisers* (New York: Harper & Row, 1958), 31, 46, 53, 54, 60–61.

19. Ibid., 26–118.

20. *The Christian Faith*, 5–12.

21. There is a significant collection of philosophical literature which argues against the possibility of non-inferential beliefs. The intellectual father of these arguments against the epistemological authority of non-inferential intuitions is Charles Peirce. See especially "Questions Concerning Certain Faculties Claimed for Man," *Collected Papers of Charles Sanders Peirce*, vol. V (Cambridge, Mass.: Harvard University Press, 1960), 135–155. For an excellent discussion of Peirce's argument against foundationalism see Richard J. Bernstein, *Praxis and Action* (Philadelphia: University of Pennsylvania Press, 1971), 174–199. For more recent statements of the argument, see Wilfred Sellars, "Empiricism and the Philosophy of Mind," *Science, Perception, and Reality* (London: Routledge & Kegan Paul, 1963), 127–196; Richard Rorty, "Intuition," *The Encyclopedia of Philosophy*, vol. 3 (New York: Macmillan,

1967) 204–212; and Richard Rorty, *Philosophy and the Mirror of Nature* (Princeton, N. J.: Princeton University Press, 1979). For a discussion of this issue with regard to religious beliefs see C. B. Martin, *Relgious Belief* (Ithaca, N.Y.: Cornell University Press, 1959), 64–94; George Mavrodes, *Belief in God* (New York: Random House, 1970); Nicholas Wolterstorff, *Reason within the Bounds of Religion* (Grand Rapids, Mich.: Eerdmans, 1976); and Alvin Plantinga, "Is Belief in God Rational?" *Rationality and Religious Belief*, ed. C. F. Delaney (Notre Dame, Ind.: University of Notre Dame Press, 1979), 7–27.

22. *On Religion*, 43, 54.

23. This phrase is used by Ronald Hepburn, "From World to God," *The Philosophy of Religion*, ed. Basil Mitchell (New York: Oxford University Press, 1971), 168–178.

24. "First Letter to Dr. Lücke," 45.

25. Ibid., 41.

26. Ibid., 40.

27. Kierkegaard's most influential work on this topic is *Philosophical Fragments* (Princeton, N.J.: Princeton University Press, 1967). Though the work is pseudonymous (Johannes Climacus), the dialectical theologians adopted the book's major concepts (e.g., the Moment, the Absolute Paradox) and attributed them to Kierkegaard's own theology. While I do not think that to be a mistaken judgment, the dialectical theologians did not give sufficient attention to the problem of pseudonymous authorship. A study of that thorny issue would be out of place in this context. I will use the name Kierkegaard to refer to the author of *Philosophical Fragments* because the "perceived Kierkegaard" is more important than the "historical Kierkegaard" for the theological story I want to tell. For three recent studies of the issue of pseudonymous authorship see John Elrod, *Being and Existence in Kierkegaard's Pseudonymous Works* (Princeton: Princeton University Press, 1975); Gregor Malantschuk, *Kierkegaard's Thought* (Princeton: Princeton University Press, 1975); Mark C. Taylor, *Kierkegaard's Pseudonymous Authorship: A Study of Time and the Self* (Princeton: Princeton University Press, 1975).

28. See particularly Karl Barth, *The Epistle to the Romans* (London: Oxford University Press, 1933). While the concept of revelation does not reach full prominence in Barth's thinking until *Church Dogmatics*, vol. I, pt. 1: *The Doctrine of the Word of God* (Edinburgh: T & T Clark, 2nd ed. 1975), the basic shape of the doctrine is deeply influenced by Barth's earlier work. While Barth's watershed volume *Anselm: Fides Quaerens Intellectum* (Richmond: John Knox Press, 1960) introduces important new elements into his thought, it does not significantly alter Barth's conception of the subjective dimension of revelation.

29. Most of the following analysis is based on Torrance's important work

Theological Science (New York: Oxford University Press, 1969). When this text is quoted, page numbers will be included in the text. Other works by Torrance are used to complement the argument of the major essay and will be cited in subsequent notes.

30. Torrance's method differs most sharply from that of Schleiermacher. Insofar as Locke seeks to assert the absolute supra-rationality of revelation his position bears some similarity to Torrance's.

31. Thomas Torrance, *Reality and Evangelical Theology* (Philadelphia: Westminster Press, 1982), 13.

32. This criticism is most often voiced by philosophers who have been influenced by Wittgenstein, but one of the most powerful statements of the criticism can be found in Jürgen Habermas, *Knowledge and Human Interests* (Boston: Beacon Press, 1971), 3–24.

33. Torrance, *Theological Science*, 106–140.

34. Torrance, *Reality and Evangelical Theology*, 14.

35. Torrance borrows from Karl Barth the distinction between God's primary and secondary objectivity. Karl Barth, *Church Dogmatics*, vol. II, pt. 1: *The Doctrine of God* (Edinburgh: T & T Clark, 1957), 3–254. Torrance, *Theological Science*, 136ff. and passim. Barth's distinction is designed to encompass both God's transcendent freedom and his gracious knowability. God in his freedom chooses to make himself known to his creatures in his secondary objectivity, Jesus Christ. Christ as the second person of the Trinity is a *reliable* though not *exhaustive* expression of God's primary objectivity, his inner-trinitarian nature. Thus revelation, God's being *ad extra*, consistently manifests God's inner nature, his being *ad intra*, without violating his sovereign freedom.

36. Thomas Torrance, *God and Rationality* (New York: Oxford University Press, 1971), 21.

37. Torrance, *Theological Science*, 164–172.

38. Ibid., 141–161.

39. Richard Rorty, *Philosophy and the Mirror of Nature* (Princeton: Princeton University Press, 1979), 157.

40. The key aspects of a foundational epistemology are as follows: 1) a set of non-inferential, self-evident beliefs which serve as the given or foundation of all knowledge, 2) a distinction between foundational beliefs and other inferential propositions, 3) a claim that foundational beliefs are justified immediately by a form of direct experience, 4) an appeal to the mental act of intuition, and 5) an assertion of correspondence between the self-evident beliefs and the language independent world.

Although these characteristics have been culled from various philosophical epistemologies, they could just as easily have been derived from Torrance's theological epistemology. His position corresponds completely to the structural characteristics of foundationalism sketched above. 1) "Theological science is . . . engaged in an unrelenting struggle to separate out from their entanglement in our experience and knowledge the elements that are *ultimately and irreducibly given* from the elements that are elaborated and constructed in our acts of consciousness" (p. viii). "The given . . . is the being of God . . . who communicates Himself to us, and it is through his self-communication and self-disclosure that He gives Himself to us" (p. 29). 2) "Existence-statements [are] . . . about matters of fact. . . . Coherence-statements [are] . . . about relations of ideas" (pp. 164–165). 3) "Existence-statements are basic and can be tested only empirically by returning to the ground of actual and primary cognitions. . . . They are statements about matters of fact which can be made only through direct experience" (p. 168). 4) "Theological activity must be regarded as a whole in accordance with our intuitive apprehension of the whole pattern of Truth. . . . Behind existence-statements there are acts of intuition in which the mind is always open to the reality beyond and cannot . . . foreclose its cognition of the existence" (pp. 129, 166). 5) "Existence-statements are acts of reference in which we experience and cognise something other than ourselves. They express our intuitive apprehension of the external world in its own form, and thus have their meaning not in themselves but in the things they denote. . . . The logic of their reference must therefore correspond to the logic of God's self-communication to man—and correspond is here the appropriate term" (p. 231).

41. Wilfred Sellars, "Empiricism and the Philosophy of Mind," 148, 168.

42. "This 'not I' is, in fact, the Spirit of God that dwelleth in me beyond the catastrophe in which 'I' in the totality of my concreteness am helplessly engulfed." Karl Barth, *Epistle to the Romans*, 290.

43. See Richard Rorty's discussion of this problem in John Locke. Rorty, *Philosophy and the Mirror of Nature*, 139–148.

44. For the purpose of comparisons I am adopting a common modern conception of the arguments as *a posteriori* proofs for God's existence in which the mind moves from a universal aspect of human experience to a conclusion concerning God's existence relying solely on the internal rationality of the argument. (See John Hick, *Arguments for God's Existence* [New York: Seabury, 1971].) In fact this way of reading the arguments may be a peculiarly modern misreading. For a defense of the rationality of the arguments as exemplifying the medieval principle of *fides quaerens intellectum*, see David Burrell, "Religious Belief and Rationality," *Rationality and Religious Belief* (Notre Dame, Ind.: University of Notre Dame Press, 1981), 84–115.

45. See Imre Lakatos' charges of irrationality against Thomas Kuhn's anti-foundational argument in the natural sciences. "My concern is . . . that Kuhn, having recognized the failure both of justificationism and falsifica-

tionism in providing rational accounts of scientific growth, seems now to fall back on irrationalism. . . . In Kuhn's view scientific revolution is irrational, a matter for mob psychology." Lakatos, "Methodology of Scientific Research Programmes," *Criticism and the Growth of Knowledge* (Cambridge: Cambridge University Press, 1970), 93, 178.

46. This example is adapted from an inconsistent triad presented by Wilfred Sellars, "Empiricism and the Philosophy of Mind," 132.

3. Theology without Revelation?

1. One reason the causative model has been attractive to some theologians is that it allows a continuation of an emphasis on predestination and / or the bondage of the will. I do not wish my appeal for freedom as a presupposition for responsible action to be understood as implying a position on freedom in relation to divine election. That question is obviously not unrelated to the issue of the prevenience of grace, but it cannot be adequately treated in this context.

2. Gordon Kaufman, *An Essay on Theological Method*, 2nd ed. (Missoula, Mont.: Scholars Press, 1979). References to this book will be given parenthetically in the text. Also, Kaufman, *The Theological Imagination* (Philadelphia: Westminster Press, 1981). References to the essays in this collection will be cited in the notes.

3. David Kelsey, *Uses of Scripture in Recent Theology* (Philadelphia: Fortress Press, 1975).

4. Charles Wood, *The Formation of Christian Understanding* (Philadelphia: Westminster Press, 1981).

5. Immanuel Kant, *The Critique of Pure Reason*, trans. Norman Kemp Smith (New York: St. Martin's Press, 1929). See especially "Transcendental Dialectic," 484-570.

6. Ibid., 488.

7. "There are two stems of human knowledge, namely, *sensibility* and *understanding*. . . . Through the former, objects are given to us; through the latter, they are thought." Ibid., 61-62. Kant, of course, never fully justified his conviction that the sensible *manifold* is *given* to understanding, a criticism raised by both Fichte and Hegel. Richard Rorty has raised this challenge most recently. "Why should we think that sensibility 'in its original receptivity' presents us with a manifold, a manifold which, however, 'cannot be represented as a manifold' until the understanding has used concepts to synthesize it? We cannot introspect and see that it does, because we are never conscious of unsynthesized intuitions, nor of concepts apart from their application to intuitions. . . . But if it is not an evident pre-analytic fact that such a manifold exists, how can we use the claim that sensibility presents us with a manifold

as a premise? How, in other words, do we know that a manifold which cannot be represented as a manifold *is* a manifold?" *Philosophy and the Mirror of Nature*, 153–154.

8. "As long as theologians suppose they are engaged in a kind of 'science' which is concerned basically with attempting to describe its 'object' in straightforward terms, much as physicists and biologists describe theirs, the issues will tend to be formulated so as to focus attention on just what the object of theology might be. . . . This way lies both obscurantism and chaos." Kaufman, *Essay*, 27-28.

9. Richard Rorty, *The Consequences of Pragmatism* (Minneapolis: University of Minnesota Press, 1982), xvi.

10. Kaufman, "Metaphysics and Theology," *The Theological Imagination*, 254.

11. Kaufman uses the words *foundation(s)* and *founded* seventeen times in the first eight pages of *Essay*.

12. Kaufman, *Essay*, 43-73.

13. Kaufman, "Constructing the Concept of God," *The Theological Imagination*, 28.

14. Ibid.

15. Kaufman, "Evil and Salvation: An Anthropological Approach," *The Theological Imagination*, 168.

16. Ibid., 167-168.

17. Kaufman, "Christian Theology and the Modernization of the Religions," *The Theological Imagination*, 199. The lack of such agreement regarding the *telos* of human life and the difficulty of adjudicating moral disagreement has led to the rise of emotivism in ethics. "Emotivism is the doctrine that . . . all moral judgments are *nothing but* expressions of preference." Alasdair MacIntyre, *After Virtue* (Notre Dame, Ind.: University of Notre Dame Press, 1981), 11. Kaufman clearly wants to avoid emotivism, but his assertion of the priority of decision makes his position formally parallel to emotivism.

18. Kaufman, "Toward a Contemporary Interpretation of Jesus," *The Theological Imagination*, 135.

19. Ibid., 127. In describing the emotivist dichotomies of Weber's thought, MacIntyre writes "Questions of ends are questions of values, and on values reason is silent; conflict between rival values cannot be settled. Instead one must simply choose—between parties, classes, nations, causes, ideals." *After Virtue*, 25.

20. Despite the fact that his sharp criticism of revelation rules out any claim to correspondence in theology, Kaufman does make one tentative move toward a kind of realism. He asks, "Does or can devotion to . . . a God constructed according to Christian criteria . . . provide us with significant and

valid orientation in the 'real world'?" His reply illustrates Kaufman's desire for stronger rational criteria than his position can deliver. "This frame of orientation must in some significant sense 'correspond' to 'how things are' and talk about God, the symbolical focus of this perspective, must represent something 'real.' . . . It would be hard to conceive how the ruling focus of a highly centered frame of orientation could be completely out of touch with that which is metaphysically real. . . . The symbol of God must in some way correspond to or represent something metaphysically real, if it is in fact true that devotion to that symbol provides proper orientation for human life." "Constructing the Concept of God," 47–48.

Kaufman's reintroduction of the notion of correspondence is certainly surprising but hardly justified given the difficulties surrounding his pragmatic criterion. If the phrase "proper orientation for human life" is, as I have argued, systematically ambiguous, depending for its content on our interpretive decisions, then an appeal to this pragmatic criterion cannot warrant a claim to correspondence. Moreover, the centeredness of a "frame of orientation" can hardly be a criterion for metaphysical reality. Paranoic delusions are nothing if not centered, but we rightly claim that persons who harbor such delusions are "out of touch with reality." I agree that Kaufman needs a stronger normative argument than he has offered, but I find his attempt to move from a pragmatic criterion to a claim of correspondence unconvincing.

21. Charles Wood, *The Formation of Christian Understanding*, 22. Subsequent references to Wood will be cited by page number in the text.

22. David Kelsey, *Uses of Scripture in Recent Theology*. Subsequent references to Kelsey will be cited by page number in the text.

23. Eberhard Jüngel, *The Doctrine of the Trinity* (Grand Rapids, Mich.: Eerdmans, 1976), xix–xx.

24. Kelsey stresses the logical priority of the theologian's imaginative construal at a number of key places in the text. "[The theologian's] decision . . . seems to be a function of a logically prior decision about how best to characterize the phenomenon over which scripture is most centrally 'authority' when used in the common life of the church" (p. 151). " 'Reasons' are never 'theological-position neutral.' They always derive their force from a logically prior imaginative judgment about how best to construe the mode of God's presence" (p. 166). "These decisions are also shaped by an act of the imagination that a theologian must necessarily make prior to doing theology at all" (p. 170).

25. The theologians Kelsey treats are B. B. Warfield, Hans-Werner Bartsch, G. Ernest Wright, Karl Barth, L. S. Thornton, and Paul Tillich.

26. The distinction is Kelsey's, p. 104. Wood does not always heed this distinction and occasionally uses the word *canon* equivocally. In his crucial concluding argument Wood asserts, "There is a *usus* of scripture which has

a prior claim to the church's attention, namely, the *usus* which establishes its canonical sense as God's self-disclosive Word. It is this canonical sense which the church has the most reason to acknowledge as the literal sense of scripture." Wood, p. 119. Wood fails to see that the canon the church holds in common is the "Christian canon," a set of formally authoritative texts which possess no determinate sense as such. When the canon is given a determinate sense, it becomes the "working canon" and then is no longer the common possession of the church.

27. For a careful analysis of the three senses of the concept *sensus literalis*, see Hans Frei, "Theology and the Interpretation of Narrative: Some Hermeneutical Considerations," paper delivered at the annual meeting of the American Academy of Religion, New York, N.Y., December 1982.

28. Hans W. Frei, *The Eclipse of Biblical Narrative* (New Haven, Conn.: Yale University Press, 1975).

29. The inability of a functional view of authority to provide rational guidance for preferential judgments within the community raises an important question about the concept of authority with which functionalism operates. If the Christian community is analogous to political communities, then it ought to hold specifiable goals in common and be able to engage in common action. "In contradistinction to mere partners, the members of a community . . . are engaged in common action whose object is qualitatively different from a sum of interdependent goals." Yves Simon, *A General Theory of Authority* (Notre Dame, Ind.: Notre Dame University Press, 1962). If Christian identity is to be communally formed, then the community itself must have a discernible identity articulated through patterns of belief and action.

Yves Simon argues that authority is the kind of rule appropriate to a community, i.e., a social organization which transcends merely personal interests by seeking the common good. A central problem for every community is how to achieve the common good when a variety of morally responsible means are available for the community's use. For a community to engage in common action a choice must be made among the alternatives. "Among the many ways of playing a concerto of Bach, several satisfy the requirements of great music, and highly qualified musicians will clash as to how the fourth Brandenburg Concerto should be played. Yet the members of an orchestra cannot be allowed conflicting interpretations of a concerto" (p. 41). Authority functions, Simon argues, precisely to adjudicate among the various apt yet often conflicting means of achieving that goal. Ironically, authority for Simon *begins* precisely at the point where the functional view of authority *ceases*, viz., in the adjudication of conflicts within the community's common life.

Simon further argues that "the need for authority as a factor in united action" (p. 45) increases in relation to the rise of greater plurality of choice. "The existence of a plurality of genuine means in the pursuit of the common good excludes unanimity as a *sufficient* method of steadily procuring unity of action. To achieve indispensable unity in common action, one method is left. . . . Everyone of us, insofar as he is engaged in the common action, will accept and follow, as a rule of his own action, one judgment thus constituted into rule for all. This [is the] rule for common action. . . . *The power in charge of unifying common action through rules binding for all is what everyone calls authority"* (pp. 47-48).

Simon's discussion, though designed as an analysis of political communities, raises some interesting questions about authority in the Christian community. Kelsey has argued that scripture, neither in its formal nor in its material uses, can function as an adjudicating authority. If the Christian church is to be a true community capable of uniting for common action, then does it require some political authority to function where scriptural authority leaves off? Can disputes concerning Christian belief and action conceivably be resolved in a community as fragmented as Christianity? Is it really appropriate to speak of the Christian church as a *community* if it is unable to engage in common action toward the common good? If there is no real Christian community, then can we speak of Christian identity as though it were a recognizable form of belief and behavior? These questions obviously cannot be discussed in the context of this project, but the issue of scripture's political authority (or lack of such) deserves much more serious attention. For an initial attempt to engage in such analysis see Stanley Hauerwas, "The Moral Authority of Scripture: The Politics and Ethics of Remembering," *A Community of Character* (Notre Dame: University of Notre Dame Press, 1981), 53-71. I first became aware of Simon's work on authority through Hauerwas' discussion in this article.

30. For an excellent discussion of the uses and abuses of the notion of incommensurability see Richard Bernstein, *Beyond Objectivism and Relativism: Science, Hermeneutics, and Praxis* (Philadelphia: University of Pennsylvania Press, 1983), 79-138.

4. Toward a Nonfoundational Theology

1. W. V. Quine and J. S. Ullian, *The Web of Belief* (New York: Random House, 1970), 131.

2. See my discussion of background belief, pp. 11-15. While holist theories of justification have held sway in analytical philosophy for more than two decades, they have only recently been introduced into discussions in the field of religion. Holist justification is put to particularly good use in two recent projects in philosophy of religion. See Basil Mitchell, *The Justification of Religious Belief* (New York: Oxford University Press, 1973) and Jeffrey Stout, *The Flight from Authority* (Notre Dame, Ind.: University of Notre

Dame Press, 1981). While a form of holism appears operative in the recent work of Hans Frei (especially in his as yet unpublished Shaffer Lectures), the only *explicit* theological use of this form of justification I am aware of is William Werpehowski, "Social Justice, Social Selves: John Rawls' *A Theory of Justice* and Christian Ethics" (Ph.D. diss., Yale University, 1981).

My use of holist justification does not commit me to the further beliefs associated with pragmatism. In particular I resist the historicist turn of Richard Rorty's pragmatism as reflected in the introduction to *The Consequences of Pragmatism* (Minneapolis: University of Minnesota Press, 1982). "When the secret police come, when the torturers violate the innocent, there is nothing to be said to them of the form 'There is something within you which you are betraying. Though you embody the practices of a totalitarian society which will endure forever, there is something beyond those practices which condemns you.' . . . There is nothing deep down inside us except what we have put there ourselves, no criterion that we have not created in the course of creating a practice, no standard of rationality that is not an appeal to such a criterion, no rigorous argumentation that is not obedience to our own conventions" (p. xlii). Rorty's conclusions require a set of anthropological beliefs about human autonomy which a Christian cannot share.

3. For a similar understanding see the works of Clifford Geertz, including *The Interpretations of Cultures* (New York: Basic Books, 1973); *Islam Observed* (New Haven, Conn.: Yale University Press, 1968); *Local Knowledge* (New York: Basic Books, 1983). George Lindbeck has recently used Geertz's notion of "thick description" to develop a "cultural-linguistic" model for religion and theology. See *The Nature of Doctrine* (Philadelphia: Westminster Press, 1984).

4. Alasdair MacIntyre, *After Virtue* (Notre Dame: University of Notre Dame Press, 1981), 207.

5. Schleiermacher argued that "the immediate utterances of the religious self-consciousness" (*The Christian Faith*, p. 81) are "fragmentary and . . . chaotic" (p. 94) and inevitably lead to contradiction and confusion. Dogmatics, as a scientific activity, provides an orderly form for these "diverse expressions of piety" by discovering that "common element" which is the "self-identical essence of piety" (p. 12). But Schleiermacher's position is ambiguous on the question of whether that essence is located *within* those diverse first-order utterances or in a deeper universal and pre-linguistic substratum. Insofar as Schleiermacher asserts the former, his method is supportive of descriptive theology. Insofar as he supports the latter, he gives aid and comfort to foundational theology.

6. "All *religious* language . . . bears the linguistic form of *re-presentation*." David Tracy, *Blessed Rage for Order* (New York: Seabury, 1978), 103.

Tracy derives that claim from the work of Schubert Ogden, *The Reality of God* (New York: Harper & Row, 1966), 33.

7. This is the way Karl Barth conceives of Christian use of non-Christian concepts. For an extended examination of Barth's procedure of theological annexation see William Werpehowski, "Command and History in the Ethics of Karl Barth," *Journal of Religious Ethics* 9/2 (Fall 1981), 298–321.

8. This formulation of the theological task is indebted to Hans Frei's discussion of Karl Barth's theology in his review of Eberhard Busch, *Karl Barth: His Life from Letters and Autobiographical Texts* in *Virginia Seminary Journal* 30 (July 1978), 42–46. Frei expands on the notion of theological redescription in two as yet unpublished works, "Theology and the Interpretation of Narrative: Some Hermeneutical Considerations" and "Jesus Christ and Interpretation," the 1983 Shaffer Lectures, delivered at the Yale Divinity School.

9. "Proslogium," *St. Anselm: Basic Writings* (LaSalle, Ill.: Open Court, 1962), 1–34. Two modern restatements of Anselm's position which I find congenial to my own are Karl Barth, *Anselm: Fides Quaerens Intellectum* (Richmond: John Knox Press, 1960) and David Burrell, "Religious Belief and Rationality," *Rationality and Religious Belief* (Notre Dame: University of Notre Dame Press, 1979), 84–115.

10. *The Web of Belief*, 127.

11. Christians ought to seek what John Rawls, *A Theory of Justice* (Cambridge, Mass.: Harvard University Press, 1971) calls "reflective equilibrium." "It is an equilibrium because at last our principles and judgments coincide, and it is reflective since we know to what our judgments conform and the premises of their derivation" (p. 20). Werpehowski, "Social Justice, Social Selves," 104–105 has a helpful discussion of the process by which such equilibrium is achieved. "A very important feature of this procedure is that a substantial amount of 'fit' between principles and judgments *as such* does not determine whether or not a 'wayward' considered judgment is to be scrapped; one must first consider how important that considered judgment is in one's total system of belief, and how it affects other beliefs that are held. For example, if all my particular considered judgments can be accounted for by a utilitarian theory *save one*, that slavery is unjust even if it *maximizes* utility, it does not necessarily and immediately follow, as Ronald Dworkin would have it, that I must scrap the wayward judgment without further ado 'if that is required to achieve the harmony of equilibrium.' On the contrary, that considered judgment, on analysis, might drive me to discover that I really hold a background theory of the person which is at odds with the background theories presupposed by the utilitarian conception. This *provisionally fixed point* of my considered judgments may, that is, lead me to revise my entire theory. The direction may even be reversed; 'we may want to change our pres-

ent considered judgments once their regulative principles are brought to light. And we may want to do this even though the principles are a perfect fit. A knowledge of these principles may suggest further reflections that lead us to revise our judgments' (Rawls, p. 49). So reflective equilibrium is obviously more than a 'narrow' harmonization between principles and judgments."

The unaddressed question in the debate over revelation is whether there *is* a conflict between the background belief in God's prevenience and the "considered judgments" which it supports. If there is no conflict then the pressures for rejecting the background belief ought to be resisted, as long as the dependent judgments are deemed to be theologically appropriate. For a useful discussion of the role of disconfirming evidence in the justification of religious belief see Nicholas Wolterstorff, "Can Belief in God Be Rational If It Has No Foundations?" *Faith and Rationality*, ed. A. Plantinga and N. Wolterstorff (Notre Dame: University of Notre Dame Press, 1983).

12. The term *restrospective justification* is borrowed from David Burrell's excellent study of the justification of religious belief, "Religious Belief and Rationality" (see note 9 above). Burrell uses the term in a more transcendental sense than I, arguing that retrospective justification can discern the regulative principle presupposed by rational inquiry. "Our use of reason to explain takes its impetus from a unity more comprehensive than any scheme can account for, much as particular discussions of justice invariably reflect a cosmic sense of justice which defies formulation. Since the more comprehensive unity cannot be forced into an explanatory scheme, one can only believe it to be the case. Yet our continued use of particular explanatory frameworks would be pointless without such a belief. . . . We begin with the very practice of explaining, only to find that such a practice presupposes belief in a first principle quite beyond its ken" (pp. 98–99). While I find Burrell's argument elegant, I do not need the transcendental turn in order to employ a retrospective justification of God's prevenience beginning from particular Christian beliefs and their supporting practices.

13. James Barr, *The Bible in the Modern World* (New York: Harper & Row, 1973), 121.

14. This was, of course, a characteristic emphasis of the so-called "biblical theology" movement.

15. Hans Frei makes a similar point in his recent work on *sensus literalis* and the interpretation of biblical narrative. "The question of 'reference' is included in hermeneutical-theological inquiry because it is solved descriptively in the case of *this* narrative (whatever may be true of others). The linguistic account, i.e., the narrative itself, renders the reality narratively. We have the reality only under the depiction and not in a language-neutral or language transcending way." "Theology and the Interpretation of Narrative:

Some Hermeneutical Considerations," p. 14. My own claims concerning God's reality and Christian convictions are developed in detail in chapter 7.

16. Most proposals of this sort have followed the original suggestion of Stephen Crites, "The Narrative Quality of Experience," *Journal of the American Academy of Religion* 39/3 (September 1971), 291–311. An excellent, though rarely cited, treatment of this issue is Brian Wicker, *A Story-Shaped World: Fiction and Metaphysics: Some Variations on a Theme* (Notre Dame: University of Notre Dame Press, 1975), especially 1–113.

17. Most of these proposals have been sparked by Hans Frei's *The Eclipse of Biblical Narrative*. An important recent work which concentrates on the literary techniques appropriate for the interpretation of biblical narrative is Robert Alter, *The Art of Biblical Narrative* (New York: Basic Books, 1981). Alter is concerned solely with narrative in Hebrew scripture and surprisingly appears unaware of Frei's work. Nonetheless, he offers sensitive literary interpretations which are rich with theological nuance. Alter does not often develop his own best theological insights, but theologians will profit enormously by reading this suggestive work.

18. See Hans Frei's description of the reformers' use of narrative, *The Eclipse of Biblical Narrative*, 1–50.

19. Stanley Hauerwas has been one of the major contributors to current discussion of narrative, but I am uncertain on which side of this great divide to place him. In intention he certainly belongs in the nonfoundational/descriptive camp. His article "From System to Story: An Alternative for Rationality in Ethics," *Truthfulness and Tragedy* (Notre Dame: University of Notre Dame Press, 1977), 15–39, written with David Burrell, offers a sustained critique of foundational notions of rationality and defends an understanding of rationality as formed by tradition, community, and narrative. In a more recent book, *A Community of Character* (Notre Dame: University of Notre Dame Press, 1981), he expresses the hope that "this book might help Christians rediscover that their most important social task is nothing less than to be a community capable of hearing the story of God we find in the scripture and living in a manner that is faithful to that story" (p. 1). And yet Hauerwas executes that intention in an ambiguous way. He rarely reflects upon the specific narrative content of scripture as the key to the Christian ethical task. When he does engage in such specific analysis his arguments are original and powerful. (See "Abortion: Why the Arguments Fail," *A Community of Character*, 212–229, especially 223–229). But more often he relies on a very general appeal to the formal qualities of narrative as defining the shape of the beliefs and practices of the Christian community. When he is arguing negatively, i.e., against foundationalism or liberalism, he regularly appeals not to the *biblical* narrative for his warrants but to nar-

rative as a category specifying the traditional and historical components of community life. When he does that his arguments can easily be understood as relying on an assumption about the "narrative quality of communal experience." I believe that Hauerwas does not want to be read in that way, but his regular reliance upon a formal view of narrative, similar to that which Alasdair MacIntyre invokes in *After Virtue*, leaves him open to the charge that his stress on narrative is merely a social-historical version of the modern "turn to the subject." I take Hauerwas to be arguing for a necessary connection between the biblical content and the historical life of the Christian community, but he has not, it seems to me, worked out the relation between the two with sufficient precision in order to fulfill his intention of granting priority to the former.

20. The following analysis is indebted to Hans Frei's detailed and illuminating discussion in *The Eclipse of Biblical Narrative*, especially, chapters 1,2,5,7, and 15.

21. See the following excellent discussions of the roles of *explicatio, meditatio,* and *applicatio* in traditional biblical exegesis. Karl Barth, *Church Dogmatics*, vol. I, pt. 2, 722ff.; Charles Wood, *The Formation of Christian Understanding* (Philadelphia: Westminster Press, 1981), 60ff. Hans Frei, *Eclipse*, speaks of *explication, application,* and *reference* as the three terms under which the shift in modern interpretation ought to be discussed. But his focus on *reference*, while elucidating the modern departure from the Reformation position, is helpful neither for the description of the reformer's position nor for a constructive alternative to the modern position. For those purposes *meditatio* is a more useful term.

22. Frei, *Eclipse*, 126–127.

23. This point is made by Stanley Hauerwas and David Burrell, "From System to Story: An Alternative Pattern for Rationality in Ethics," *Truthfulness and Tragedy*, 15–39.

24. See Paul Ricoeur's helpful discussion of this point in " The Narrative Function," *Hermeneutics and the Human Sciences* (Cambridge: Cambridge University Press, 1981), 274–296.

25. Frank Kermode, *The Sense of an Ending* (London: Oxford University Press, 1967), 18.

26. "That the concordant tale should include irony and paradox and peripeteia, that making sense of what goes to make sense should be an activity that includes the acceptance of inexplicable patterns, mazes of contradiction, is a condition of humanly satisfactory explanation," ibid., 163. In his more recent book, *The Genesis of Secrecy* (Cambridge, Mass.: Harvard University Press, 1979), Kermode stresses far more the dissonance and obscurity of narrative.

27. See Alter, *The Art of Biblical Narrative*.

28. See Frei, *Eclipse*, 10.

29. Alter, 21.

30. Ibid., 147–154.

31. For an extended account of this point see Hans W. Frei, *The Identity of Jesus Christ* (Philadelphia: Fortress Press, 1975) 112–115.

32. See especially Stuart Hampshire, *Thought and Action* (1959; reprint Notre Dame: University of Notre Dame Press, 1983) and P. F. Strawson, *Individuals* (London: Methuen, 1959). The intention-action model is put to good theological use by Hans Frei, "Theological Reflections on the Gospels' Account of Jesus' Death and Resurrection," *The Christian Scholar*, 49/4 (Winter 1966), 263–306 and *The Identity of Jesus Christ*. See also David Kelsey, *The Uses of Scripture*, 46–50 where he illuminates Barth's conception of the person by showing its similarities to the intention-action model. For a full length treatment of the importance of the intention-action sequence for conceptions of God's agency see Thomas Tracy, *God, Action, and Embodiment* (Grand Rapids, Mich.: Eerdmans, 1984).

33. MacIntyre, *After Virtue*, 203.

34. This term is obviously related to the notion of "promissory narration," which Christopher Morse unpacks with such skill in his excellent study *The Logic of Promise in Moltmann's Theology* (Philadelphia: Fortress Press, 1979). Moltmann himself suggests that revelation can profitably be reconceived under the category of promise in *The Theology of Hope* (New York: Harper & Row, 1967). I am indebted both to Moltmann's original suggestion and to Morse's clarification of the logic of promise and narrative. For a related use of these two notions see Robert Jenson, *Story and Promise* (Philadelphia: Fortress Press, 1973).

5. God's Prevenience: The Logic of Promise and Agency

1. *Sacrorum conciliorum nova et amplissima collectio*, ed. J. D. Mansi (Venice, 1759 ff.), 8:712ff., appended affirmations. Quoted in *Christian Dogmatics*, vol. 2 ed. Carl Braaten and Robert Jenson (Philadelphia: Fortress Press, 1984), 126.

2. For the notion of "conviction set" see James Wm. McClendon, Jr. and James M. Smith, *Understanding Religious Convictions* (Notre Dame, Ind.: University of Notre Dame Press, 1975), 96–106.

3. While there are surely more issues at stake in Christian aptness than the grounding of a theological position in scripture, I take such grounding to be the minimal condition for Christian aptness. I am in agreement with those theologians David Kelsey analyzes, for whom "scripture" is "ingredient" in Christian identity. Kelsey, *Uses of Scripture in Recent Theology* (Philadelphia: Fortress Press, 1975), esp. 164–167.

4. I use this notion, ordinarily associated with pragmatism, in order to emphasize the nonfoundational character of theology's inquiry into the warrants for Christian truth-claims. While I affirm the progressive character of justification, I also want to argue that there are procedures for settling beliefs and justifying claims to truth. The concept of "warranted assertability" stands opposed to foundational theories of truth but not to the notion of justified true beliefs.

5. John Dewey, *Logic: The Theory of Inquiry* (New York: Henry Holt, 1938), 8–9.

6. Julian Hartt, "Theological Investments in Story: Some Comments on Recent Developments and Some Proposals," *Journal of the American Academy of Religion* 52/1 (March 1984), 117–130. Hartt's essay is followed by two responses: Stephen Crites, "A Respectful Reply to the Assertorical Professor," 131–139 and Stanley Hauerwas, "Why the Truth Demands Truthfulness: An Imperious Engagement with Hartt," 141–147. Hartt then engages his critics in "Reply to Crites and Hauerwas," 149–156.

The exchange is important not only because it treats important issues in the theological use of narrative but also because it illustrates the confusion surrounding current discussions of truth in religion. Hartt raises some hard questions about the relation between "truth and truthfulness in story," asking particularly whether "aesthetic truthfulness [is] the strongest and most reliable bridge to actuality?" (p. 126). Hartt's critical challenge, however, relies on a sharp logical distinction between "the expressive" and "the fact-assertive (assertoric)," which he further correlates with the distinction between belief and truth. In his clever and insightful reply Crites show how questionable those distinctions are. "Let us ponder this distinction a little. The former, I take it, is a statement about the believer, the latter about a putative fact. But I should have thought that a statement of belief refers both to the subject and to the object of belief" (p. 132). Crites goes on to ask whether the creedal statement that Jesus was raised from the dead is "true in a merely symbolic sense, as the content of a purely expressive act on the believer's part, or is it a fact? . . . Hartt's alternatives put me in the position of a man who is asked whether he would prefer to be shot or garroted. Aren't there some other options? Something less deadly perhaps?" (p. 132). But when Crites proceeds to say, "that God raised [Jesus] from the dead is not a factual statement at all" (p. 133), then all of Hartt's original worries resurface. Clearly some view of truth-claiming is needed which does not rely on a *false* dichotomy between belief and truth and yet allows for the recognition of historical and ontological claims to truth in the context of the Christian confession.

7. Richard Bernstein, *Beyond Objectivism and Relativism: Science, Hermeneutics, and Praxis* (Philadelphia: University of Pennsylvania Press, 1983), 18.

8. George Lindbeck, *The Nature of Doctrine: Religion and Theology in a Postliberal Age* (Philadelphia: Westminster Press, 1984), 68. Lindbeck is seeking a view of truth-claiming which avoids the impasse illustrated by the Hartt-Crites-Hauerwas exchange (see note 6). While his own view of religious truth-claiming inclines toward the "truthfulness" option, he is more attuned to the religious importance of historical and ontological claims than either Crites or Hauerwas. Lindbeck's discussion, though quite schematic, marks an important advance in the treatment of these issues.

9. See Barth's discussion of "The Nature of the Word of God" and "The Knowability of the Word of God" in *Church Dogmatics.* vol. I, pt. 1: *The Doctrine of the Word of God*, 2nd ed. (Edinburgh: T & T Clark, 1975), 125–247. For two critical discussions of this issue in Barth see, Donald Evans, "Barth on Talk about God," *Canadian Journal of Theology*, 16/3–4 (1970), 175–192 and Christopher Morse, *The Logic of Promise in Moltmann's Theology* (Philadelphia: Fortress Press, 1979), 60–65.

The position I am recounting here characterizes Barth's early works, particularly *The Epistle to the Romans* and *Church Dogmatics*, vol. I, pt. 1: *The Doctrine of the Word of God* and vol. II, pt. 2: *The Doctrine of God*. There is another strain in Barth's thinking which is evident particularly in *Church Dogmatics*, vol. 3, pt. 2: *The Doctrine of Creation* and throughout vol. IV: *The Doctrine of Reconciliation*. In those volumes Barth reckons more seriously with the relation of human speech as God's creation to the use of that speech as the vehicle for God's revelation. This renewed appreciation for the form of human language is not unrelated to Barth's discovery of the significance of narrative form for biblical interpretation. For an interpretation of Barth which disputes the Evans/Morse view, see William Werpehowski, "Divine Commands and Philosophical Dilemmas: The Case of Karl Barth," *Dialog* 20 (Winter 1981), 20–25. Note especially Werpehowski's use of the notion "open-textured concepts."

Despite this important second strain in Barth, he never used these later insights to reformulate his doctrine of revelation. Consequently an unresolved tension remains at the heart of Barth's thinking on this question. His earlier work, with its simpler dichotomies, has been more accessible, especially to theologians in the English-speaking world, and has, for good or ill, exercised enormous influence. It is this earlier view which I am disputing.

10. Karl Barth, *Church Dogmatics*, vol. I, pt. 1: *The Doctrine of the Word of God* (Edinburgh: T & T Clark, 1975), 166.

11. Martin Luther, *Lectures on Galatians, 1535*, vol. 26 of *Luther's Works* (St. Louis: Concordia Publishing House, 1963), 29.

12. Martin Luther, "The Babylonian Captivity of the Church," *Word and Sacrament III, Luther's Works* (Philadelphia: Muhlenberg Press, 1959), 42.

13. For a brief but insightful discussion of this issue see, Robert Jenson, "Pneumatological Soteriology," *Christian Dogmatics,* ed. Carl Braaten and Robert Jenson, 125-134.

14. Ibid., 128.

15. "Apology of the Augsburg Confession," *The Book of Concord,* ed. and trans. Theodore G. Tappert (St. Louis: Concordia Publishing House, 1959), 107-168.

16. Ibid., 108.

17. Ibid., 113.

18. Luther, *Lectures on Galatians,* 72-73.

19. Jenson, *Christian Dogmatics,* 131.

20. "Apology of the Augsburg Confession," 112-113.

21. *Lutheran Book of Worship* (Minneapolis: Augsburg Publishing House, 1978), 69-70. Similar prayers are present in the Anglican rite. Cf. *The Book of Common Prayer* (New York: Seabury, 1977), 368.

22. This distinction is made by J. L. Austin, "Performative Utterances," *Philosophical Papers* (Oxford: Clarendon Press, 1961), 238. Austin develops his "speech-act theory" at length in *How to Do Things with Words* (Cambridge: Harvard University Press, 1962).

23. For a brief but cogent analysis of the liturgical function of the eucharistic prayer see Robert Jenson, *Visible Words,* (Philadelphia: Fortress Press, 1978), 95-104.

24. This notion was brought to my attention by David Burrell, "Religious Belief and Rationality," *Rationality and Religious Belief* (Notre Dame, Ind.: Notre Dame University Press, 1979), 86. His sources are C. K. Grant, "Pragmatic Implication," *Philosophy* 33 (1958), 303-324 and P. F. Strawson, *Introduction to Logical Theory* (New York, 1952) on "presupposition," 175-179.

25. McClendon and Smith, *Understanding Religious Convictions* (Notre Dame: Notre Dame University Press, 1975), 7.

26. For this notion, see Paul Ricoeur, *Interpretation Theory: Discourse and the Surplus of Meaning* (Fort Worth: Texas Christian University, 1976), 29.

27. For a full analysis of the conditions for "nondefective" promising see, John Searle, *Speech-Acts: An Essay in the Philosophy of Language* (Cambridge: Cambridge University Press, 1970), 54-71. Searle's nine conditions for nondefective promises and five rules of semantics are reproduced in full by Christopher Morse, *The Logic of Promise in Moltmann's Theology* (Philadelphia: Fortress Press, 1979), 72-74.

McClendon and Smith. *Understanding Religious Convictions,* 49–83, have developed a speech-act theory of religious language which advances beyond the work of Austin and Searle. See especially their analysis of the conditions of nondefective speech-acts under the categories, "preconditions, primary conditions, representative conditions, and affective conditions."

28. McClendon and Smith, 59.

29. *Lutheran Book of Worship*, 56. Cf. *The Book of Common Prayer*, 321, 353.

30. *The Book of Common Prayer*, 360.

31. *Lutheran Book of Worship*, 56.

32. Langdon Gilkey, "Ontology, Cosmology, and the Travail of Biblical Language," has shown how the biblical theologians' concept of revelation foundered on their incoherent notion of "God's acts." These theologians were unable to distinguish between the initiative of God and the faith of the community because they lacked "a theological ontology that . . . put intelligible and credible meanings into [their] analogical categories of divine deeds and of divine self-manifestation through events," Gilkey, 203. Subsequent attempts to reconstitute concepts of God's agency and acts, particularly by Gordon Kaufman and Schubert Ogden, have been undermined by their dependence on forms of mind-body dualism. (See Thomas F. Tracy, "Enacting History: Ogden and Kaufman on God's Mighty Acts," *Journal of Religion*, 64/1 [January 1984], 20–36.) A coherent account of God's agency is an indispensable part of a coherent doctrine of revelation. My own discussion of the logic of discourse concerning agents is indebted to Thomas F. Tracy, *God, Action, and Embodiment* (Grand Rapids, Mich.: Eerdmans, 1984).

33. Tracy, *God, Action, and Embodiment*, 22.

34. Ibid., 3-6.

35. The term is used by Gilbert Ryle, *The Concept of Mind* (New York: Barnes & Noble, 1949), chap. 5. See Tracy's discussion, pp. 6-8.

36. Tracy, *God, Action, and Embodiment*, 4.

37. Ibid., 12.

38. Ibid., 20.

39. See Tracy's discussion, 73f.

40. Tracy draws a helpful distinction between "story-relative" and "story-bound" identifications. "Story-relative identification" as defined by P. F. Strawson, *Individuals: An Essay in Descriptive Metaphysics* (London: Methuen, 1959), 18, is "identification within his story; but not identification within history." That is to say, it is identification purely within the imaginative framework of a narrative, independent of the issues of historical reference or ontological truth-claiming. Tracy rightly points out that "story-relative identification in this pure form is clearly of no help to the theologian who does not want to reduce his talk of God simply to an imaginative structure disconnected from the world of particulars in time and space" (p. 75). Consequently, he suggests the alternative notion of "story-bound identification" in which God "is identified as an actor introduced within a story. But

this story . . . is not left as a piece of elaborate fantasy. Rather, it purports to be the story of our lives and our history. The setting of the story is continuous with the world within which the rest of our references are made, and the events it narrates coincide with events we can identify in our shared field of reference. . . . Reference to God is story-bound insofar as it is dependent upon a network of supporting claims that, taken as a whole, set the context within which we can identify God. . . . Far from being isolated from the rest of our references, this story embraces as many of them as it can, relating them all to the central referent of the story: God" (p. 79).

41. Searle, 60.

42. Austin, *How to Do Things with Words*, 117.

43. Austin deals with these effects under the notion of the "perlocutionary act." Ibid., 109–132.

44. "Apology of the Augsburg Confession," 112–113.

6. The Promising God: The Gospel as Narrated Promise

1. Hans Frei, "Theological Reflections on the Gospel's Accounts of Jesus' Death and Resurrection," *The Christian Scholar* 49/4 (Winter 1966), 263–306 and *The Identity of Jesus Christ* (Philadelphia: Fortress Press, 1974) has pioneered this use of intention-action models in theology. But Frei insists on the necessity of a dual mode of analysis which employs both an intention-action and a self-manifestation model of selfhood. The latter form of analysis is necessary, Frei argues, to indicate the ultimacy, elusiveness, and persistence (see "Theological Reflections," 280–283 and *Identity*, 94–96) of "the ascriptive center or focus of intentional activity," i.e., "that to which both states of consciousness and physical characteristics are ascribed" ("Theological Reflections," 280). He also argues that the latter model allows the description of "the unbroken continuity of identity through its changes" (*Identity*, 44) in a way not possible with the intention-action model.

Though I am indebted to Frei's ground-breaking work, I find his argument for the necessity of the self-manifestation model unconvincing. (Frei himself expresses some reservations about this model in the Preface to *Identity*, x.) The intention-action model, employed in the service of a story-bound identification, appears to account for all the elements which the self-manifestation model is designed to elucidate. Alasdair MacIntyre seems to me exactly right when he says, "Personal identity is just that identity presupposed by the unity of the character which the unity of a narrative requires. Without such unity there would not be subjects of whom stories could be told." *After Virtue* (Notre Dame, Ind.: University of Notre Dame Press, 1981), 203. The "ascriptive center" is simply that one to whom traits of character are applied when patterns of behavior are deemed to be sufficiently *persistent* as to be characteristic. If we are seeking formal tools of personal identification, the intention-action model seems to allow talk of the "ascriptive center" and thus of the self's persistence and ultimacy. Whether a self is also elusive can only be determined by its narrative-particular description. In order to account for the self's elusiveness we do not need to reflect on "the fact that one's own acts *now* cannot become objects of knowledge to oneself until they have receded into the past" (*Identity*, 95). However interesting such speculation might be it seems necessary neither for the task of personal identification nor for the broader task of theology.

Finally my claim of inclusiveness for the intention-action model must be judged by the model's usefulness in defining the identity of God and Jesus Christ as depicted in the biblical narrative.

2. For a provisional attempt to do this for Old Testament narratives, see Dale Patrick, *The Rendering of God in the Old Testament* (Philadelphia: Fortress Press, 1981).

3. I agree with Jack Dean Kingsbury that "Son of God" is the key title in the Gospel of Matthew. See especially, *Matthew: Structure, Christology, Kingdom* (Philadelphia: Fortress Press, 1975), 40–83. I will attempt to defend that claim by emphasizing the literary structures which provide the *narrative continuity* within Matthew's Gospel. As a historical critic Kingsbury focuses on the more discreet form-critical units in order to demonstrate the pre-eminence of the title "Son of God." I am not so much interested in defending the pre-eminence of the title as in showing its relation to Matthew's narrative identification of Jesus Christ.

4. For a discussion of realism or verisimilitude in narrative prose see Robert Scholes and Robert Kellog, *The Nature of Narrative* (New York: Oxford University Press, 1966), esp. 82–159 and J. P. Stern, *On Realism* (London: Routledge & Kegan Paul, 1973).

5. Most commentators deny this connection, because, they argue, "no moral stigma was attached to these women in Jewish tradition." Francis Wright Beare, *The Gospel According to Matthew* (New York: Harper & Row, 1981), 65. Nonetheless, Matthew's inclusion of them is striking, and their role as aliens and outcasts is more plausible given the importance of that literary and theological motif throughout the Gospel.

6. On Matthew's use of the term *dikaiosyne* see Gerhard Barth, "Matthew's Understanding of the Law," *Tradition and Interpretation in Matthew* (Philadelphia: Westminster Press, 1963), 138–139.

7. In contrast to the willingness of James and John to leave their father is the unnamed "disciple" who wants to delay his discipleship so that he might bury his father (8:21–22).

8. In contrast to the metaphorical blindness of the inhabitants of Jerusalem, Matthew depicts the two physically blind men of Jericho as

recognizing Jesus as "Son of David" (20:31), whereupon their sight is restored.

9. See Zechariah 14:21. "And there shall be no longer a trader in the house of the Lord of hosts on that day."

10. Contemporary interpreters must exercise extreme care in interpreting these passages, for they have been the source for much Christian anti-Judaism. See Charlotte Klein, *Anti-Judaism in Christian Theology* (Philadelphia: Fortress Press, 1977). Matthew's Gospel is written at a time when Christianity was an emergent Jewish sect, contending with other elements in Judaism as rival claimants to the authentic Jewish tradition. The polemic within Matthew cannot be transferred to a situation in which Christianity has become a clearly disinct and numerically dominant religious tradition. For two studies of the problem of the anti-Judaism in Matthew see Lloyd Gaston, "The Messiah of Israel as Teacher of the Gentiles: The Setting of Matthew's Christology," *Interpreting the Gospels*, ed. James Luther Mays (Philadelphia: Fortress Press, 1981), and George W. E. Nickelsburg, "Good News/Bad News: The Messiah and God's Fractured Community," *Currents in Theology and Mission* 4/6 (December 1977), 324–332.

11. For a recent interpretation of this story, see Elizabeth Schussler Fiorenza, *In Memory of Her* (New York: Crossroads, 1983).

12. Is there an echo here of the three temptations of Satan in 4:1–11?

13. The final "Hear him" comes from Deut. 18:15. For a more complete account of the Old Testament imagery in this passage, see R. H. Gundry, *The Uses of the Old Testament in St. Matthew's Gospel*, Nov-TSup, 18 (Leiden: Brill, 1976), 36–37.

14. This emphasis is captured in the traditional distinction between the immanent and economic trinity. See pp. 137–140.

15. Albert Schweitzer, *The Quest of the Historical Jesus* (New York: Macmillan, 1961), 370–371.

16. The most thorough study of Matthew's use of Old Testament quotations and allusions is Hubert Frankenmoelle, *Jahwebund und Kirche Christi*, NTAbh 10 (Münster: Aschendorff, 1974).

17. See chapter 5, pp. 108–111.

18. An excellent recent discussion of the doctrine of the trinity is Robert Jenson, *The Triune Identity* (Philadelphia: Fortress Press, 1982).

19. Hans Frei, *Identity*, makes this point particularly well. "In his passion and death the initiative of Jesus disappears more and more into that of God; but in the resurrection, where the initiative of God is finally and decisively climaxed and he alone is and can be active, the sole identity to mark the presence of that activity is Jesus. God remains hidden, and even reference to him is almost altogether lacking. Jesus of Nazareth, he and none other, marks the presence of the action of God" (p. 121).

20. See Jenson, 103–159.

21. This formulation of the perfection of God's agency is from Thomas Tracy, *God, Action, and Embodiment* (Grand Rapids, Mich.: Eerdmans, 1984), 244.

22. Matthew makes this point with Jesus' prayer in 11:27. See my discussion pp. 132ff.

7. Promise and Prevenience: Revelation as the Doctrine of God's Identifiability

1. For a more complete exegetical account of this movemnt within the narrative discourse see chapter 6, pp. 135–136.

2. "The sense correlates the identification function and the predicative function within the sentence, and the reference relates language to the world." Paul Ricoeur, *Interpretation Theory: Discourse and the Surplus of Meaning* (Fort Worth: Texas Christian University, 1976), 20.

3. See Ricoeur's discussion of the "interlocutionary act," ibid., 14–19.

4. Ibid, 20.

5. This is a contemporary restatement of Luther's insistence that "promise and faith necessarily go together." Faith does not *constitute* a promise but rather shows that a particular linguistic act has been *heard* as promise and believed. Faith is thus necessary if a promise is to be a successful interlocutionary act.

6. Ricoeur, 29-30.

7. "That someone refers to something at a certain time is an event, a speech event. But this event receives its structure from the meaning as sense." Ibid., 20. Ricoeur then adds the sentence, "No inner mark independent of the use of a sentence, constitutes a reliable criterion of denotation." While I do not disagree with that statement, I am seeking to show how in the interpretation of biblical narrative sense not only precedes but anticipates its own reference, and thus how the text creates its own context of use (see pp. 000-000). I am arguing that the shape and content of biblical narrative provide reliable criteria of denotation precisely as they suggest the appropriate context for their own interpretation.

8. The distinction between "the given" and "inner representations" is present, e.g., in the epistemologies of both Locke and Kant. According to Locke the "impressions" given *to* the mind are represented *by* the mind as ideas. Simple ideas are those which correspond to the given impressions and which the mind knows by intuition, that immediate form of knowing which requires no rational reflection. Kant, of course, dispensed with the notion of unsynthesized impressions but maintained the distinction between "the given" and "inner representations" by distinguishing the intuitions of sensibility from the concepts of understanding. Kant's assertion that intuitions precede concepts is grounded in a more basic assumption that the sensible

manifold is given to the mind, which in turn synthesizes and unifies the manifold. Though Kant argues that knowledge always results from the synthesizing activity of the mind (thus we cannot know things-in-themselves), his assertion that the unity of knowledge is *constructed* by the mind is based on the assumption that the sensible is both given and manifold. But if sensations can be known only as they are synthesized, then on Kant's own principles we can know, and consequently can say, nothing about their pre-synthesized state, including whether the sensible is given or constructed, manifold or unified. Thus the distinction between "the given" and "inner representations," though perpetuated by Kant, is not justified within the context of his own theory of knowledge.

9. Those modern theologians who adopt some version of the "method of correlation" seek, as I do, to steer a middle course between the more radical options represented by Torrance and Kaufman. Such theologians operate with three assumptions, only one of which I find persuasive. First, they recognize that if human access to God is to be possible then *relation* and not *separation* must be the ultimate category under which the divine-human situation is conceived. That, it seems to me, is an eminently sensible assumption.

Second, since they operate within the framework determined by Kant's "turn to the subject," they seek to ground that relation both ontologically and epistemologically in human subjectivity. Ordinarily theologians of correlation acknowledge the ontological separation of subject and object in ordinary experience but posit a realm of experience ("feeling," "ecstasy," "limit-experiences") in which the dichotomy is overcome. Such theologians accept the epistemological model as the appropriate framework within which thinking about revelation is to be carried on but seek to show how revelation makes manifest the hidden depth of human subjectivity. Because human beings have lost touch with their own religious depths, revelation must be given to the human subject in a way which does not disrupt but reaffirms the ordinary structure of human experience. I have stated my objections to this understanding of revelation in detail in chapter 2 (pp. 24–31, 43–46) and chapter 4 (pp. 73–78). Despite their intuitive sense for the necessary primary of relation, theologians of correlation continue to accept the epistemological model as the basic framework within which revelation must be conceived and thus struggle unsuccessfully with the conceptual puzzles that model dictates.

Third, the method of correlation assumes that relation to God is the natural human state, and theologians who use that method seek to demonstrate that fact through the use of neutral philosophical and hermeneutical tools. The modern secular person, they argue, can be shown to be *homo religiosus* through an analysis of common human experience. The arguments which purport to show the universal religiosity of the modern or post-modern person usually fall considerably short of persuasive demonstration (see, e.g.,

David Tracy's attempt to argue that "limit-to" experiences are disclosive of a "limit-of" or ground of our experiences of contingency. *Blessed Rage for Order* [New York: Crossroads, 1978], 102–109).

Theologians who adopt this approach often stress the inescapable pluralism of the modern theological situation but seek, nonetheless, a universally valid argument in order to establish the truth-status of key Christian claims. Thus correlationists continue to devise transcendental arguments which seek to discern the ground of the possibility of human religiousness. Such arguments ought to be viewed skeptically for two reasons. One, it is not at all clear that a transcendental argument of this sort can be developed independent of the conceptual confusions of epistemological foundationalism. Two, even if the arguments could be given self-consistent formulation, they justify the truth-status of only the most general of religious claims. The concrete doctrinal statements of religious communities, since they do not possess the requisite universality, cannot be construed as truth-claims. Though they may be intelligible and meaningful, they cannot be true or false.

I am not convinced that this limitation of the category "truth" does justice to the claims of particular religious communities. There is a danger that limiting truth-status to the most general and universal claims perpetuates an unwarranted "myth of universality." Most post-Enlightenment theologians have sought to replace the shattered consensus of Christendom with a general argument of universal validity. While there may no longer be intellectual and cultural consensus concerning the possibility of religious belief, such agreement ought to be re-established, these theologians reason, on the basis of a logically necessary transcendental argument. Insofar as that argument presupposes elements of concrete Christian belief it has often served as the basis for claims of the superiority of Christianity to other particular religious traditions (e.g., Schleiermacher, *The Christian Faith,* paragraphs 8–10; Tillich on the superiority of the symbol of the cross, *The Dynamics of Faith* [New York: Harper & Row, 1957], 98, 125). When the argument possesses utter generality it must perforce deny the truth-status of all particular religious claims, thereby relativizing the claims of all religious communities. (For an analysis of the dangers of this view of truth for religious dialogue, particularly between Christians and Jews, see Ronald F. Thiemann, "G. E. Lessing: An Enlightened View of Judaism," *The Journal of Ecumenical Studies* 18/3 [Summer 1981], 401–422.) The former option continues a dangerous tradition of Christian imperialism toward other religions. The latter option implicitly denies that disagreements between religious traditions are properly understood to be conflicts of truth-claims. (For an analysis which shows the implausibility of that view, see William A. Christian, *Oppositions of Religious Doctrines* [New York: Herder & Herder, 1972].) In either case the appeal to universality seems less than fruitful.

While I share the conviction of the theologians of correlation that God and humanity ought to be conceived as primarily or ultimately in relation, I find the method of correlation itself to be minimally helpful in developing and explicating that insight.

10. I am arguing that the ontological distinction between Creator and creature is an *implication* of a Christian doctrine of revelation (the doctrine of God's identifiability) rather than its *presupposition*. Christian theology is made possible by the conviction that the God identified in biblical narrative is in a relation of promise with the Christian community. In explicating the identity of the God of promise, one recognizes that the God who is Father of Jesus Christ is Yahweh, God of Israel, creator of heaven and earth. Thus the one who is *pro nobis* in Jesus Christ is identified as the creator who is ontologically other and thus *extra nos*. Christian theology thus begins from the identification of God in Jesus Christ and seeks to specify his identity further with reference to those "temporally" prior narrative descriptions which are implied by the uniquely individuating identification of God as the Father of Jesus Christ. The logic of theology need not (and ought not) follow the temporal structure of biblical narrative. The decisive Christian belief is that God is identifiable in Jesus Christ. Theology which begins from that conviction and seeks to understand its implications both for the further identity of God and for a life of Christian faith and discipleship is appropriately "Christocentric."

11. On the Catholic side see Avery Dulles, *Models of Revelation* (New York: Doubleday, 1983).

12. Michael Polanyi, *Personal Knowledge* (Chicago: University of Chicago Press, 1958), 214.

13. Martin Luther, *Lectures on Galatians*, vol. 26, *Luther's Works*, ed. Jaroslav Pelikan (St. Louis: Concordia Publishing House, 1963), 72–73.

Name Index

189

Subject Index